T0302155

# PARTICIPATORY BUDGETING IN EUROPE

Can participatory budgeting help make public services really work for the public? Incorporating a range of experiments in ten different countries, this book provides the first comprehensive analysis of participatory budgeting in Europe and the effect it has had on democracy, the modernisation of local government, social justice, gender mainstreaming and sustainable development. By focusing on the first decade of European participatory budgeting and analysing the results and the challenges affecting the agenda today it provides a critical appraisal of the participatory model. Detailed comparisons of European cases expose similarities and differences between political cultures and offer a strong empirical basis to discuss the theories of deliberative and participatory democracy and reveal contradictory tendencies between political systems, public administrations and democratic practices.

**Yves Sintomer** is professor for political science at Paris 8 University, and Senior Fellow at the Institut Universitaire de France. He is visiting professor and associated researcher at Neuchâtel University, Lausanne University and Bask Country University. He is doctor of political and social sciences (European University Institute, Florence) and works in a research supervision capacity (Paris 5 University).

**Anja Röcke** is Assistant Professor of Sociology at the Institute for Social Sciences at Humboldt University, Berlin. She studied in Berlin and Paris and achieved her doctoral degree at the European University Institute in Florence.

**Carsten Herzberg** is Senior Researcher at the nexus Institute – a think tank for participatory politics and cooperation management in Berlin. He studied Political Science and holds a German-French PhD.

# PARTICIPATORY BUDGETING IN EUROPE

## Democracy and Public Governance

*Yves Sintomer, Anja Röcke
and Carsten Herzberg*

Routledge
Taylor & Francis Group

LONDON AND NEW YORK

Original French Language Edition – Les Budgets Participatifs en Europe; Des Services Publics au Service du Public
Yves SINTOMER, Carsten HERZBERG, Anja RÖCKE
© Editions LA DECOUVERTE, Paris, France, 2008, 2015.

This translated edition first published 2016
by Routledge
2 Park Square, Milton Park, Abingdon, Oxon OX14 4RN

and by Routledge
605 Third Avenue, New York, NY 10017

First issued in paperback 2021

*Routledge is an imprint of the Taylor & Francis Group, an informa business*

© 2016 Yves Sintomer, Anja Röcke and Carsten Herzberg

Publisher's Note
The publisher has gone to great lengths to ensure the quality of this reprint but points out that some imperfections in the original copies may be apparent.

*British Library Cataloguing in Publication Data*
A catalogue record for this book is available from the British Library

*Library of Congress Cataloging-in-Publication Data*
A catalog record for this book has been requested

ISBN 13: 978-1-03-209799-2 (pbk)
ISBN 13: 978-1-4722-6789-8 (hbk)

Typeset in Garamond
by Apex CoVantage, LLC

Translated from the French by Judith Hitchman

# CONTENTS

# CONTENTS

# ILLUSTRATIONS

## Figures

## Tables

# NOTES ON THE AUTHORS

**Yves Sintomer** is professor for political science at Paris 8 University and Senior Fellow at the French University Institute. He is invited professor at Lausanne University, associated researcher at Neuchâtel University, and external professor at Bask Country University. He is doctor of political and social sciences (European University Institute, Florence) and has a Habilitation to supervise research (Paris 5 University). He has also studied at Paris 8, Paris 10, Frankfurt/Main, and Harvard University. He has been invited Professor at Catania University (Italy), Louvain-La-Neuve University (Belgium), Goethe University Frankfurt/Main and Tsinghua University (Beijing), and invited Scholar at the European University Institute (Florence), the Institute for Social Research (Frankfurt/Main), and the Ash Centre for democratic governance and innovation (Harvard Kennedy School). He has been deputy-director of the Marc Bloch Centre (Berlin). He has written various books and articles on participatory and deliberative democracy, on political representation, and on French and German political sociology. His writings have been published in 18 languages.

**Anja Röcke** is Assistant Professor of Sociology at the Institute for Social Sciences at Humboldt- University, Berlin. She studied in Berlin and Paris and achieved her doctoral degree at the European University Institute in Florence with a thesis on 'Framing Citizen Participation. Participatory Budgeting in France, Germany and the United Kingdom' (published with Palgrave, 2014). Her research deals with participatory democracy and democratic innovations, social theory and the concepts of conduct of life ('Lebensführung') and of 'optimisation' (enhancement).

**Carsten Herzberg** is Senior Researcher at the nexus Institute – a think tank for participatory politics and cooperation management in Berlin. He studied Political Science and holds a German-French PhD. His topics of research are: local democracy in Europe and Latin America, the modernisation of public administration, and social movements. He has written several books on participatory budgeting, amongst which was the first German monograph on the Porto Alegre experience. Currently, he is working on the participation of citizens and workers in public utilities in the context of remunicipalisations in the water and energy sectors.

# FOREWORD TO
# THE ENGLISH EDITION

This book was previously published in French, German, Italian and Spanish. When it was written, the financial and economic crisis had not yet modified the international hegemony of neoliberalism. Global financial capitalism had not shown so clearly its limits. The economic power had not shifted so crudely away from the old continent. In 2015, this time seems far away. The legitimacy crisis of representative regimes in the old continent has sharpened. The world has deeply changed.

For the first time since the fall of the Berlin Wall, in Spain, in Iceland, in Greece and elsewhere, huge European social movements have claimed 'true democracy', institutional innovations, citizen participation in government. In the US, Occupy Wall Street has gone in the same direction. Participatory budgeting is part of this story. It inspired some of the proposals of the Spanish movement '15-M', the Iberian equivalent of Occupy Wall Street, which in 2011 reclaimed: 'Real Democracy Now!' ('Democracia Real Ya!'), and was able to develop sophisticated methods of horizontal deliberation. Democratically controlling both the markets and public authorities is even more crucial than it was. Modernising public services, with the people and for the people, remains more than ever a compelling issue. Although participatory budgeting has suffered setbacks in some European countries (such as Italy, Spain or the United Kingdom), it significantly developed in others, most notably in Poland, Germany and Portugal. Elsewhere in the world, it also continues to expand. However, European experiments are facing huge challenges in times of public debt crises and the retrenchment of increasing parts of the population from the political arena. Up to now, most cases were top-down processes that focussed on limited issues and involved limited amounts of money. They had ambiguous social, ecological, ethnic or gender impact and did not alter the global balance of power. Nevertheless, they did change some dimensions of the everyday life of a large number of citizens and civil servants and in some cases even triggered broader political and administrative reform processes.

The authors of this book tried to analyse both the positive innovation that participatory budgeting represents and the limits it faces in Europe. Their hope is that the story so far is only the beginning of a broader learning process, that participatory budgeting will overcome its limits and contribute to the democratic revolution that is required in the 21st century. They would be satisfied if this book could modestly contribute to this movement.

# ACKNOWLEDGEMENTS

This book is the outcome of a joint research project funded by the Hans-Böckler Foundation on the theme of 'Participatory Budgets in a European Comparative Approach. Prospects and Opportunities of the Cooperative State at the Municipal Level in Germany and Europe'. It has been produced with the assistance of: Hans-Böckler Foundation, Marc Bloch Centre (Berlin), Humboldt University Berlin, ACI programme 'Consultation, Participatory Democracy and Social Movements' (French Ministry of Research), PICRI project 'Local Participatory Procedures in Ile-de-France and Europe: Towards a Technical Democracy?' (Ile-de-France region), programme 'Dilemmas of Participatory Network Planning. Sustainability, Democracy and Planning in France, the Netherlands, Spain and Sweden', URBAN-NET/PUCA/Paris 8 University, Research Centre CRESPPA (CNRS/Paris 8 University).

The project was led by Yves Sintomer in collaboration with Carsten Herzberg and Anja Röcke. The administrative director was Hans-Peter Müller (Humboldt University Berlin). Responsible at Hans-Böckler Foundation were Volker Grünewald and Karsten Schneider.

The team comprised the following researchers and countries:

Belgium: Ludivine Damay and Christine Schaut (Centre of Sociological Studies, Saint-Louis University, Brussels);
France: Marion Ben-Hammo and Sandrine Geffroy (Paris 8 University), Julien Talpin (Research fellow at the CNRS, Paris, Lille 2 University);
Italy: Giovanni Allegretti (coordinator, Centre for Social Studies, Coimbra University), Pier Paolo Fanesi (Macerata University), Lucilla Pezzetta (La Sapienza University, Rome), Michelangelo Secchi (Milano State University), Antonio Putini (University of Reggio Calabria), and Paolo Filippi (Venice University);
Netherlands: Hugo Swinnen (Verwey-Jonker Institut, Utrecht);
Poland: Elżbieta Plaszczyk (School of Public Administration Lodz) and Dorota Dakowska (Strasbourg University);
Portugal: Luis Guerreiro (Palmela town) and Giovanni Allegretti and Nelson Dias (Algarve University)
Spain: Ernesto Ganuza Fernandez (Andalusian Institute for Social Studies, Córdoba);
United Kingdom: Jez Hall (PB Network).

Our partners are also co-authors of some parts of the book. In Part II of this work, Sections 1 and 2 of Chapter 4 were written together with Ernesto Ganauza for the former and Giovanni Allegretti, Pier Paolo Fanesi, Michelangelo Secchi and Lucilla Pezetta for the latter; Sections 2 and 3 of Chapter 5 were written together with Marion Ben-Hammo and Julien Talpin, respectively; Sections 1 and 3 of Chapter 6 were written together with Ludivine Damay and Christine Schaut for the former and Luis Guerreiro and Giovanni Allegretti for the latter; and Sections 1 to 4 and 5 of Chapter 8 were written together with Jeremy Hall for the former and Elzbieta Plaszczyk and Dorota Dakowska for the latter.

The arguments set out here have been presented at a large number of seminars, conferences and workshops, whether academic or organised by practitioners, in Western and Eastern Europe, North and South America, Asia and Africa. The comments and criticisms we received enabled us to correct some errors and considerably enriched our reflections. Without our team of researchers, who have worked with us over several years, we would never have been able to realise a work on this scale. We would particularly like to thank Giovanni Allegretti for his constant contributions to the project and to Jez Hall who contributed considerably to the English publication. The text for this English version of our book on participatory budgets in Europe was, with the exception of the British chapter, translated by Judith Hitchman, revised by James Patterson. For the elaboration of the graphics we received help from Ilaria Scartazi. Lisa-Flor Sintomer prepared the typescript for the English edition.

Some of the ideas presented here are based on prior research carried out with Marie-Hélène Bacqué. Loïc Blondiaux's regular comments made a significant contribution to improving the quality of our analyses. We would also like to thank Leonardo Avritzer, Sergio Baierle, Ismael Blanco, Luigi Bobbio, Sophie Bouchet-Petersen, Yves Cabannes, Geraldo Campos, Catherine Colliot-Thélène, Cécile Cuny, Donatella della Porta, Luciano Fedozzi, Joan Font, Véronique Giraud, François Hannoyer, Hugues Jallon, Heinz Kleger, Pascale Laborier, Fabian Lemmes, Aldamir Marquetti, Catherine Neveu, Tiago Peixoto, Muriel Pic, Jacques Picard, Franklin Ramirez, Henri Rey, Pierre Rosanvallon, Felix Sanchez, Eloisa Santos, Boaventura de Sousa Santos, Bryan Wampler, Alexander Wegener and Michael Werner for their contributions and support, and Lisa-Flor Sintomer for her editing work.

# INTRODUCTION

Twenty-five years after the fall of the Berlin Wall, for the first time in history, most of Europe is gathered under common institutions that are based on representative democracy and the rule of law. A shared democratic culture is beginning to emerge, in spite of the major differences that still exist, particularly between East and West and between the North and the South. While most direct political exchanges between actors from different countries take place within the national institutional arena, the main European public spheres tend to discuss issues in increasingly similar terms, as can be seen in the main European newspapers (Eder 2007). Since the beginning of the 2000s, the European Parliament has played an increasingly important role; political parties and trade unions have coordinated their European-level activities more and more closely; social forums have enabled direct communication between civil society actors; a protest movement emerged in the European economic crisis. The question of developing alternatives to neoliberal capitalism is discussed in the whole continent, although with different variations.

## Discontent with Democracy

Nonetheless, the discontent is growing among citizens, together with the rejection of politics as currently practised by the continent's elite. The European project seems paralysed, torn between varying conceptions and threatened by national or even nationalistic sentiments. Parallel to the new engagement of citizens, in almost all countries, political systems face voter disillusionment or crises of legitimacy. Traditional representative democracy no longer appears capable of dealing with new challenges: increasing social inequalities, ecological crisis, xenophobic and authoritarian tendencies, the provincialising (Chakrabarty 2007) of Europe in the new world order. In many places, the idea of Europe seems unable to mobilise the energies and trust of citizens. The current problems of the European integration undermine the idea that elected representatives can find adequate solutions for society's needs. Everywhere, abstention is on the rise; citizens' faith in political institutions and politicians is declining; party membership is decreasing, in terms of both quantity and intensity of identification, and this affects strongly the traditional parties. In a parallel move, institutional participatory procedures have multiplied since the beginning of the 1990s and citizen participation is on the political agenda. Everywhere, citizens use the social media for new forms of activism. This is a development that does not seem merely circumstantial, but probably marks a long-term trend. The reasons are hard to decipher. On the one hand, major socio-cultural changes have fostered demand for an increasingly democratised political system. Politics cannot remain unaffected by the widespread development of education, the crises in most authoritarian structures (from the patriarchal family to school, political parties and research laboratories), more equal gender relations, the development of public discussions on science and technology, the emergence of an information model based on networks rather than top-down integration, the replacement of the Taylorist model and the collapse of economic models based on authoritarian planning. Completely out of step with these developments, the world of politics is becoming increasingly professional and inward-looking, despite the fact that some political actors have seized upon these issues to score points against those who continue to cling to traditional ways of thinking.

Expectations are not, however, universally in favour of more democratic ways of doing politics. Authoritarian tendencies are also emerging: companies seem less open to the idea of codetermination or workers' participation than they were in the 1980s; there is an increasing emphasis on security; and the far right and xenophobic parties are making significant gains in a number of places. This is due to several factors: uneasiness due to the acuteness of the social and economic crisis; the increasing inequality in the capitalist system of the 21th century (Picketty 2014); the apparent powerlessness of politicians when faced with economic globalisation and the global market; institutional inadequacy in handling the scale of current challenges; the loss of traditional identities without the appearance of new clear reference points; and the calling into question of the ambivalent effects of 'progress'. Here again, political actors seize upon these themes to distinguish themselves from their opponents and to exploit reactionary opinions.

The loss of credibility of traditional models is not a new political phenomenon: the post-1968 demonstrations; the revolutions that produced the fall of Southern European dictatorships in the 1970s; and those that produced the downfall of the Communist regimes in the 1980s, all called authoritarian and paternalistic social relations into question. The idea of 'doing politics differently' followed the emergence of issues related to self-management, new social movements, green and alternative currents and then the alter-globalisation movement, although these movements' political practices are often far removed from their rhetoric. Traditional bureaucracy has been brought into disrepute by the failure of 'Real socialism' and was then further discredited by the rise of neoliberal globalisation. Public service users' increasing discontent and public authorities' tendency to 'speak on behalf of' user or patient associations also enhanced this trend. Of course, modernisation and reform are often euphemisms wielded to extol the virtues of the minimalist state and attack social benefits. Nevertheless, increased problems related to traditional forms of public action and politics seems more and more difficult to contain in most Western democracies. A significant trend has emerged in the past decades, characterised by increased calls for citizen participation in public policy, closer relations between users and managers and increased dialogue between the institutional political system and the rest of the population. These calls have come from social movements and from within the political system, as well as from both international organisations and their critics. Far from mere political or administrative rhetoric, these calls are in line with the expansion of new institutional procedures of citizen involvement and developments in legal standards. A 'deliberative imperative' (Blondiaux and Sintomer 2002) is emerging – to a greater or lesser extent, depending on the country – together with a push to increase participation.

## The 'Rue Jourdain' Example

Participatory budgeting is distinct from other new participatory instruments, because of both its rapid spread and the political reactions it has produced. The procedure – which involves non-elected citizens in making decisions on public finances – was invented in Porto Alegre and very rapidly spread through the rest of Brazil and Latin America. A few years later, it spread to Europe and the rest of the world. It is now advocated by the alter-globalisation movement, the World Bank and the UN, as well as radical NGOs, political parties from all political camps, political foundations and administrative managers. Is this merely a passing trend or a fundamental shift that will produce radical changes in administrative and political practices?

There are many explanations for the success of participatory budgeting. First and foremost, the Porto Alegre procedure seems to have found a way of reinventing politics and redistributing resources in favour of the most disadvantaged. In addition, it is well known that money is at the heart of everything, and that budgets are key in local authorities' functioning. Enabling citizens to participate in drawing up the budget, even if in a limited manner, is therefore highly symbolic, particularly during periods of financial squeeze. Thirdly, it is a tool that has the potential to bypass parochialism: the most widespread participatory approaches are generally limited to a specific neighbourhood or area of public policy and the people involved often tend to defend very specific interests.

This was the case in the French city La Rochelle, for example, at the beginning of the 2000s, when the members of a neighbourhood committee asked for a no-entry sign to be placed at one end of the Rue Jourdain. Those present at the meeting were almost unanimous in denouncing the problems caused by traffic driving down the street and, after looking into the request, the town's technical department judged it reasonable and put up the sign as requested. The measure, however, resulted in some unexpected effects: part of the traffic went through the adjacent neighbourhood instead, which led their committee to ask for a no-entry sign too, this time to be placed at the other end of the Rue Jourdain. The technical department and local politicians discussed the matter and decided to accede to the new request as well, given that the Rue Jourdain was far from being a main street. The street was now completely closed to traffic and was used as a prime example to justify politicians' oft-repeated view that 'involving ordinary people in setting out public policy is certainly important, but should not be taken too far and the different roles in the process should be respected. Residents should look out for their specific interests and politicians should uphold the common good and therefore retain a monopoly over decision-making. Failing this, there would be a decrease in the common good and an irrational increase in specific interests'. Participatory budgeting would appear to provide a way of overcoming the 'Rue Jourdain example'. There are no question marks hanging over the good will of local politicians in the La Rochelle neighbourhood committee system: they are genuinely convinced of the importance of participation and have been highly enthusiastic in its implementation. However, while the result is undeniably illogical, is it the methodology or citizens' short-sightedness that is to blame? When participation consists of a series of vertical discussions between decision-makers and residents, without the latter being able to exchange ideas with other neighbourhoods, is it not inevitable that they find it difficult to develop an overall perspective? If, on the other hand, citizens are asked to deal with the overall budget and justify to their peers why a certain request has more legitimacy or urgency than another, participatory budgeting would appear to produce a model that runs counter to the Nimbyism[1] that characterises the 'Rue Jourdain example' (see Figure I.1).

At least part of the reason why participatory budgeting Porto Alegre-style appear able to contribute to social justice and public service modernisation, therefore, is that citizens are urged to compare their situation with that of their peers; take an interest in overarching political choices; and get involved with the issues at the heart of the administrative process. These approaches seem likely to produce both bottom-up and top-down modernisation. This is a significant advantage at a time when purely managerial models, such as those initially proposed by international organisations, are being increasingly called into question. They may even prove as attractive to international consultants who are concerned with ensuring that money distributed is put to good use as

---

1 NIMBY is an acronym for 'not in my back yard'.

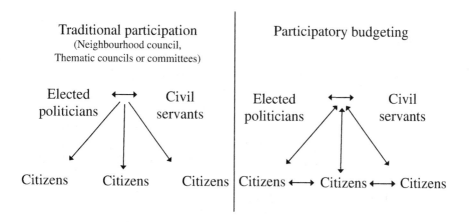

*Figure I.1* Traditional participation and participatory budgeting

*Source:* authors' elaboration

they are to activists who believe that 'another world is possible'. The success of participatory budgeting is in no small measure due to this unexpected convergence between widely differing actors.

However, is a procedure that is the result of such highly divergent expectations not destined to be engulfed in confusion? The fact that participatory budgets have been tried out in a wide variety of different contexts and the different forms they have taken could lead to the various procedures being linked only by highly superficial elements. A cursory examination of the development of this process in Europe appears to yield a diversity that makes it very difficult to reach any overall conclusions. On which concrete procedures are European participatory budgets based? Who are the actors involved and what are their ideological and theoretical frames of reference? Aside from political rhetoric, what are the actual effects of these experiments? Can an overall conclusion be drawn? In alter-globalisation circles, many saw participatory budgeting as the foundations upon which to build an alternative to neoliberalism. Some German foundations, on the other hand, viewed them as a politically neutral way of producing administrative modernisation, whereas some critical sociologists and radicals said that they merely distract citizens' movements from real issues and integrate those involved into a subordinate role in the system, thereby legitimising the status quo. Where does the truth lie? However they are interpreted, can participatory budgeting be considered symbolic of a 'new spirit' blowing through public institutions (Bacqué, Rey and Sintomer 2005)?

It is these questions that the present book aims to answer. We believe that this assessment of participatory budgets – which covers the first decade of their emergence, spread and functioning – can contribute to establishing a vision of the similarities and differences between the political cultures, legal frameworks and institutional contexts of different European countries that is both all-encompassing and detailed. Participatory budgets are a lens through which the partly contradictory developments in the political system, public administration and democracy at the start of the twenty-first century can be studied. What does the future hold? Is the development of participation not just one facet of the emergence of an 'audience-' or 'opinion-based democracy' (Manin 1995) dominated by demagogy, media manipulation, charisma and depoliticisation? Or, on the other hand, is it the first sign of a 'democratisation of democracy' through more flexible, collective and less hierarchical decision-making procedures? Could it lead to a more balanced, less party-machine and administration dominated form of democracy? Is this something that is common to 'old' and 'new' Europe and which includes Latin and Nordic countries, countries marked by French-style republicanism and those that follow the Anglo-Saxon tradition? Is it something that the 'Rhineland', liberal and Scandinavian models all share? To reach the heart of the matter it was necessary to carry out a close examination of all the European countries involved, using methodologies that would cut through political discourse and proclamations of good intentions.

## The Research

This book is part of a dynamic and developing field of study. The past decades have seen a huge increase in studies of participatory democracy in Britain, Europe and the world, spanning a range of very different issues, disciplinary approaches and objectives. Initially, these were mainly monographs or comparisons dealing with two or three areas. A second phase enabled the comparison of a variety of sites (Font 2001, Fung and Wright 2001, Bacqué, Rey and Sintomer 2005, Dias 2014). However, these comparisons faced the problem that the research upon which they were based had been carried out using a wide variety of different methodologies, concepts and categories (Font, Della Porta, Sintomer 2012). The research was heterogeneous and this it made more difficult to produce cumulative outcomes and comparisons. The aim of this book is to contribute to a new phase in the development of participatory research; in other words, to carry out integrated assessments that are not limited to local effects and national contexts, thereby enabling the construction of a general overview (Smith 2009; Font, Della Porta, Sintomer 2014). To this end, we have based our work on the results of the previous phases and other similar attempts that dealt with Brazil or Latin America (Avritzer 2002, 2009, Cabannes 2003, 2006). Our research did, however, come up against a lack of empirical information: unlike those working on areas such as the welfare state or education, we were unable to rely on pre-existing sets of comparable data. We were therefore obliged to both produce the data and interpret it, at one and the same time. Also, most of the processes assessed are very recent and still under way, which explains why some of our arguments have been left as hypotheses.

This first comparative continent-wide study on participatory democracy is centred on the first decade of European participatory budgets, which are among the most innovative participatory procedures today. This gave us a focus for our research, through which we could achieve a better understanding of local democracy in Europe and of democracy as a whole. The idea was to look at the European construction from a different angle, raising the issue of the convergences and differences between different national models from a specific starting point. This enabled an analysis of a wide variety of different relations: that is, between the state and the market; the institutional political system, the network of associations and social movements; politics and the administration; and public service modernisation, the defence of the status quo and privatisation.

During several years, our study considered over 250 participatory budgets that existed in 2010 in a dozen (mainly Western) European countries, as well as a few experiments that were similar in nature. Seventeen researchers of eight different nationalities were directly involved, while many other colleagues were involved in an indirect manner. Our fieldwork was based on four concentric circles. The first, which was the heart of our work, involved ethnographic research and comprised long stays in the respective places of concern, participatory observation of interactions that were key to local social and political life, and deep-rooted knowledge of political-institutional and cultural context. This was carried out in twelve places in five different countries.[2] The second circle comprised in-depth studies based on at least two visits to the place in question, observation of interaction, and in-depth semi-structured interviews with local politicians, administrators, association members and, where appropriate, others (foundations, NGOs and so on); and the systematic gathering of quantitative and qualitative data on the political, financial, economic and urban situation of the town concerned, as well as on the participatory model itself (through questionnaires that were common to all the locations). In some cases, questionnaires were also handed out to participants. On each occasion we worked with researchers from the country in question, in order to reach a better understanding of the socio-political context in which the participatory experience was taking place. The second approach was used in thirteen local authorities in eight different countries.[3] The third circle was

---

2 This included France (Morsang-sur-Orge, Poitou-Charentes, Saint-Denis), Germany (Berlin-Lichtenberg, Rheinstetten), Italy (Grottammare, Pieve Emanuele, Rome XI, Venice), Spain (Cordoba, Puente Genil), United Kingdom (Salford).

3 These were Belgium (Mons); Finland (Hämeenlinna); France (Bobigny, Pont-de-Claix, Paris 20th district) ; Germany (Emsdetten, Esslingen, Hilden); Netherlands

merely a 'looking glass case': a single case whose purpose was to provide greater clarification of the object of our research.[4] In this case, the investigation was not carried out as fully or systematically. Finally, the outer circle comprised those processes which we only studied via secondary literature, the Internet and telephone interviews.[5] The analysis and interpretation of the empirical material is based on circle one and two; we used the other two circles as complements to back up our hypotheses and 'test' the ideal-type models.

\* \* \*

In order to answer the questions raised in this introduction and to ensure coherence with the research programme set out above, we proceed in three parts. Part I consists of a cross-cutting analysis that looks at the context in which European participatory budgets emerged and explains their development. Moreover, it presents a typology of six participation models that includes participatory budgeting, but also other participatory instruments. Its goal is to assess the effects, strengths, weaknesses and scope of participatory processes in Europe as well as the relations between participatory democracy and administrative reform, social justice and changes taking place in the political system. In this first part, we will answer the following series of questions: How can we explain the simultaneous development of participatory budgeting in such diverse contexts? Is there convergence between the various approaches and do they belong at all to the same political phenomenon? What is the social and political meaning of these developments? Part II provides a more detailed analysis of twenty participatory budgets in the 2000s, setting them in their national contexts and highlighting their similarities and differences. This will enable us to provide a detailed picture of the different models of participation set out in Part I. Part III deepens our cross-cutting analysis by focusing on three types of impacts of participatory budgeting: managerial, social and political. This analysis serves as springboard for a general discussion about the challenges and outcomes of citizen participation. Our conclusion summarises the results set out throughout the work and raises pragmatic issues related to the specific nature of the 'British' model of citizen participation and democracy in general. A glossary placed at the end of the book contains the most important technical terms we use throughout.

---

(Utrecht); Spain (Albacete, Seville); Poland (Plock), United Kingdom (Bradford).

    4 This was the city of Palmela in Portugal.

    5 For an overview, see Sintomer, Herzberg, Röcke 2005.

# PART I

# THE RETURN OF THE CARAVELS

The history of participatory budgeting is still young, but nevertheless astonishing. The procedure was invented in the late 1980s in Porto Alegre and just fifteen years later there were hundreds of examples spread across Latin America. By 2005 it had been adopted by 55 European towns. Five years later there were more than 250 participatory budgets and at the end of 2012, between 474 and 1317 (this large difference is due to the fact that in some cases, and especially in Poland (see Figure 1.3, p. 23), it is difficult to get reliable data on how exactly or whether at all the process is still working). Traditionally, complex products such as democratic constitutions and mass political parties, were invented in Europe or North America before being exported to the rest of the world. This is perhaps the first time that an institutional innovation has travelled from South to North and a procedure invented in Latin America imported into Europe. It could be described as a 'return of the caravels'. But what exactly are the caravels bringing with them? Given the different national and continental contexts, are European participatory budgets comparable to those in Latin America? How far can they be considered a single phenomenon? Does participatory budgeting represent nothing more than a fashionable terminology, or is it instead a slogan only used by a restricted number of political actors?

To answer these questions, we will start this first Part by systematically taking stock of the current situation in order to obtain a better idea of the scope, forms and reasons behind the procedure. We will make an initial diagnosis, then begin to tell the story of and explain the puzzling phenomenon that is participatory budgeting. The big question is: what conclusions can be drawn from the procedure's remarkably rapid spread? Chapter 1 enables us to take stock of developments since participatory budgeting was invented in Porto Alegre, going from prior experiences in other Brazilian towns to its arrival in Europe during the early 2000s. We will also provide a precise definition of participatory budgeting as we understand it, for the purposes of this investigation. The second chapter looks into the factors that explain the launching of participatory budgeting experiments in Europe. It also tackles the issue of the convergence of these various processes in Europe, as well as looking at local institutions and approaches. For this purpose we will be obliged to deal with the question of comparative research. Chapter 3 goes beyond the mere process of participatory budgeting in that it presents a general typology of citizen participation. It is only at this point that we will be in a position to undertake a more concrete assessment of the wide variety of participatory budgeting processes in Europe without risking getting lost in the almost infinite number of local shapes it may take.

# 1

# 'IT ALL BEGAN IN PORTO ALEGRE ...'

In the late 1980s, a team representing the radical left was elected to the Porto Alegre Town Hall. (Porto Alegre is one of the largest cities in the south of Brazil, with a population of 1.3 million inhabitants.) This was the time when the country was going through the final stages of a transition to democracy. This transition had lasted a good ten years, starting with the major struggles of the working class in the second half of the 1970s, and followed by the introduction of a very progressive constitution in 1988. Brazil is today one of the top ten economic powers of the world; it is also one of the countries with the greatest social inequalities. The fight to overthrow the dictatorship combined social claims with a demand for democracy. The State of Rio Grande do Sul, of which Porto Alegre is the capital, has always had a special relationship with the federal government. It has often been politically opposed to it, and has a history of progressive currents; there is less social inequality there than in the rest of the country and, conversely, the management of public affairs tends to be better.

## 1. The Porto Alegre Experiment

In the 1980s, one of the most important waves of urban social movements occurred in Porto Alegre (Avritzer 2002). As in other major cities, there had been a population explosion over recent years, caused by the rural exodus. This had led to a big increase in the slum areas (favellas). There was enormous need and the old habits of favouritism had reached their limits. The Workers' Party (PT), led at national level by Lula (who was to be elected President of Brazil in 2002) had strong local support. The PT has a history of trade union struggles (of which Lula himself had been a part) and includes progressive Christian currents organised in grassroots Church communities and imprinted with liberation theology. Moreover, a large number of experienced left-wing and extreme left activists (such as Dilma Youssef, who succeeded to Lula at the head of Brazil in 2010) joined the movement, which was very important in the formation of the party. In Porto Alegre the most radical currents were particularly well represented.

When the Popular Front, constituted around the Workers' Party, took over the Town Hall in 1988, they were confronted by a Town Council with a majority of opposition parties. The Brazilian political system is a presidential one at both municipal and federal level, and the executive and the legislature are elected separately on the basis of direct universal suffrage. It was also to cope with this cohabitation, and not only in order to introduce an extremely radical programme (initially conceived on the basis of the 'double power concept'), that the executive launched a participatory structure that enabled non-elected citizens to take part in budgetary decision-making (Fedozzi 1999, 2000). This process was strongly marked by the Marxist revolutionary tradition, but the 'soviets' were organised in neighbourhoods rather than in factories. This was the basis for creating the pyramid of delegates, with explicit reference – for the most part mythical – to the Paris Commune of 1871. There was no crossover between state and civil society organisations in Porto Alegre. They were both totally independent and the participatory space was built around new institutions that facilitate cooperation between the associative structures (NGOs) and the town executive. (The legislative body was only marginally involved, although its approval was required, at the end of the day, to adopt the final budget.) The procedure that was implemented was the result of a compromise between the initial proposals made by the Workers' Party and those that emanated from the associative movement; moreover, it was the outcome of a learning process that continued until 1992, which is when the Popular Front was voted in for a second time (Baiocchi 2005, Wampler 2010).

During this period, the local government successfully managed to stabilise the city's financial situation, taking advantage of national reforms which granted more financial support and autonomy to local governments. The tax system was reformed, with more means redistributed to social policy. The civil service at municipal level also underwent a deep reform, and while the existing staff progressively abandoned the idea of an immediate revolution in favour of the prospect of more progressive management, participatory budgeting gradually acquired its key characteristics. By 1992 these had become stable. Participatory budgets were initially conceived, thanks to a window of opportunity, by actors who had no exact ideas about what they were trying to do (Abers 2000). They benefited from a series of converging circumstances such like the movement of democratisation in Brazil, the reform of local finance, the fall of the Berlin Wall and the subsequent discrediting of bureaucratic socialism.

Participatory budgeting showed itself to be a highly original process that was both coherent and functional. Centred on municipal investments, it is anchored in two dimensions. The first is geographical: each territory defines its own priorities and discusses them with its neighbours. The second is thematic: every town council department has its own meetings and committees. By developing a joint vision via territories and themes, it is possible to develop a transversal vision that reaches from the micro-local level of neighbourhoods to the city as a whole. Many meetings are held in the neighbourhoods. They are more or less formalised and make it possible to discuss needs in a very detailed manner. At district level, annual general assemblies take place, and permanent participatory forums allow projects to be prioritised, implemented and followed up. At town level, the Participatory Budget Council meets several times a month and delegates finalise the synthesis of these proposals, negotiate them with the municipal authorities and define the rules of the game for the following year. Assemblies are open to all volunteers and, although the neighbourhood associations play a major role through their ability to mobilise, they have no statutory privileges.

The delegates to the District Forums and Participatory Budget Council are closely linked to their grassroots and have a 'semi-imperative mandate'. Throughout the year, a carefully organised cycle is used to maintain and develop the quality of discussion, the follow-up of decisions and mobilisation of citizens. The overall process is structured by very precise rules that are discussed anew every year and which are largely determined by the citizens themselves. Prioritising and ranking of projects is carried out by a weighted voting system that takes specific populations and infrastructure needs into account, as well as the ability of public services to meet those needs. It is thanks to these formalised criteria for distributing resources that participatory budgeting enables the implementation of social justice, combined with a majoritarian logic (projects that meet the redistributive criteria and which gain the greatest support are ranked highest). There is also a certain democratisation of the technical choices via the intense discussions that the delegates have with the town engineers. All in all, the power granted to participants is considerable, and they also have great procedural independence. All investments are subjected to a joint decision-making process between the executive and the participatory structure; the respective weight of these partners varies, according to the field under consideration. The Participatory Budget Council plays only a consultative role in the remainder of the budget, although its influence remains significant (Allegretti 2003, Genro and De Souza 1998, Gret and Sintomer 2004, Herzberg 2002).

It is significant that the working class was actively involved and appropriated this instrument (Granet and Solidariedade 2003). Even if there was a quantitative limitation, the level of participation increased from one year to the next: the main cycle of district assemblies brought together about 1,000 people in 1990. This increased to 14,000 in 1999 and peaked at 17,000 in 2002. The 'demonstration effect' is that of a process that convinced an increasing number of citizens of its usefulness. What is even more remarkable is the social composition of participants: whereas the working class has traditionally been marginalised from politics, it is massively present in participatory budgeting. Working class participation makes up the vast majority, with women attending the assemblies more regularly than men. Moving up the levels of the participatory pyramid, these characteristics change and the weight of men and upper socio-professional categories of the working class – as well as of those with time to spare (the unemployed, for example) – tends to increase. The Participatory Budget Council does, however, reflect the overall population of the city: far more, at any rate, than the Town Council or the leadership of local parties.

Initially, the ideological frames of the promoters of the experiment mainly underlined the need to 'reverse priorities' for the benefit of the most needy and to 'democratise democracy' via participation. The two objectives are supposed to be linked: participation should enable the working class to promote their own interests and end the appropriation of the state by the dominant classes. Progressively, a third objective was added, namely the prospect of 'good governance' based on the improved local administration that resulted from the fight against favouritism, the internal reorganisation of administrative services and the rapid and more systematic inclusion of people's needs in public policies. These ambitions were partly realised (Gret and Sintomer 2004). Establishing clear rules for the distribution of resources and the public nature of discussions clearly improved the transparency of the budgetary process, reduced patronage networks and encouraged better accountability on the part of political leaders and civil service managers. The fact that the working class was mobilised and the criteria for redistribution to the poorest neighbourhoods based on social justice (Marquetti, de Campos and Pires 2008) meant that daily life in the outlying zones was transformed. The lower classes felt a sense of symbolic recognition as legitimate actors, their real weight in the decision-making process was considerably increased and the participatory budget enabled the creation of a 'plebeian public sphere' (Baierle 2006). The latter was also supported by the emergence of a new, partially institutionalised power, separate from the legislature, the executive and the judiciary.

The project faced a series of challenges, such as how to increase participation with regard to issues that go beyond short-term considerations, or the risk of progressive co-optation of civil society activists into the political system, or the danger that routine could replace an initially innovative dynamic. The institutional political system was only very partially transformed by the participatory experience, and the power struggles within the PT were no different from those in traditional organisations. Nevertheless, until the early 2000s, the experiment appeared to be a powerful process, and the government was re-elected three times, which is exceptional in Brazil. The participatory budget was recognised by such international institutions as the World Bank and the UN Habitat programme and was applauded by the Left both in Brazil and internationally. In January 2001, the first World Social Forum took place in Porto Alegre; it was to be followed by three others in subsequent years (2002, 2003 and 2005). The city became the capital of the alter-globalisation movement, and seemed to have assumed its leadership, as proclaimed in the slogan 'another world is possible'. Other left-wing Brazilian towns emulated the process sooner or later, and in 2002 Lula's successful election as president was based largely on the previous success story of these local governments. It appeared to be a well-deserved victory.

## The Porto Alegre Participatory Budget Following the Defeat of the Workers' Party

At the end of 2004, the Workers' Party went into the local elections without having developed any significant alliances with other parties, and was heavily defeated in Porto Alegre. Their management model had progressively run out of steam, and the modernisation of civil services that had started at the beginning of the 1990s appeared to have broken down. The town council's ability to take action was seriously reduced as the outcome of a serious financial crisis. This crisis was partly caused by the restrictions on the transfer of funds from the federal government, partly by the running costs incurred by the departments and infrastructure introduced in the 1990s (BIRD and BM 2008) and partly by the difficulties involved in planning a strategy for local economic development.

The multiplication of trends and in-fighting within the Workers' Party, the difficulty encountered in building political alliances, the defection of some of the leading officials to the federal government following Lula's victory in the presidential elections and the disappointment with the moderate political approach adopted by Lula felt by the more radical strands of the electorate constituted the final blow in a country where it is rare for any party to remain in office for four terms.

Throughout this period, participatory budgeting experienced difficulties. The people responsible for its implementation were unable to achieve any significant evolution of what they considered to be 'the' ultimate model, and didn't bother much to learn from other processes. Focusing on the investment budget led to a failure to take the real overheads resulting for the introduction of new services or the construction of infrastructure into account. This blind spot continued to aggravate the financial crisis that led to ever-greater delays in implementing the projects that had been accepted. This all caused the local authorities to renege on their initial objectives of transparency. The process of parties co-opting participatory budgeting delegates was introduced, while the number of participants in general assemblies at district level and thematic assemblies fell significantly, dropping from 17,200 in 2002 to 13,300 in 2004.[†]

---

*Note:* [†]This figure remains significant compared to institutional politics. By way of comparison, in 2008 fewer than 4,400 activists voted in the internal Workers' Party primaries to designate a party candidate for the post of mayor in local elections.

Nevertheless, the new team elected to the town hall, a heterogeneous coalition ranging from the centre-left to the hard-core right wing, committed itself during the election campaign to maintaining what people for the most part had come to consider an achievement of the Workers' Party government. As a result, most people involved considered that it was not participatory budgeting that had been discredited by the elections, but rather the Workers' Party (Fedozzi 2007).

Despite the uncertainties and the hesitancy of the new local authorities to make a political commitment, participatory budgeting continued after 2004, operating in more or less the same way. The profound change in political culture among the most active parts of the working class population of Porto Alegre appears obvious (Fedozzi 2007). Nevertheless the new team progressively restricted the field of investment affected by participatory budgeting and the rate of implementation for the projects selected dropped to an average of 18 per cent in 2005 and 2006 (Cidade 2007). Political in-fighting also began to seriously upset the internal workings of the participatory process. After slight progress in the first year, participation continued to drop, falling back to the 1997 level, while the modification of the internal regulations that authorise the re-election of members to the Participatory Budgeting Council led to serious restrictions on the renewal of members (this rate was 60–70 per cent in the 1990s, but only 35 per cent in 2006–2008).

Despite a real continuity in the formal device and in the numbers of participants (Fedozzi et al. 2013), a major threat to the process is the risk of formally continuing while voiding it of the initial content. The new local government intends to undermine the central role it plays and to include it in a broader process of 'local solidarity governance'. This approach, which is strongly influenced by the neo-corporatist and multi-stakeholder participation models (see Chapter 3), puts citizens on an equal footing with other actors, including companies, foundations, churches, NGOs, universities and para-public bodies. The introduction of this new project entails the risk that the objectives of reversing social priorities and of developing a plebeian public sphere may disappear. This is why the most incisive actors perceive this development as a 'conservative revolution', which threatens the very meaning of the model (Cidade 2005). Even if participatory budgeting remains an instrument of the working classes, it would be subordinate to other logics (for example, that of the market economy) and could play only a compensatory role. The future remains unsure. Are we witnessing a progressive petering out of the experiment that originally created the reputation of the process of participatory budgeting? Will we see the renewal of the original project in a new form? Or will a new model become permanently implemented under the auspices of the international institutions?

## 2. The Spread of Participatory Budgeting in Brazil and Latin America

Participatory democracy, social justice, improved management of public affairs: the programme seemed promising and encouraged emulation. Other towns in Brazil came first, with the participatory budget becoming the flagship of the Workers' Party and radical NGOs. The process was progressively legitimised and became widely recognised and mentioned in national legislation. During the 2001–2004 term of office, over 200 participatory budgets were implemented in Brazil; only half of these were in cities where the Workers' Party had been elected to the Town Hall and 43 per cent of the Brazilian population lived in cities where a participatory budget had been implemented. This proportion was higher in the largest towns (Marquetti 2005). In 2008, 9 of 14 cities of over one million inhabitants had implemented participatory budgeting (Avritzer and Wampler 2008). The movement spread progressively to the rest of Latin America (Cabannes 2006, Sintomer et al. 2012a, b).

Gradually, the Porto Alegre participatory budget became the model for a great many actors. Part of this success was due to the fact that it was not just an idea: the precise rules of implementation that had been tried, tested and improved over a period of time represented an 'institutional kit' that could be imported, adapted and modified to suit other contexts (similar to the way in which the American and French constitutions were disseminated throughout the nineteenth and twentieth centuries). There was plenty of interactive pedagogical material to support this dissemination, and in the space of one or two meetings, citizens, civil servants and activists could fairly easily get a grasp of how the system works in practice, as well as learn the ground rules (Cabannes 2004b). There were many opportunities for exchange at regional or continental level which enriched the attempts to improve, innovate or quite simply to adapt the system to local specificities. A process of 'hybridisation' was born, combining participatory budgeting with tools for participatory strategic planning, traditional forms of self-organisation of indigenous communities, forms of community development (supported by international cooperation in the poorest areas of the continent), gender mainstreaming as theme or with specific policies aimed at supporting rapidly developing minority groups, again under the influence of NGOs and international cooperation.

Given this exponential development, the socio-political logic that underpins the participatory budget institutions varies widely in Brazil, Latin America and the world, even if it is impossible to draw up a clear overview, as no systematic studies based on a reliable method are available. Certain divisions do come to light, however. One of these concerns the decision-making or purely consultative nature of the process. Another opposes those experiments based on participation of individuals, such as in Porto Alegre to those that favour organised group- or community-based participation. A third concerns the importance of the themes and resources discussed in the budget (which can vary from small sums to amounts that can determine the future of the entire community). A fourth opposes a bottom-up process to other approaches in which there is no such control. A fifth concerns the degree of formalisation and institutionalisation of the procedure (Cabannes 2005). Whether or not the participatory structure clearly has a concrete interface with the authorities is also important, as is the question of whether there are mechanisms aimed at encouraging the participation of those groups that tend to be excluded from the political system (blacks, indigenous people, women). Undoubtedly the most important division concerns whether or not there is grassroots mobilisation capable of feeding into the institutional process. In many places, the participatory budget is introduced top-down and has led to only a partial rapprochement with civil movements. This has enabled more efficient management of local affairs and greater awareness of the local population's needs, but has not led to the democratisation of political affairs (Avritzer 2002), let alone the creation of a plebeian public sphere.

Despite all these differences, the participatory budget is an instrument of the poor, almost everywhere, and they are more involved than either the middle or the upper classes. It encourages people with 'no voice' to speak up. It frequently has a genuine redistributive impact that is the outcome of the mobilisation of the working classes and the formal rules that encourage social justice and sharing of resources (Marquetti, de Campos and Pires 2008). The towns that have introduced the participatory budget manage to improve basic infrastructure – for example, introducing running water and sanitation – and also to fight poverty more efficiently, also when their results are compared to other local governments where the Workers' Party was in power but where a participatory budget was not introduced (BIRD and BM 2008). This participatory procedure sometimes helps to improve the material and symbolic conditions of minority groups. Almost unfailingly, at least when the process is the result of genuine political will and not mere lip service, it constitutes an instrument of good governance and helps to limit corruption, favouritism and waste. It encourages better control over public action and greater thoughtfulness about efficiency. At the political level, the outcomes are more varied, and there is no guarantee of the sustainability of the process at local level: many cases fall by the wayside when the initial team loses an election. These difficulties have not stopped exponential growth in the popularity of participatory budgeting in Latin America, however; its inclusion in the legislation of several countries has been a supporting factor.

## 3. What is Participatory Budgeting?

As of 2001, the year of the first World Social Forum, European actors used the term 'participatory budgeting' to categorise the experiments that they were conducting. There was a year on year increase, even if on a lesser scale than in Latin America. To summarise and evaluate these efforts, observers come up against an issue of definition: how to undertake rigorous research and avoid comparing what is not comparable? In general, participatory budgeting is a process that enables non-elected citizens to participate in the allocation of public money. In Europe, however, even more than in Latin America, participatory budgeting is based on many different procedures and, as we shall see, the influence of the Porto Alegre model is far less direct. This makes it difficult to provide a *purely empirical definition*, as it does not enable us to define the procedures that should be included in or excluded from the comparison; nor does it differentiate participatory budgeting from other participatory mechanisms, be they traditional or innovative. Certain processes that are called 'participatory budgeting' by their promoters would not be considered as such by others, and conversely, certain processes that do not lay claim to the name could without a doubt be considered as such in other circumstances. A *nominalist definition*, limited to recording categories of actors, is therefore impossible as soon as one moves beyond the framework of a single case or single country analysis. It would be possible to take a decision concerning the controversial meaning of 'participatory budgeting', but the present work aims first and foremost to analyse emerging trends in the development of local democracy in Europe rather than proposing an ideal model. In this context, *a normative definition* appears therefore to be unsuitable. An *objectivist or essentialist definition* aiming at a scientific definition of what really constitutes a participatory budgeting does not appear to be legitimate, either. The history of science shows us that ideas and categories used by people to understand the world around them are social constructions and this rule applies equally to researchers (Desrosières 2000).

The solution that we have adopted is based on the Weberian approach: we propose an essentially methodological definition of European participatory budgets. In the present work, processes that correspond to the criteria that we have developed will be called 'participatory budgeting' in order to carry out a rigorous and sufficiently homogenous comparison of what are otherwise very different experiments. Our definition needs to include the criteria necessary to carry out a targeted and coherent comparison and we shall limit ourselves to these criteria alone. The objective is heuristic: to achieve a sufficiently broad definition that will allow us to analyse a considerable number of processes (particularly those that claim to be participatory budgets), but at the same time to avoid experiments that could dilute the originality and relevance of this study. Armed with our own definition we shall be able to undertake a critical dialogue that is scientifically well-informed with the actors in the field.[1]

---

1 The definition provided here owes a lot to G. Allegretti and E. Ganuza.

Generally, a participatory budgeting is a process that enables non-elected citizens to take part in prioritising or allocating public funds. In studying European experiments, five additional criteria need to be taken into consideration.

1. Participatory budgeting deals with financial and/or budgetary issues.
2. The city level, or a (decentralised) district with an elected body and some power over administration, has to be involved.
3. It has to be a repeated process.
4. It must include some form of public deliberation within the framework of specific meetings/forums.
5. There needs to be some accountability on the output.

Three other aspects have to be taken into consideration in this discussion. First, certain processes may correspond more than others to our definition. Nor have we considered the size of the city to be a decisive factor in our defining criteria. Participatory budgeting can be implemented in territories of all sizes. Obviously a very different logic applies depending on whether we are talking about a town of several thousand inhabitants or one of hundreds of thousands, but this is not a factor that we shall be taking into consideration. As the definition of a state does not depend on number of population (there are states with few thousand people, whereas others are composed of millions, even billions), the definition of participatory budgeting does not depend on size of town. Finally, the criteria that we have selected refer first and foremost to the procedure that is implemented. They say little or nothing about the real dynamics of participatory budgeting or its social, political and administrative impacts. Concentrating on the procedural aspects will help us to highlight the characteristics and a certain homogeneity of the subject under consideration. The procedures and impacts of European experiments of participatory budgeting are, as we shall see, too variegated to be included in a general definition.

## 4. The Development of Participatory Budgeting in Europe

Armed with a coherent definition that enables us to establish a framework for the processes that we are going to compare, we can now start to measure the development of participatory budgeting on the Old Continent. The figures are impressive. In 1999 you could count the number of experiments on the fingers of one hand, and Europe seemed to be far behind Brazil. In 2002, there were over twenty cases. By 2005, 55 participatory budgets had been introduced and the movement was growing. In 2010, some projects had come to a halt, but subsequently regained dynamism. Overall, there were between 474 and 1317 projects in 2012 (Sintomer et al. 2013).

The diffusion of participatory budgeting has concerned many different kinds of town. Whereas there was only one local authority of 100,000 inhabitants involved in 1999, four had committed to this procedure by 2002 and 17 by 2005. (The largest of these was Seville, in Andalusia, with a population of 700,000.) That same year Paris, Berlin, Rome and London each had at least one district in which participatory budgeting had been introduced, and Lisbon set up a process in 2007. Two regions – Poitou-Charentes (France) and Latium (Italy) – have established a self-proclaimed process and counties in France have actively supported towns in their jurisdiction to implement participatory budgeting institutions. Many cities of fewer than 15,000 inhabitants have also introduced the process. And since 2014, Paris became, with more than two millions inhabitants, the largest city with participatory budgeting in Europe. All in all, there is great diversity between the municipalities in question.

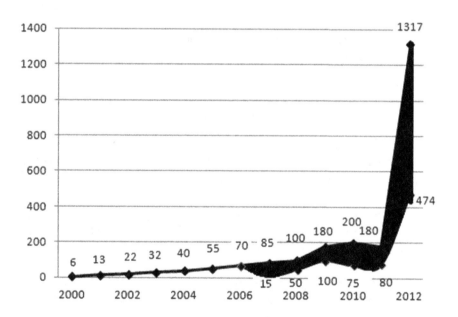

Figure 1.1 Number of participatory budgets 2000–2012
(minimal and maximal number)

Source: authors' elaboration

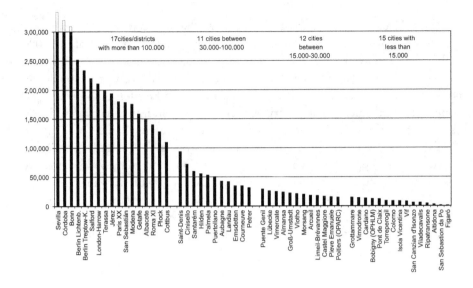

*Figure 1.2* Population of cities/districts with participatory
budgeting in Europe (2005)

*Source:* authors' elaboration

Far from being concentrated in one or two countries, the phenomenon has spread geographically. Originally, participatory budgeting started in Southern Europe and Germany. France, Italy and Spain were the most important countries until 2005. In 2012, Portugal (16–18 cases) surpassed France (5–10 cases). In Germany (70–93 cases), participatory budgeting has also increased in the 2010s; this is due to internet-based procedures. In Northern Europe, the United Kingdom (10–15 cases, with a much higher number of processes that local actors consider as participatory budgets) is another important participatory budgeting country. With the notable exception of Poland (324–1102 cases), there are only few participatory budgets in Eastern European countries. However, in Russia (10–14) participatory budgeting projects may spread in the future.

Existing procedures in Switzerland should also be taken into account, and although we have not taken them into consideration, some of them no doubt fall under the definition that we have provided (Feld and Kirchgässner 2001). In terms of the number of inhabitants concerned, Spain was the clear leader before 2011, as participatory budgets had been implemented in major cities there. In 2005, over two million inhabitants were involved, as opposed to barely a million in Germany and about 500,000 in France and in Italy. In the latter two countries participatory budgeting has firstly been introduced mainly in small or medium-sized cities, before to gain regions.

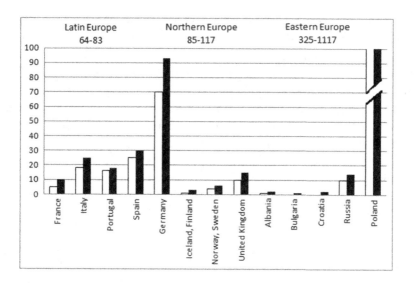

*Figure 1.3* Participatory budgets per country (minimal and maximal number) in 2012

*Source:* authors' elaboration

These data allow us to view the importance of the phenomenon in its true context. Although there was exponential growth, only about two hundred local authorities were involved in 2009 out of tens of thousands in the European Union. Even in Spain, where participatory budgeting had developed most extensively before 2010, the towns where the process has been introduced only accounted for about 5 per cent of the overall population in 2005 – which is not a huge figure in comparison to Brazil, even if it is far more than in other European countries, where only 1 or 2 per cent of the population was involved in 2009. One exception may be Poland's rural districts, which are now legally obliged to implement participatory budgeting.

At first sight and on a purely quantitative basis, it is difficult to grasp the parameters that might provide a clear profile for the cities in question. We have already seen that size is not a factor. Nor are history or geographical situation: some places have a history going back several centuries, whereas others were built in modern times; and there are central cities and national capitals, but also suburban towns.

Socio-economic situation is not a decisive factor that they share, either: on the Old Continent as a whole, the phenomenon is not specific to flourishing cities or, on the contrary, to towns whose financial situation is particularly difficult: some of the local authorities we analysed were highly indebted, others well-off. While some cities have large populations of immigrants (approximately 25 per cent of the inhabitants of Bobigny, Bradford or Saint Denis are foreigners), other towns are more homogeneous in terms of ethnic origin, as is the case with most Spanish and German municipalities.

This very varied panorama is representative of European local government in general, and provides us with a picture of its extraordinary diversity. At the socio-economic level, the differences between towns are essentially local in nature and only partially related to the national context. Significant variations exist in certain countries, but also within states and even within the same city. There is not, however, a general trend in Europe specifically fostering the emergence of participatory budgeting, for example, when the situation is difficult (by 'scraping the bottom of the barrel' on a consensus basis) or, conversely, when the situation is comfortable (and there is 'a cake that can be shared out').

Although the degree of legitimacy of the political system appears highly variable from one place to another (the rate of participation in municipal elections varies between 32 per cent in Płock and over 70 per cent in Italian municipalities, while Saint-Denis and Bobigny score a little under 50 per cent), the political profile of a given town does appear to be a decisive explanatory factor. In 2005, the overwhelming majority of European cities with participatory budgeting were left-wing: one out of every two mayors was a Social Democrat, a little over one-third were communist or members of the alternative left and barely 7 per cent of the projects were led by liberal right or conservative mayors.

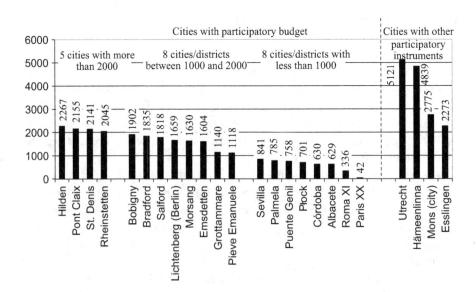

Figure 1.4 Municipal budget per citizen in selected cities/districts around 2005 (euros)

Source: authors' elaboration

Total municipal debt in relation to total municipal budget in selected cities/districts

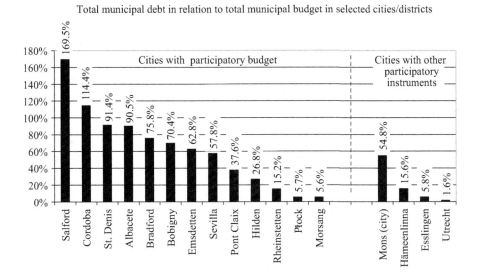

*Figure 1.5* Municipal debts/municipal budgets around 2005
*Source*: authors' elaboration

When we take coalitions into consideration, the weight of communists and the alternative left is reinforced, because they were often responsible for initiating participatory budgeting in left-wing authorities. If these figures are compared with the number of cities that were under the two leading movements of the left, the relative importance of the communists and the alternative left is even stronger. The Greens played only a marginal role in this development even when they are minority members of coalitions. Initially, they brought their influence to bear on these questions only in Catalonia (where they developed an alliance with the ex-Communists), as well as in Italy. It was only from 2007 in Germany that they really started to have an impact.

The overall domination of the left has tended to lessen over time, and towns governed by conservative parties are now progressively providing an increasing share. Of course, differences can be discerned from one country to another. In the case of France and Portugal, the communists initially represented the driving force, while in Spain or in Italy – where the deputy who introduces the project was often communist, with a social democratic mayor giving his or her stamp of approval – their weight was essentially equivalent to that of the socialists or Social Democrats. Germany and, to a lesser extent, the UK and Poland represent a very different trend, as participatory budgeting there is driven equally by the left and the right, and this variable does not appear as a

25

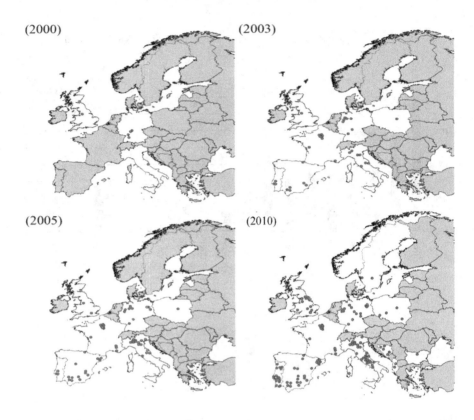

(2000)    (2003)

(2005)    (2010)

*Figure 1.6* Maps 1–4. The geographical distribution of
participatory budgets during the 2000s

*Source*: authors' elaboration

relevant factor in explaining the existence of the process. Nevertheless, in the
countries that entered the game at a later date, such as Sweden, Albania and the
former Yugoslavian states, it is the right that is in the majority.

All in all, it is not the socio-economic profile or size of the town, the urban
context or the degree of legitimacy of the political system that would initially
appear to be most propitious for the development of participatory budgeting,
but rather the embedding in the left, and even more so the presence of a
coalition that includes communists or alternative left. This is hardly surprising,
given the origins of the process, invented in a city with a radical left-wing
government and the impact of the first Brazilian experiments on the alter-
globalist movement. This still leaves the political factor unexplained, however,
partly because the attitude of the left to participatory approaches is far from
uniform, and many currents – from the most moderate to the most radical –
have a distinctly paternalistic orientation. Why then have an increasing number

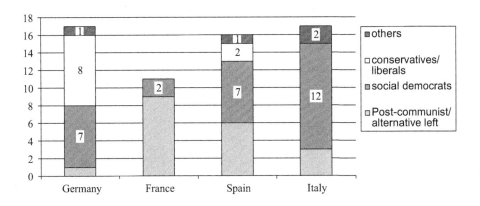

*Figure 1.7* Political affiliation of mayors in cities with
participatory budgeting (1998–2005)

*Source:* authors' elaboration

of left-wing towns in Europe become so interested in a practice imported from
the South, which is in itself a most unusual occurrence? Why did the process
catch on quickly in Spain and in Italy, to a lesser extent in France, Germany or in
the United Kingdom, but was slow to do so in the Scandinavian countries, which
are bastions of the traditional European left?[2] It is not easy to understand what
specifically characterises the cities that have become involved in the process of
participatory budgeting, while others, often geographically or politically close
to them, have not followed suit. In order to understand the exponential growth
of participatory budgeting in Europe, as well as its current limits, we need to
broaden the picture and analyse what other factors might help to explain the
converging phenomena of several dozen towns on the Old Continent, and also
follow up on how this instrument has been disseminated.

---

2 Although the participatory budget is increasingly under discussion in Norway,
Finland and even more so in Sweden, where several towns committed to introducing
the process in 2008, there is a five- to ten-year gap with the Mediterranean countries of
Southern Europe.

# 2

# EUROPEAN CONVERGENCE?

One explanation for the increasing popularity of participatory budgeting can be found by analysing the structural or functional changes that, at a macro-sociological level, could favour its emergence. We have already seen that the explanation cannot be based on general socioeconomic factors. Should we therefore look at institutional factors, such as the construction of the European Union, which would encourage an overall convergence between local European democratic systems and, in particular, the development of a participatory trend?

## 1. Low Levels of Convergence between Local Political Systems

At first sight, this explanation appears to offer only very partial support to our analysis. This can be demonstrated by a counter-example: the UK was (at least under the previous Labour governments) the country where national legislation most encourages citizen participation in public policy. However, over the past two decades regulatory and legislative developments in this area had generally been used by national governments to restrict the powers of local councils, which were already relatively weak (Wilson and Game 2002). This is in sharp contrast to the situation in Finland, where the spread of participatory procedures is part of a widespread movement to consolidate an already significant local autonomy (Kettunen 2003). In France, local democracy has also been institutionalised following a series of decentralisation laws. We should therefore be careful not to put too much emphasis on European convergence, according to which decentralisation and participation are developing hand in hand.

The first point to be made is that European local authorities differ greatly and this heterogeneity can be clearly observed in scientific analyses. It is extremely difficult to find reliable comparative data on municipalities in Europe. Figures from budgets managed by local authorities generally refer to heterogeneous institutions and comparative works are either limited to two or three countries, or merely juxtapose independent monographical national studies.

Countries vary greatly with regard to the average sizes of their municipalities. Some, such as the UK, have few municipalities (less than 500) with large populations (an average of 130,000), whereas others, such as France, have an enormous number of communes (over 35,000) that are often very small (an average of 1,700 inhabitants). Between these two extremes are intermediate cases, such as Spain, Italy and Germany (each with between 8,000 and 12,500 municipalities). In many Western European countries, the number of municipalities began to be dramatically reduced in the 1960s in a nationally imposed consolidation process. Germany, for example, went from 24,000 to 12,500 and Belgium from over 2,600 to less than 600. The goal was to produce economies of scale and improve the functional effectiveness of local public sector action by targeting larger geographical areas.

In addition, the competences of European local authorities also vary greatly and they have very different amounts of power. Here, the real issue is less the importance of their resources, particularly fiscal, than the financial amounts that local authorities are free to spend without their use and the range of powers they can exercise being ring-fenced by the central state. Analytically and institutionally a distinction can be made between cases in which municipalities have no autonomy – often the case in dictatorships, such as most Eastern European countries before the fall of the Berlin Wall, Spain under Franco and Portugal under Salazar; those where municipalities have little autonomy (France before 1982, the United Kingdom during and after Margaret Thatcher); those that have greater scope for action but where intermediate levels of power between local authorities and the central state produce competence-sharing with regard to local matters or even place local municipalities under the authority of regional authorities (traditionally the case in Germany, but also a feature in Italy, Spain, Belgium and, to a lesser extent, France and Poland); and finally those where local authorities have significant autonomy and comprise the only local level of government with significant power (the Nordic countries and the Netherlands). The situation is further complicated by the fact that political autonomy and functional power (which enables local governments to act effectively) do not always go hand in hand. English local authorities, for example, are both politically and functionally weak. This results from the competition produced by the multitude of bodies that only partially depend – or not at all – on their authority and have competences in specific areas. Swedish and German municipalities, on the other hand, have significant political power and the functional means to exercise it, while the French intermediary-based model comprises politically powerful communes with little functional power (Wollmann 2007).

The European Union has imposed a minimum level of convergence, as set out in the European Charter on Local Self-Government of 15 October 1985. As a result, situations characterised by a complete absence of self-government disappeared from the continent with the transitions to democracy of Southern and Eastern Europe. Furthermore, while no predominant model has emerged, there has been an almost generalised movement towards decentralisation, to the benefit of local authorities. Only Great Britain under Margaret Thatcher, and to a lesser extent Italy under Silvio Berlusconi, have demonstrated a tendency to recentralise at the expense of municipalities. There is also enormous variety in the internal political organisation of local authorities. At one extreme are purely 'monistic' systems, where there is no independent executive political power and the head of the administration is a management figure subordinate to the local parliament (the Nordic model and, to a lesser extent, the traditional model in Great Britain, where the mayor, rather than running the government administration, simply chairs the local council as a kind of *primus inter pares*). At the opposite extreme are purely 'dual' systems where, based on a presidential model, the mayor and municipal councillors are elected separately. Here local executive power is in the hands of the mayor and is entirely separate from local legislative power (this model is rarely found in Europe but is dominant in North and South America).

Between these two extremes are various intermediate models. In some cases, the mayor is appointed by the local council and not directly elected by the people, but holds actual executive power. This system was traditionally widespread in continental Western Europe and is still the model in France, Spain, Belgium, the Netherlands and the Czech Republic. In other cases the mayor is directly elected by local citizens and not by the local council and therefore has a distinct form of legitimacy and his own executive power. However, this 'dualism' is tempered by the fact that the municipal executive branch includes deputies who are appointed by – and responsible to – the local council. This model was extended across the whole of Germany, is predominant in Eastern Europe and is also similar to the situation in Italy in that, while the directly elected mayor appoints the executive, he or she can be dismissed by a vote of no confidence in the Municipal Assembly. The panorama is further complicated by the fact that the actual powers of the executive are often greatly superior to those expressly laid down in the law.

Recent years have been characterised by a strong trend towards strengthening the power of mayors and, to a lesser extent, pressing for their direct election by local citizens (Bäck, Heinelt and Magnier 2006). Most Eastern European countries, Germany and Italy have thus moved towards models that are more or less 'dualist', with the possibility now also locally available in the United Kingdom. While other countries have not modified their systems, it is striking that there is no movement in the opposite direction: that is, towards parliamentary-style municipal systems that would reduce the powers of the mayor. With a certain time lag, local authorities are therefore following a strong trend in Western democracies, which have tended to strengthen the power of the executive over the legislative branch, producing an increasing personalisation of power.

Finally, different political cultures make matters even more complex. In all European countries in which participatory budgeting has been implemented the left/right divide remains an important factor, even though often interspersed with divisions based on the national situation. Nevertheless, the meaning of the notions 'right' and 'left' is subject to heated debates and these alignments are often a smaller part of people's identities than in the past. In addition, electoral systems and political traditions have a significant influence on local dynamics, where the predominant way of thinking may be consensual (Finland, Belgium); highly divergent (Poland); favouring wide coalitions that transcend the right/left divide; case-by-case coalitions (Germany); alternating coalitions from the left or right of the political spectrum (France, Italy, partially Spain); or finally, systems that are essentially two-party (Great Britain until 2010).

## 2. Crisis of Legitimacy and Changes in Representative Democracy

The institutional panorama of local political systems is therefore extremely varied. Much as on the socioeconomic level, this diversity is predominant and, without taking a closer look at developments, it appears difficult to isolate one factor that would clearly lead to the emergence of participatory budgeting.

Nevertheless, in addition to this institutional diversity there is certainly at least some convergence between the various dynamics that underlie political systems. On the one hand, representative democracy has become entrenched as a constitutive framework. On the other hand, European political systems face an increasing legitimacy deficit, which is more or less marked depending on the country (Tocal and Montero 2006). In many local areas, or even entire countries, it is not rare to find only one-third of the adult population participating in local elections. Due to an increasing lack of confidence in them, politicians now frequently come near the bottom of popularity lists. In the United Kingdom and France, the number of political party activists has decreased by half over the past two or three decades and this is by no means exceptional. This disengagement is particularly marked among the working classes, who are more likely to abstain or register a protest vote. Their likelihood of belonging to an organisation is diminishing. Mass political parties and trade unions have been dramatically affected, although to varying degrees depending on the country. This is clearly an issue in all countries where participatory budgeting has emerged, however. The category 'working class' seems to be increasingly losing impact in terms of collective mobilisation. It produces less and less of a feeling of belonging, but without being replaced by other encompassing categories, leaving highly fertile ground for populist authoritarian tendencies and xenophobic trends.

Bernard Manin (1997) has clearly demonstrated how party-based democracy is a variation on representative government. To provide it with a proper definition and distinguish it from other types, such as direct democracy, Manin proposes four criteria: (i) the election of governments at regular intervals; (ii) the independence of those elected in the decision-making process vis-à-vis their electorate, balanced by (iii) the independence of public opinion vis-à-vis the government; and, finally, (iv) the subjection of decision-making to public debate. Seen in this way, representative government is very different from 'pure democracy' in which citizens can exercise real power. We can agree with Bernard Manin when he says, together with the founding fathers of the French and North American Republics of the late eighteenth century, that modern representative government is a mixed regime: aristocratic, because it gives real power to an elite that is different to, and largely independent of, the people; and democratic, because this elite is elected (and re-elected, as the case may be), its power is, in principle, subject to the laws it issues (the rule of law), those governed are free to hold opinions that are contrary to those of the government and the government is obliged to justify its decisions in public. Historically, this has produced three major types of representative government. The first, which was established during – and outlasted – the time of tax-based suffrage, was based on the domination of important persons (*'notables'*) and the central role of parliament in political life. The second was linked to mass-membership parties, which drew their strength from the inclusion of the working classes in the representative system and concentrated the substance of decision-making power.

The third model – 'audience democracy' or 'opinion-based democracy'[1] – is what is emerging today. This new form of representative government is characterised by the central role played by the media in political life. Under the influence of communication consultants and polling agencies, politicians are induced to move away from the traditional political stage and toward other platforms: television, for example, has more of an impact than party conferences. People are thus partially freed from the supervision of political systems and are 'free' to vote for candidates who are not put forward by traditional parties, thereby putting their fate in the hands of new kinds of governing figures: media moguls, star journalists, communication specialists, pollsters and so on, as well as those politicians who have worked out how to take advantage of the new rules of the game. The trend is away from a situation of bureaucratic domination over the system and towards media domination, which relies more on charismatic qualities.

Discussion of the crisis of democracy is as old as democracy itself. Is it therefore possible to see the current period as one in which audience or opinion-based democracy is dominant? Should different or contrasting evidence not also be looked at? With European integration and the increasing interdependence of geographical areas – of which globalisation is but one dimension – it is in fact the role of political representation as a whole that seems to be called into question. There is an increasing belief that we are seeing

---

1 It partly resembles to the 'post-democracy' analysed by Colin Crouch (2004).

a shift from government to governance (Scharpf 1999). Emphasising this term implies seeing audience democracy as the visible side of a development that includes an increase in decision-making methods that are independent of the representative regime, in that they are not based on elections. This development is contributing a reduction in the credibility of traditional forms of political representation, whose scope for objective action appears to be increasingly restricted – while non-political, particularly business-related, pressure groups have always unofficially influenced public decision-making through lobbying. The multiplication of non-elected legal or expert structures and the proliferation of autonomous inter-administrative agencies or committees that are, to a greater or lesser extent, free from democratic control (the most recent example being three American rating agencies that influence the fate of entire states) produces a perception of a democratic deficit among the population. In this situation, a mere roll-back to the old situation would not satisfy the demands of the population for more participation. An alternative would be to implement new procedures, which involve the population in decision-making. The current situation is increasingly contested, which is why it is becoming more and more difficult to keep ordinary citizens outside the decision-making process. At a transnational level, the Council of Europe has played a pioneering role, becoming aware very early on that this new situation required the increasing involvement of social movements in decision-making. The European Union was slower in picking up on this development, but most international bodies now extol the qualities of 'participatory governance' and this seems to provide an entry point through which civil society actors could become more involved.

While social movements have always been important in European democracies, nowadays they are less likely to be affiliated to party groupings and can act more independently. In addition, many social movements have, during the past two or three decades, developed more horizontal and consultation-based forms of organising and mobilising. These forms are difficult to interpret when looked at within the framework of representative government, as this is based on vertical power relationships. Part of the success of the alter-globalisation movements of the early 2000s is, in fact, that they reflect the relative independence of associative forms of civil society vis-à-vis the institutional political system (Della Porta 2007) and the increasing power of new forms of organisation and coordination. This is demonstrated by the 'forum form'; it aims, in a consensual manner, to enable debate that includes a right of reply and to boost the establishment of networks, while refuting the representative logic according to which individuals speak in the name of others to announce a programme, launch a rallying cry or decide upon a course of action. At the same time, it offers opportunities for individuals to coordinate their actions: the most high profile example of this was the demonstration of the Arab Spring in 2011. Coordinated by social media networks, young people organised the occupation of Tahir Square in Egypt's capital. Even though this event took place outside EU borders, it has massively influenced the organisation of protest in Europe (and beyond). For example, social media has played a central role in the Occupy movement that took off in November 2011.

Institutional participation is an area that is potentially removed from audience democracy and it is making a space at the crossroads between technocratic governance structures and the actions of social movements. The multiplication of institutionalised participatory mechanisms demonstrates the extent to which this area has developed over the past couple of decades. A significant ideological change is taking place, which entails acknowledging the value of discussion, debate, consultation and participation. This is producing a 'new spirit' of modern public action, similar to Luc Boltanski and Eve Chiapello's (2005) 'new spirit of capitalism', which has been developing over the past twenty years. While the contrast between rhetorical ambition and modest implementation is often striking, this normative change in public action and its link to policy-making must be taken seriously (Blondiaux and Sintomer 2002).

The development of anti-authoritarian orientations within social movements and of institutionalised participatory mechanisms is stimulating a fresh look at the history of modern democracies. Democracy's 'participatory trend' (Sintomer 2011a) is not merely a criticism of representatives' common propensity to dispossess those they represent of the power with which they have been entrusted. Rather, it rests on a different ideal; that of a radical democracy in which citizens have a real capacity to govern, where the government's independence is minimised and in which spaces for collective autonomy are maximised. Nevertheless, it would be taking things too far to say that this participatory trend is now being renewed through the development of European participatory budgets. Following the defining moment that was Porto Alegre, are we really seeing the start of a wave of democratisation, or should the opposite be inferred: should this trend be seen as a secondary or marginal dimension of a form of governance that is dominated by commercial actors, or even an aspect of the increasing spread of audience democracy?

## 3. Local Governance and Participation

We cannot really answer these questions without carrying out a detailed assessment of current experiments. One observation, however, stands out with regard to neoliberal globalisation. According to several members of the radical left, participatory budgeting has emerged as a reaction against neoliberalism, and indeed demonstrates that 'another world is possible'. It is true that globalisation affects the context in which participatory budgeting takes place. Everyone is aware of its effects, from privatisation to the increasing affirmation of commercial rationales and financial capitalism. Nevertheless, globalisation takes different shapes in different geographical areas. There would seem to be no immediate correlation between the unequal spread of participatory budgeting in Europe and the strength of the impact of globalisation. Very globalised towns are not necessarily those that develop participatory budgeting, and vice versa. If there is a correlation, it is no doubt more related to the impact of criticisms of neoliberal globalisation. This is a point we will come back to, but this explanation is based on contingent actors' strategies rather than a macroeconomic structure.

An important part of the explanation is related to the way in which the development of participatory approaches is linked to changes in local governments. A structural factor does, in fact, seem to have a direct impact on the development of participatory mechanisms: at the level of public administration, there is significant convergence between countries, despite their different points of departure. Everywhere, traditional public administration is being questioned and put on the defensive. A wide-ranging reform movement is taking place, inspired by company management structures. On the one hand, it implies the increasing use of commercial mechanisms, such as the introduction of profitability as a criterion, the sub-contracting of certain tasks, competition between private and public service providers, the constitution of publicly-owned companies with private legal status and the multiplication of public–private partnerships and privatisations. Here the influence of neoliberal globalisation is obvious. Another area of reform is related to internal administrative modernisation. This is characterised by a reduction in the levels of hierarchy, changes in budget accounting methods, with more importance being given to analytic accounting and product- or objective-based budgeting, cross-cutting dimensions and transversal cooperation between administrations, and new ways of managing staff, with increasing personalisation of careers. This double trend – theorised as New Public Management – can be observed almost everywhere (Wollmann and Marcou 2010, Bouckaert and Pollit 2004). At the same time, in very different contexts, interaction with citizens increasingly appears essential for public action and citizen-users' participation is expected to contribute to management effectiveness. Theories on this issue are proliferating, with a vast array of mechanisms aimed at putting them into practice: user feedback mechanisms, quality charters, guidelines to involve users in the management of some facilities, the delegation of public services that can even include community development (complete transfer of assets), meetings enabling face-to-face discussion between officials, politicians and residents, the use of new tools such as the Internet, and so on. By turning towards citizens and making use of their contributions, administrative modernisation should be both more effective in terms of services provided and more responsive, due to the external pressure exercised by civil society (Bacqué, Rey and Sintomer

2005). This trend is present in certain New Public Management theories, such as the Third Way of administrative modernisation, together with tendencies to turn towards the market and internal reform (Reichard 2001).

It can therefore be seen that there is some European-level convergence with regard to administrative reform, and participation is one of its dimensions. It would be impossible to understand participatory budgeting properly without this context. In addition, an overarching assessment of the development of local governments in Europe over the past two or three decades brings several salient trends to the fore. Local authorities have been the object of wide-ranging reform (Reynaert 2005). The former members of the Warsaw Pact have been particularly affected by this and the question of whether or not there is convergence at European level produces a very different answer depending on which side of the East/West divide is under discussion (Wollmann 2007).

An internal comparison within Western Europe produces a very diverse scenario. There are five general trends, with rhythms and states of development that vary greatly between countries: maintenance of the diversity of institutional models; increasing prevalence of market-based rationales (while several countries or local authorities are resisting this trend, the increasing pressure to produce a return on public sector activities is extremely strong at the local level); internal managerial reforms of the administration; increasing mayoral powers (with the exception of the Nordic states and, in part, England); and the development of participatory instruments. An internal comparison within Eastern Europe shows that convergence here is far more marked, in terms of both the institutional model and the rhythm of political-administrative reform. Finally, a comparison between Western and Eastern Europe also shows significant convergence, with the new European Union member states generally moving towards the Western European model (or rather, models).

At this stage it is difficult to see to what extent the development of participatory approaches in general – and participatory budgeting in particular – is linked (or not) to other trends in local government reform. Four questions emerge, however.

i. A definite affinity is emerging between administrative modernisation and participation with regard to procedural legitimacy. Can participatory budgeting therefore be reduced to a simple management and governance tool and does it lack a political dimension (for example, the 'democratisation of democracy')?

ii. Does participation develop better where the political executive and local council are one; in dual systems where the municipal executive and municipal assembly are two separate bodies; or in mixed systems? In Europe, the Scandinavian countries long had no experience of participatory budgeting but things began to change fairly rapidly in

Sweden, starting in 2007. Participatory budgeting also developed in the UK, where local councils are institutionally very powerful in comparison to local executives. By contrast, Latin America demonstrates that participatory budgeting is at least compatible with 'dual' systems. There is therefore nothing to suggest that either of these situations is more conducive to participatory budgeting.

iii. Is there a logical link between decentralisation and participation? While the two movements would appear to go together, there are, as previously pointed out, counter-examples (for example, the United Kingdom) and decentralisation can also produce a plethora of small local despots.

iv. In Europe, like elsewhere, participatory mechanisms are most often promoted by the executive and are sometimes frowned upon by the legislative branch. In addition, de facto concurrence can often be observed between reinforcing the legitimacy and powers of the mayor and the implementation of participatory mechanisms. At a national level, participatory democracy is seen as following the same logic as appointing election candidates through primaries (whether internal to parties or open to supporters) rather than through the political apparatus, as both developments produce a reduction in the power of party machines and the legislative branch. Does this lead to a fundamental convergence, with audience democracy enabling charismatic leaders to communicate directly with the electorate? Or, in contrast, do electing a mayor through universal suffrage and, more generally, the increased personalisation of power imply a domination of personal charisma that is the antithesis of genuine participatory democracy, thereby reducing the delegation of power?

## 4. Connected Histories

Generally speaking, it seems that the wave of European participatory budgeting should be seen as the meeting point between the democratisation of local democracy and the modernisation of local administrations, but the links between the two sides of the equation are as yet far from clear. It is difficult to isolate sufficient numbers of unequivocal structural factors that convincingly explain this simultaneous development that has taken place in very varied sociopolitical contexts. This is why certain interactionist perspectives suggest that participatory budgeting in fact results from the largely coincidental convergence of a series of events, each of which is unique. However, this explanation seems unsatisfactory from a comparative perspective: while it is true that no experience is identical, it is striking that some ingredients (discourses, processes, power relations and so on) can be found in many examples. More interesting is the theory that this is a historical movement spread through transfers, loans and exchanges, with analysis essentially required to trace its genealogy.

European participatory budgets clearly took off after 2001. Previously, their number could be counted on the fingers of one hand and there were few new processes taking place. Since 2001 their development has been rapid and constant. However, the year 2001 did not mark a significant shift in the macro-social context and trends. It was a political event, the organisation of the World Social Forum, that suddenly projected the idea of participatory budgeting into Europe, rather than a structural break with the past. Prior to the end of the millennium, there was very little interest in the Brazilian experience on the Old Continent. With the emergence of the alter-globalisation movement, it took just four or five years for the capital of Rio Grande do Sul to become a symbol of change. Now, many activists and politicians have travelled there, or organised visits to Europe for Porto Alegre's leaders. These actions are yet more effective because, as in Latin America, participatory budgeting is presented as a procedural toolkit as well as a political ideal. The book by Tarso Genro (2001), elected mayor of the town for the second time in 2000, articles written by activists and, a little later, scientific or semi-scientific articles or books all contributed to this diffusion process.

Five kinds of actors contributed to the spread of participatory budgeting in Europe. Left-wing political parties played the initial role, through the municipalities that they controlled. Communist and post-communist organisations faced an urgent need to renew their programme and practices following the collapse of the Soviet model, and needed to distance themselves from bureaucratic management methods. As part of this, interest in the procedure used by Porto Alegre was initially carried by a handful of more open activists, then later became part of a general policy of left-wing parties, particularly in Italy and Spain and, in a weaker sense, also in Germany. The social democratic left has been more partially affected: it is mainly certain individuals within the party that are in favour of participatory budgeting, the most prominent being Hazel Blears in the UK, Elio Di Rupo in Wallonia and Ségolène Royal in France. At local level, activists that are most open to alter-globalisation-related themes were often those that are also interested in the procedure invented in Porto Alegre. As already stated, European green parties and the far left have played a marginal role, unlike sister organisations in Brazil to which several mayors that run towns in which participatory budgeting takes place belong. Finally and logically enough, no European party from the (far) right of the political spectrum has taken this procedure on board: only a few liberal and conservative party activists are interested in these ideas.

Social movements and activist associations are a second type of actor, but due to several factors they have had less of an impact in Europe than political parties. The most obvious point is that implementing participatory budgeting requires a decision from local authorities. In addition, political parties have played a more important role in the alter-globalisation movement in Europe than they have in Latin America. This is particularly the case in Italy and France, the countries that hosted the first two European Social Forums. Finally, a significant minority of activist associations involved in the alter-globalisation movement have an anti-institutional perspective that makes them distrust any management mechanisms, whether participatory or otherwise. The way in which the activist left is capable of linking up with the institutional left varies from country to country. Where there is more positive interaction, there is generally a positive effect on participatory budgeting. It is only in fairly exceptional cases, such as Albacete in Spain, that associations were, right from the start, as important in the process as politicians.

As already highlighted, other actors outside the local context – such as international organisations and experts – did not initially play the role in Europe that they had played in Latin America. Nevertheless, the World Bank is more and more active in Eastern Europe and it was World Bank initiatives that led to participatory budgeting being introduced in Albania and some states of the former Yugoslavia. Here it is even believed that this process could be applied at the national level. In Germany, it was foundations that played a major role, and the emergence and development of participatory budgeting could not be understood without reference to their influence. NGO activities were particularly effective in the United Kingdom: one of them, the Community Pride Initiative (it later became the PB Unit and then the PB Network), which is closely linked to the community-based movement, carried out intensive lobbying on the issue based on its interest in the Porto Alegre experiment. It received the support of Oxfam (also one of the main supporters of the World Social Forum) and, through close cooperation with certain key individuals working for the previous national government, has been involved in the set-up of a national network on the subject. In the same way the Portuguese NGO In-Loco organised workshops and provided expertise on participatory budgeting and contributed significantly – in cooperation with the *Centro Estudos Sociais* of the University of Coimbra – to the dissemination of new examples in Portugal.

The role of international bodies is much less relevant in Europe than in Latin America. Initially, the United Nations, the World Bank, the European Bank for Reconstruction and Development (BERD) and the Organisation for Economic Cooperation and Development (OECD) played only minor roles. Direct action by the European Union is non-existent, although the call for URB-AL projects that it launched to boost horizontal cooperation between European and South American local governments produced a Porto Alegre-led group in 2003 on the theme 'Local finances and participatory budgeting'. In Europe, this network principally comprises Spanish and Italian municipalities and contributes to legitimising participatory budgeting, mainly by playing a supporting role. The impact of national networks of towns that have decided to innovate in the field of municipal management, such as *Nuovo Municipio* in Italy and 'Municipalities of the future' in Germany, are direct and more fundamental. We will be looking at them in more detail in the second part. In addition, some regions have played an active role by fostering the establishment of communal experiments.

Finally, we should be careful not to underestimate the emergence of a group of participation professionals, made up of local government employees who are expert in new techniques (which are beginning to be part of their training), as well as trainers and coordinators who specialise in this rapidly expanding area and who work in research departments and specialised NGOs. Activist research has also made a major contribution by providing knowledge, analysis and expertise, and contributing to the implementation of mechanisms in a more specific manner through action research-based approaches. The rapid and extensive internationalisation of networks of researchers working on the issue has enabled them to exercise their social responsibility by having a strong influence on the course of events, particularly in Italy, Spain, Portugal and the United Kingdom.

## 5. A Paradox

Historians have underlined the importance of connecting national histories in order to produce a global view without sacrificing the analysis of micro-interactions (Subrahmanyam 1997, 2011). In the French-German program of the *histoire croisée* (intertwined history), one major idea of which is to link structural comparison and transfer studies, has been providing an original path for comparative research (Werner and Zimmermann 2004). Just as our brief overview indicates, each participatory experience implies a coinciding set of specific factors and events that make it a kind of 'miracle' requiring analysis. Nevertheless, the reason why actors who are committed to this path are so often successful, in such a variety of different contexts, also requires explanation. Why have these 'miracles' mushroomed? Without overlooking the chance factor, it is necessary to provide explanations that go further than the history of transfers or the juxtaposition of local contexts. Structural or macro-sociological aspects – such as administrative modernisation, the rise of neoliberal ways of thinking, the political system's crisis of legitimacy and local government reforms – have already been brought up.

A further point needs mentioning, because it becomes obvious in a general overview of the situation: European and Latin American participatory budgeting have very different social characteristics. This would seem to point against the relationship with the alter-globalisation movement mentioned above. In fact, the people who participate in these processes in Europe are, in the vast majority of cases studied (twelve processes out of eighteen), middle- and upper working-class. In a minority of cases (five out of eighteen), participatory budgeting involves mainly the middle classes. In just a few cases (two out of eighteen), it involves mainly the working class.[2] In Europe, participatory budgeting perhaps has a slightly more lower class make-up than the majority of participatory mechanisms, but it is the middle and upper working classes who set the tone. The lower working class, who has largely switched off from institutional political action, is barely involved in participatory structures. This is also true for other subaltern groups. In the majority of processes, young people, those on the margins of society and immigrants barely participate more than they do in the conventional system and it is only in a small minority of cases that tailored voluntarist policies have been able to change the situation. In terms of sociological representation, participatory approaches suffer the same imbalances as representative democracy, although less markedly.[3]

This objection is strengthened by the fact that European participatory budgets are much less frequently the product of grassroots mobilisation than their Latin American counterparts. In the vast majority of cases analysed (sixteen out of nineteen),[4] it was a top-down process with very weak grassroots mobilisation. Cases in which participatory budgeting is the product of simultaneous top-down and bottom-up dynamics (three experiments out of nineteen) are much rarer than in Latin America and cases in which the process is established following grassroots mobilisation are practically non-existent. While there is widespread demand for participation in European societies, this demand is not characterised by wide-ranging movements that have latched on to the idea of participatory budgeting.

To sum up, this overview of European participatory budgeting has shown us that, in this area as in others, the path to innovation is a long and tortuous one: the mechanism invented in Porto Alegre spread mainly through the alter-globalisation movement, at least in the first decade, but has not triggered widespread social mobilisation and does not enjoy significant grassroots support. It is too early to say whether this will produce a contradiction between a transfer process that is mainly conveyed through the alter-globalisation left and a structural context that is unfavourable to the reproduction of the Brazilian socio-political dynamic. However, this paradox and uncertainty lead us

---

2 These numbers, as well as those in the next paragraph, refer to the years around 2005, when the empirical research for this project was carried out.

3 Even women, whose participation is generally far greater than their presence in institutional politics, hit a 'glass ceiling' when they reach the summit of the participatory pyramid (where there is one). This can be found in both Brazil and its neighbours.

4 According to the type of data, the number of analyzed case studies can vary from eighteen to nineteen.

back to the other initial question: can European participatory budgeting – and participatory instruments in general – be seen as an element in the affirmation of an alternative to neoliberal globalisation? Here again, before providing a definitive answer we must step back and explore real cases. This is the object of the second part of the book. Only then – in the third part – will we be able to apply a cross-cutting analysis and draw an overall conclusion.

# 3

# SIX PARTICIPATORY MODELS

Before carrying out a detailed analysis of various experiments of participatory budgeting in Europe, we feel it is necessary first to provide readers with a conceptual road map. In a broad comparative survey, given that each case is unique, there is such diversity that there is a serious risk of getting lost on the way. Understanding detail can come at the cost of developing an overall understanding. In order to help us on our road, we gradually constructed a typology that provides identifying characteristics, similar to the method used in another field by those analysing different types of welfare state and capitalism.

How did we set about this task? Having taken the measure of the diversity of the existing procedures, we needed to constitute semi-abstract models using a Weberian approach. We shall therefore not be developing an empirical typology by grouping concrete cases placed in boxes in a figure. The ideal-types we develop correspond to the axes of a conceptual map on which one can situate empirical cases. As with a road map, you do not usually travel due North, South, East or West, but the existence of these cardinal points means you do not get lost. In this case we have based our work on six series of criteria to define this typology.[1]

*Context.* The analysis of the national cases has shown how context influences the concrete dynamics of participatory budgeting. Even when this analysis aims to emphasise factors linked to agency, it needs to consider the respective contexts. The same procedure and the same political determination will produce very different effects, depending on the socio-political context in which they are implemented.

*Normative frames.* It is difficult to deny the importance of the normative dimension, irrespective of whether this is explicitly expressed or whether it transpires from the normative frames that guide actions without the actors necessarily being aware of them (Röcke 2014). We therefore aimed to clarify the declared goals of citizen participation: for example, administrative aims (modernisation of public action, proximity management and so on) or social goals (social justice, social inclusion, solidarity, gender equality and so on). Finally, over and above the declared objectives or goals, it is important to understand

---

1 See Sintomer, Herzberg and Röcke (2008) for a corresponding typology relating to participatory budgeting only.

the normative frames of action (for instance, participatory democracy or community empowerment).

*Procedures.* Procedures alone are not enough to build an overall typology; we need also to consider how the process actually works. Political theory has, in recent years, underlined the importance of procedural rationality in democratic processes, whereas sociology has used procedures to study the way in which interactions are grounded in know-how and the material world. In a given socio-economic context and with reference to a similar normative frame, participative dynamics can vary greatly, depending on the methodology used. What are the main approaches used in these six participatory 'worlds'? Processes may have decision-making abilities or be based on selective listening (cherry-picking). In some cases, the rules are transparent, in others not. Procedures may (or may not) confer participants with real decision-making capacities as well as a great deal of autonomy, and it may or may not lead to the beginnings of a new kind of institutional power, a fourth power that reaches beyond the traditional division of power.

*Dynamics of collective action.* As we will see in the second part of this work, the meaning of participatory instruments depends essentially on whether a broad social mobilisation does or does not exist. For the construction of ideal-types, we therefore consider it necessary to include the logics of action that are partially rooted in the context and partially contingent. We also need to take the macro-actors into account (social classes, social movements), as well as the local actors involved in the implementation of citizen participation. Participatory instruments vary considerably depending on the type of actors that participate, and their dynamics depend on whether they are rooted in a social movement or whether, on the contrary, they have been initiated top-down. The extent to which civil society is organised is, in this respect, far from secondary; a process that formally grants procedural autonomy to non-state actors can prove ineffectual unless actors are genuinely involved. A participatory approach takes on a very different form depending on whether it aims at the participation of social sectors, organised citizens, active citizens, ordinary citizens or all citizens – and also depending on whether it has been initiated by political parties, foundations, NGOs or international organisations. There are other important questions, too, such as how the participatory instruments deal with social conflicts, to what extent they are consensus-oriented and whether or not they enable a countervailing-power to emerge.

*The relationship between conventional politics and participatory instruments.* They may be non-existent and in no way interwoven, or be so only to a small extent, particularly when participation is being used only as a managerial technique with no political impact. One may also be substituted for the other when participation develops on a parallel path to that of conventional politics and absorbs energy that would, in another context, be devoted to this aim. Conversely, participation may be instrumentalised to the advantage of conventional politics and thus have a knock-on effect of remobilising people to this end. Finally, certain scenarios can lead to a combination of two types of commitment, with a virtuous circle that mutually reinforces mobilisation in conventional and non-conventional politics (Rey 2005).

*Strengths, weaknesses, challenges.* The strengths, weaknesses and challenges of the six participatory models are first evaluated in terms of a logic that is internal to each of the models, although they also draw on the comparison between different ones. This emphasises the fact that the ideal-types built in this way have an impact that is both normative and cognitive, similar to the concept of the public sphere developed by Jürgen Habermas, or the scientific field in the work of Pierre Bourdieu (Sintomer 2011b).

According to these criteria, we can then distinguish between six different participatory models in Europe. They are as follows: participatory democracy, proximity democracy, participatory modernisation, multi-stakeholder participation, neo-corporatism and community development (Sintomer et al. 2012a). These six models allow us to draw a conceptual map of citizen participation in Europe, and to situate and illustrate the position of participatory budgeting and other participatory processes.

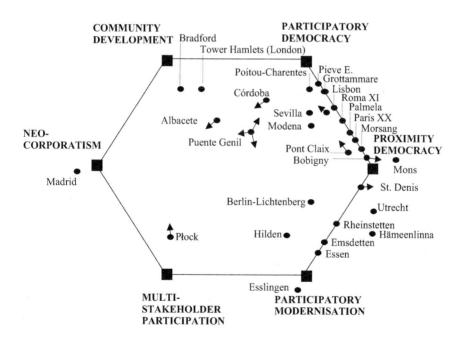

*Figure 3.1* Typology of participatory models in Europe (with the example of participatory budgeting, 2005–2010)

*Source:* authors' elaboration

## 1. Participatory Democracy

We have chosen to call the first model 'participatory democracy'. It is marked by the simultaneous emergence of a fourth power (via the decision-making powers conferred on the process by local authorities) and a countervailing power (by the mobilisation of civil society that is supported by the new institutional structure and that accepts the idea of cooperative conflict resolution). In this model we can observe the greatest potential repercussions in terms of social justice or political effects. It is based on the participation of the working class and not just the middle classes, thereby creating an emerging plebeian public sphere. This creates a positive equation between conventional and non-conventional politics, as the dynamics of the two can combine. On the Old Continent as outside Europe, it first represented an attempt to promote an alternative to neoliberalism. We can therefore expect to find that it is generally implemented by 'progressive' town halls, particularly in places where alter-globalist currents bring pressure to bear on institutional left-wing forces. At present, this is the model that is most frequently grounded in participatory budgeting rather than other instruments.[2] This concerns primarily Latin America. In Europe, it has had its greatest influence in Spain and in Italy.

The term 'participatory democracy' is often used as a catchword, referring to the majority of approaches that in some way bring non-elected citizens together in the decision-making process, even if this is purely consultative. We decided to give the notion a narrower meaning: for us, it means that traditional mechanisms of representative government are linked to direct or semi-direct democratic procedures – in other words: non-elected inhabitants (and their delegates who are invested with a 'semi-imperative mandate') have *de facto* decision-making powers, although *de iure* the final political decision remains in the hands of elected representatives.

This is the meaning that most contemporary social scientists have attached to the term, and it constitutes the normative frame for our first participatory ideal-type (alongside anti-authoritarian socialism). We shall also return to the fact that this ideal-type is the one that appears to us to be the most politically and philosophically stimulating, as it queries the 'fetishism of representation' without, however, leaving aside representative authorities. It also enables good quality decision-making, combines participation with social justice and, in this way, contributes to making the idea of citizen participation more credible. In the context of participatory budgeting, this model is linked to processes where projects are ranked by criteria of distributive justice and where they have formal

---

2 Partial exceptions are randomly elected citizen assemblies that elaborate propositions (for example on electoral reform like in British Columbia) that are then put to the electorate-at-large in a referendum.

rules. The meetings at the neighbourhood level are open for every interested citizen or organised groups; delegates are elected for the city level. In contrast to proximity democracy, the discussions go beyond the micro-local level and include projects of city-wide importance.

Despite these advantages in terms of the democratic content, historical and sociological analyses have demonstrated that this model can work only under specific circumstances, and that other models are therefore more appropriate in certain contexts. Each model presents its own strengths and weaknesses that can be evaluated only on the ground. The strength of participatory democracy is that it combines a strong, autonomous, influential civil society with a transformation of political institutions that aims to reinforce their legitimacy. The weakness is that it requires many favourable factors (particularly a strong political determination and independent civil society that is prepared to cooperate with the local authorities). It is unstable if confined to local level only. The main challenges include how successfully to link participation to the modernisation of civil services, avoiding the risk of co-opting the mobilised members of civil society into the institutional framework (which would cut them off from their own grassroots), and reaching beyond town level to have a more global impact.

## 2. Proximity Democracy

The key characteristic of the second model is that it showcases proximity in the double sense of geographical closeness and increased communication between citizens, civil services and local authorities, while leaving the main decision-making powers in the hands of the latter. Proximity democracy is grounded in informal rules and leaves civil society with only marginal autonomy. Over and above ideological rhetoric, it constitutes more of a deliberative modification of republicanism than an inroad into participatory democracy in the more precise sense of the term. In proximity democracy, the state is powerful at local level, but civil services are not necessarily involved in a strong process of administrative modernisation, and the participatory processes take place essentially at neighbourhood level.

Left-wing towns commit more easily to proximity democracy than right-wing ones, but there is no clear dividing line. Due to the lack of criteria that would enable resources to be redistributed for the benefit of the most disadvantaged dominated groups, proximity democracy is not an instrument of social justice, even if it does guarantee some degree of solidarity (for example, by limiting real estate speculation or introducing policies of urban renewal). As the process is merely consultative and civil society does not have much independence, there is no likelihood of a fourth power or expression of a countervailing power emerging. Proximity democracy is essentially a top-down movement, even though the working class is sometimes involved in the process. In the context of participatory budgeting, the process essentially addresses individual volunteer citizens, but NGOs play a considerable unofficial role; other participatory processes may use random selection to select participants. It would be hard for proximity democracy to generate any remobilisation within the framework of conventional politics, at least at micro-local level, because it really deals only with 'small things'.

In the case of participatory budgeting, this model is related to procedures that include the mere consultation of citizens, or a discussion and decision about small neighbourhood funds (without any link to the city-wide level). This model is particularly influential in France and Portugal. It is undoubtedly the most widespread model in Europe; next to some participatory budgets, it includes neighbourhood funds and neighbourhood councils. The main strength of proximity democracy is that it enables improved communication between citizens and policymakers to take place on micro-problems. Its weaknesses lie in the essentially arbitrary way in which policymakers 'selectively listen' to cherry-pick people's proposals; in the fact that it fosters parochial perspectives; and in the instrumentalisation of civil society by existing institutions. The challenge it faces is especially that of ensuring that participation effectively serves social policy, as well as improving the quality of decision-making, and combining proximity with the modernisation of civil services beyond neighbourhood level.

## 3. Participatory Modernisation

The key trait of the third model is that participation is merely one aspect of the modernisation of civil service, in a context in which the state is trying to modernise in order to become more efficient and legitimate and to resist the pressures to privatise (the German civil service trade unions have adopted the slogan 'Become competitive rather than go private'). Viewed from this angle, the participatory process is top-down, is not political and has only consultative value. Civil society has only limited independence and there is no space for either a fourth power or for a countervailing power.

What is at stake here is quite different: participation is first and foremost linked to good management and is aimed at increasing the legitimacy of public policies and, indirectly, of local politics. The quality of decision-making and of deliberation is relatively limited, because these projects are generally based on techniques that are similar to opinion polls and limited to aggregating opinions rather than stimulating discussion. The people involved are mainly middle class, except when procedural measures are used to improve the sociological diversity of the participants. The participatory process is essentially aimed at ordinary citizens, and it is here that we most commonly find the practice of random selection. The role of Porto Alegre is small or even non-existent, and there are other, more distinct influences (such as that of Christchurch in New Zealand). More generally, the normative frames on which this model is based are closer to the participatory versions of New Public Management than the utopia of participatory democracy as an alternative to neoliberal globalisation.

Relating this model to participatory budgeting, this approach is particularly common in Germany. Municipal authorities of very different political affiliations have introduced participatory budgeting procedures that are linked to this model to a greater or lesser extent. In the last years, participatory budgeting has also been linked to austerity policies: people are invited to make proposals for savings or have to discuss saving proposals made by the government. Participatory modernisation can draw on a wide range of participatory projects and approaches, ranging from mechanisms that enable feedback from users, to quality charters or councils that involve users in the management of local services or institutions. Approaches close to the ideal type of participatory modernisation have thus developed in a variety of contexts, particularly in Northern Europe.

The strength of this third model is the close link between the modernisation of civil services and participation, and the fact that cross-bench political consensus can easily be achieved. The flipside is that there is only a low level of politicisation, which makes it difficult to introduce certain broad questions, particularly that of social justice; processes close to the model tend to be purely managerial in nature. With regard to participatory budgeting, they often involve a citywide consultation about public finances. In the most extreme cases of this approach, this can represent nothing more than a legitimation cloak for decisions (on savings or others) that have already been made before. The challenges of this model include how to increase the participation and autonomy of civil society and develop a genuine political dimension (instead of becoming a merely technocratic procedure) in order to provide politics with renewed impetus.

## 4. Multi-stakeholder Participation

The main characteristic of the fourth model is that the citizens who take part constitute just one of the many different actors, together with private enterprise and local government. In this model, local politics appears to have only limited room to manoeuvre, compared with economic forces. The approach is not strongly politicised and the major development issues of local politics can be discussed only peripherally (if at all). Although participatory procedures may well have decision-making powers, they remain caught in a top-down approach that does not enable a countervailing power to emerge.

Rather than an emerging fourth power, participatory instruments of this type represent an enlargement of governance mechanisms (whereby private economic interests gain an institutional influence in the decision-making process). In the multi-stakeholder participation, civil society is weak and has little autonomy, even if the rules of the decision-making process are clearly defined. It is essentially middle class individuals who take part, and the projects are aimed at active citizens or NGOs, who are supposed to be the spokesmen of local residents. International organisations such as the World Bank or the United Nations play an important part in dissemination. In this model, participation often serves policies that have incorporated the constraints of neoliberal globalisation: in the best case it represents only a small weight with which to counter these forces. The dominant normative frame is a hybrid of the rhetoric of governance and the theme of citizen participation. Even though the initial frame is that of an economic and managerial perspective (more markedly so than in the other models), this participatory model may locally have a limited impact in terms of reinforcing social cohesion and improving the legitimacy of the political organisers of the process.

As far as participatory budgeting is concerned, this model exists only in Eastern Europe. Processes are set up by partnerships involving for instance local governments, international organisations and private enterprises. Meetings are not open to the public, but only to those the donor(s) selected; they also provide the funding. With regard to other participatory instruments it has considerable influence in the Anglo-Saxon world and beyond, particularly in the context of programmes of international organisations of development cooperation. Its strength is that it is well adapted to contexts with a strong market, and it directs private funding to projects of general interest. Of course, it also includes private companies that are fundamental to local development but which tend in other ideal-types to remain outside the participative process. However, this comes at the cost of private enterprise having the upper hand in a process in which they have voluntarily become involved (and on condition they clearly profit from their involvement), whereas civil society is limited to a subordinate role and is not able to question the dominant economic and political framework. Furthermore, there is no structural connection between participation and modernisation. The challenges facing this model are how to link participatory instruments with the core business of municipal politics: that is, to stabilise the financial flows on which they depend (these flows are precarious and do not operate under clear legal constraints); to balance the weight of the various stakeholders involved in the process, and to open up to topics that are relevant to them; and to counter the pressure to transform NGOs and associations into para-governmental organisations or semi-commercial entities.

## 5. Neo-corporatism

The distinctive trait of the neo-corporatist model is that local government plays a strong role by surrounding itself with organised groups (NGOs, trade unions and employers' associations), social groups (the elderly, immigrant groups and so on) and various local institutions. In this model, government aims to establish a broad consultation with 'those who matter' and tries to achieve social consensus through the mediation of interests, values and demands for recognition by the various factions in society. Participatory budgets influenced by the neo-corporatist model have somehow developed in Spain. In this model, the political leanings of local governments vary, as does the dynamics of modernisation of the civil service. The normative frames are linked to neo-corporatism and certain variations of the concept of governance.

In the neo-corporatist model, the participatory rules may be formalised, while the quality of deliberation is variable. In most cases, local corporatist processes are essentially consultative. Even though civil society does play a considerable role in them, their procedural independence is fairly limited, and they are essentially top-down processes. This is why the emergence of a countervailing power – or of a fourth power – is unlikely to occur. The outcome is more a case of reinforcement of traditional participation than a virtuous circle of conventional and non-conventional participation (or the substitution of the former by the latter). At national level, the classic neo-corporatist approaches, particularly those used to manage the health care system, often work in very different ways: they may be highly formalised, have real decision-making authority and confer decision-making powers on the social partners.

In terms of participatory budgeting procedures, the neo-corporatist model (which heavily influences local Agenda 21s and participatory strategic plans) is not widespread in Europe today. It has had only a certain influence in Spain, where the blend with the Porto Alegre approach has given birth to forms of associative democracy. The reinforcing of the mechanisms of sectorial participation in various aspects of municipal civil services might lead to the development of original forms of participatory budgeting, however.

International organisations play a considerable role in disseminating this model. Its main strengths are the linkage between the main organised structures of society, which facilitates social consensus around certain aspects of public policies. However, it is characterised by asymmetrical relationships of power and non-organised citizens are excluded. The main challenges are linking participation and modernisation, avoiding co-optation of associations or NGOs (that may become cut off from their roots) to public management, or going beyond a simple cherry-picking approach and successfully discussing the most controversial matters.

## 6. Community Development

The dominant characteristic of the sixth model is that participation is aimed fundamentally at the phase of project implementation, in a context that dissociates municipal politics and a strong participatory process driven as much by a bottom-up dynamic as a top-down one. The margins for representative politics are fairly small in this ideal-type. The fourth institutional power and countervailing power that emerge are therefore not closely linked to local institutions, which is an aspect that distinguishes community development from the participatory democracy model. The influence of Porto Alegre is more indirect because it has become blended with older local traditions. There are fairly clear procedural rules and a relatively high quality of deliberation. The most active participants are those involved in running the community organisations (in Europe, often the upper fraction of the working classes or middle classes). The role of NGOs is often decisive, with participation being aimed at disadvantaged or marginalised groups with a view to inclusive action rather than at an overall form of distributive justice. In a configuration such as this, the partial substitution of non-conventional participation linked to community activities for conventional participation (party membership and voting in elections) is fairly likely to develop.

In the field of participatory budgeting, this model is based to a great extent on processes using community funds. Community Development means that participants (often members of NGOs or local community groups) are addressed as joint managers that nearly autonomously organise the process and decide about the funding for local projects. In contrast to multi-stakeholder participation, it is the participants and not the donors who determine the rules of the process. In Europe, this approach has been mainly developed in the United Kingdom. In other countries of the Global North, particularly in Canada (in the town of Guelph) and in many countries in the Global South, this model influences many incarnations of participatory budgeting, but also other participatory processes. The political inclination of local government is not a decisive factor; the normative frame is one of empowerment, but also of liberal socialism, left liberalism and sometimes the traditions of local communities, particularly of indigenous ones. This participatory model has clear advantages in a context in which local government is weak and where, conversely, civil society has genuine independence and a real tradition of organising that enables the community sector to manage local projects by themselves. The weakness lies in the fact that it is difficult to build an overall vision of the town, as well as the tenuous links between participation, modernisation of the civil service and institutional politics. The challenges that the model faces include trying to keep the management of community organisations free from managerial influence and to stop them from turning into para-public bodies; moreover, processes of this type need to look beyond the micro-local level and contribute to the transformation of institutional politics.

Table 3.1 summarises the main elements of each of the six participation models.

Once again, we wish to remind the reader that these ideal-types are mostly intended to better identify the different kinds of participatory devices that exist in Europe. The various case studies show a high degree of creativity and in practice one can observe the 'hybridisation' of processes: in fact, this tends to develop further due to increasing transversal exchange and political, associative and scientific networking.

At the end of this first part, we see that due to this diversity, explaining the emergence of participatory budgeting in Europe is not simple, because there is so much diversity. This mosaic adds another dimension to the puzzle of the institutional variations and highly contrasting socio-economic contexts in Europe. There is a marked contrast between those processes that transfer powers to civil society (at least on paper) and those that carefully maintain the separation between elected representatives – considered the sole guardians of the common good and therefore of decision-making – and citizens, who are to be listened to, but who are not considered capable of taking an overview, or at any rate of taking decisions. There are other variable parameters: only certain projects followed the example of Porto Alegre in including a social dimension, for example by the use of criteria of distributive justice or affirmative action. The link between the participatory budget and the local institutional system also varied from one model to another.

Before we go into the issues in greater depth and outline the challenges, dynamics and impacts of participatory budgeting and of citizen participation in general, we need to carry out a more systematic study of empirical developments. This is the content of Part II. The reader will become acquainted with many case study illustrations as we go down this road. Thus, what so far is only an explanatory skeleton, will be 'filled with life' in the next part. It is only later, when we reach the Part III, that we shall attempt to reconnect to the discussion about general characteristics of citizen participation as it is entailed in the ideal-type typology and discuss the overall impacts and significance of participatory budgeting and other participatory instruments.

Table 3.1 Key characteristics of models of citizen participation in Europe

| | 1. Participatory democracy | 2. Proximity democracy | 3. Participatory modernisation | 4. Multi-stakeholder participation | 5. Neo-corporatism | 6. Community development |
|---|---|---|---|---|---|---|
| **Context** | | | | | | |
| Relationship between state, market and third sector | Central role of state | Central role of state | Central role of state | Hegemony of the market | Central role of the state | Hegemony of the market, assertiveness of the third sector |
| Political leaning of local government | Left-wing | Variable (initially left-wing for participatory budgeting) | Variable | Variable | Variable | Variable |
| **Normative frames and declared objectives** | | | | | | |
| Normative frames | Participatory democracy, post-authoritarian socialism | Communication-oriented version of republicanism, urban renewal policies, deliberative democracy | Participatory version of New Public Management | Participatory governance | Neo-corporatism, participatory governance | Empowerment, libertarian traditions, left-wing liberalism |
| Goals (administrative, social, political) | Inclusion of user knowledge, social justice, democratisation of democracy | Inclusion of user knowledge, renewal of social relationships, inclusion of deliberation to representative democracy | Modernisation of civil services, social peace | Public–private partnerships, inclusion of user knowledge, citizens considered clients, input from NGOs, social capital, economic growth | Inclusion of user knowledge, input from NGOs, consensus and social cohesion | Public services delegated to community sector, inclusion of user knowledge, empowerment, affirmative action, delegation of power to community level |
| **Procedures** | | | | | | |
| Rules, quality of deliberation | Clearly defined rules, good quality deliberation | Informal rules, deliberative quality weak or average | Rules may be clear, weak deliberative quality | Clearly defined rules, average to good deliberative quality | Rules may be clear, variable deliberative quality | Rules may be clear, average to high deliberative quality |

| | | | | | | |
|---|---|---|---|---|---|---|
| Procedural independence of civil society | Strong | Weak | Weak | Weak | Variable | Strong |
| Decision-making powers or consultative in nature | Decision-making powers | Consultation | Consultation | Decision-making powers | Variable | Decision-making powers |
| Fourth power | Yes | No | No | No | No (at local level) | Yes |
| **Collective action** | | | | | | |
| Weight of civil society in process | Strong | Weak | Weak | Weak | Fairly strong | Strong |
| Top-down vs. bottom-up | Top-down and bottom-up | Top-down | Top-down | Top-down | Top-down | Top-down and bottom-up |
| Main categories of citizens targeted | Active organised citizens | Active organised citizens | Ordinary and active citizens | Organised citizens (in association with companies) | Organised citizens (alongside employers' unions and local institutions) | Organised citizens |
| Consensus vs. cooperative conflict resolution; countervailing power | Cooperative conflict resolution Countervailing power | Consensus No countervailing power | Consensus No countervailing power | Consensus No countervailing power | Consensus No countervailing power | Cooperative conflict resolution Countervailing power |
| Link between conventional and participatory politics | Combination | Instrumentalisation of participatory politics supporting conventional politics | Weak (participation is a management tool) | Weak (participation is a management tool) | Strengthening of traditional participation | Substitution (participation develops outside conventional politics) |
| Key area of influence (for participatory budgets) | Spain, Italy | France, Belgium, Portugal | Germany | Eastern Europe (Poland) | Spain | United Kingdom |

Source: authors' elaboration

# PART II

# 'TWO, THREE ... MANY PORTO ALEGRES?'

A few decades ago, Ernesto 'Che' Guevara called for 'Two, Three, Many Vietnams'. The slogan was a good one: obstinate Vietnamese resistance to the dominant global power was a banner under which radical movements could rally and carried echoes of Cuba, the other anti-imperialist experience. The call to multiply these kinds of experiences aimed to establish an international front that could support them, prolong their existence and draw lessons from 'exemplary procedures'. Throughout the world, these developments fostered hopes of the advent of a new, fairer world. Without wishing to take things out of proportion, have we not seen a similar development as the alter-globalisation movement tried to spread the participatory process that was invented in its 'capital', Porto Alegre? As we have seen, participation has been a fundamental feature of the powerful wave of social transformation that has marked Porto Alegre, to the benefit of the lower classes. More than many others, this movement appears to embody the slogan 'Another world is possible!' This slogan has also been present in the Occupy movement and its protest against social and economic inequalities. Hence, we ask: could the anti-imperialist protest of the 1960s be reproduced in other contexts and on different scales?

Things are, of course, complicated. While criticism of US interventionism and war-mongering is still topical, the reference to Vietnam now appears outdated and romanticised. 'Real-life Socialism' is dead and the model put forward in a different age now appears delusional. Porto Alegre's participatory budget is therefore interesting because there is less of a gap between theory and practice (Avritzer 2002, 2009, Baiocchi 2005, Gret and Sintomer 2004, Wampler 2010). In addition, while the alter-globalisation movement is at least partly of 1960s 'anti-imperialist' descent, its vision of the world has been profoundly renewed. Armed struggle has been discredited to the point that the Porto Alegre Charter, the basic document of the alter-globalisation movement, bans *guerrilla* organisations from membership of the World Social Forum. Democratic procedures, widely disparaged by the radical fringes of 1968, have been re-evaluated and are today one of the cornerstones of the radical Left's projects for renewal, which goes at least some way towards explaining the prominence of participatory budgeting. Rather than a reference to the Cuban revolution and the guerrilla fighters' descent on Havana from the Sierra Maestra, the changes taking place are the result of a link between the independence of radical social movements and progressive management procedures. In addition, the scale is entirely different: ordinary people regularly saw images of Vietnam on television and heard about it on the radio and in the newspapers. The opposite is true of participatory budgeting, which is well-known in Europe only in relatively narrow political and academic circles.

Aside from a common heritage and similarities between past and present, to what extent is the metaphor relevant? Will participatory budgeting go down in history as a procedure of major significance or will it merely mark the local history of a few hundred towns in Latin America, Europe and the rest of the world? Will it represent more than a political trend or a temporary variant on the modernisation of public action? Could it become widespread in the European context or, at least, become an innovation that is widely known about? To answer these questions, we will provide a detailed analysis of the main experiments of the 2000s. Only then will we be able to develop answers to our initial questions: How can the sudden appearance of participatory budgeting in Europe be explained? To what extent is there convergence or divergence between participatory experiments? What is their scope and significance? How do national and local contexts affect the process?

In presenting the results of our investigation, we follow the order of the six ideal-type models of citizen participation established in Part I, Chapter 3. Thus, we begin with two countries, Spain and Italy, where participatory budgets are closest to the participatory democracy model derived from the Porto Alegre experience (Chapter 4). We then move on to the French case (Chapter 5), where democracy and citizen participation are usually based on the idea of proximity. The Belgian, Dutch and Portuguese experiments (Chapter 6) will allow us to determine the extent to which proximity democracy represents a springboard or a trap to civic engagement. In Germany and Finland (Chapter 7), citizen participation is less political in nature. Moreover, it has been used first and foremost with the aim of participatory modernisation. Participatory budgets in Poland come closest to the multi-stakeholder participation model, whereas we find hardly any case that would correspond to the model of neo-corporatism. The model of community development is present in many British examples of participatory budgeting. As both the United Kingdom and Poland have been strongly affected by neoliberal policies, and as participatory budgeting in both countries is torn between the logics of citizen empowerment and citizen disempowerment through the creation of non-democratic management boards, we decided to present them together (Chapter 8).

# 4

# PORTO ALEGRE IN EUROPE?

## (Spain and Italy)

In Italy and, even more so, in Spain, participatory budgeting is most clearly inspired by the Porto Alegre experiment, which is why these cases led us to elaborate on the model of participatory democracy presented in Part I of the book. The idea of involving citizens in budgetary redistribution is usually linked to the transfer of decision-making powers to civil society and the promotion of social justice, and participants can often influence the rules of the process. This does not, however, imply that citizens are directly involved in implementing selected projects. Porto Alegre has had a fairly direct influence in these two Mediterranean countries through the World Social Forums. Another, more lasting means of influence have been visits and projects that took place prior to the 'Local Authority Forums', at which progressive mayors and politicians met on the margins of the World Social Forum, as well as through the URB-AL network. This cooperation programme aimed at Latin American and European local authorities comprises, in particular, a network on 'Local Finance and Participatory Budgeting', coordinated by Porto Alegre. Most of the participating local councils came from Spain and Italy (Cabannes 2003). As we saw in Part I, it is in these two countries that European participatory budgets initially have developed the furthest. Have they actually managed to reproduce the Brazilian system? And how have they been able to graft it on to the existing, more traditional forms of participation?

## 1. Spain: All Power to the People?

In comparison with most other Western European countries, Spanish democracy is still in its infancy. Neighbourhood committees played an essential role in the transition following the fall of the Franco dictatorship. They gave rise to wide-ranging social mobilisation on urban issues that was highly important at the time and provided a secure legal framework for the activities of opposition activists. From the 1980s onwards, most local politicians emerged from these committees. However, the committees declined over the years and their institutional recognition did not prevent stagnation in their functioning, as well as a decrease in the number of participants. For the past two decades, they have seen competition from other local movements dealing with new issues, such as gender relations, immigration or the environment. Nevertheless, they almost always warrant a mention in regulations on participation that local authorities can adopt pursuant to framework legislation on local councils. The city of Barcelona here served as a model, with several local councils taking inspiration from regulations on participation that the Catalan city adopted in 1986. During the 1990s, several advisory councils were set up on issues such as culture, education or social issues, enabling municipal service providers and leaders to discuss options within their area of competence with organised civil society. Decision-making power remained, however, in the hands of local government, and the organisation of committees, often less than transparent, favoured the appearance of patron–client networks. In this context, marked by non-elected citizen associations' intense but relatively rigid approaches to public decision-making, participatory budgeting was seen as a breath of fresh air that had the potential to boost the entire system of local participation.

One of the specific features of Spanish local authorities is that their tasks vary depending on their size. They are all responsible for certain basic services such as water supply, collecting household waste, public lighting and repairing road surfaces, but larger towns have additional responsibilities. As we saw in Part I, the mayor is generally elected by the municipal council. The law on large towns has changed the situation of communes (Ballesteros 2004): their independence has been strengthened and the establishment of districts has had a significant impact in terms of internal decentralisation and the use of participatory approaches.

While the first participatory budget-style initiatives date back to the 1980s[1] it was a further two decades before the first real participatory budgets took shape. Tomás Villasante (1995, 2002), a researcher, eco-socialist and Izquierda Unida (IU) (United Left) activist, is considered their spiritual father. Fostering a transfer of knowledge between Latin America and Spain through research-action approaches, he and his team were involved in some of his country's most remarkable experiments. Among the pioneering towns, Rubí in Catalonia and Cabezas de San Juan in Andalusia saw their participatory budgets end when the local council changed its political hue after the first term of office (Ganuza and Álvarez de Sotomayor 2003). Nevertheless, the number of participatory budgets rose from three in 2001 (date of the first World Social Forum) to 14 in 2005, before reaching around 50 in 2010. As we have already seen, over 5.2 per cent of the Spanish population lived in a commune with participatory

---

1 Without being labelled as such, proto participatory budgets were established in 1982 in Tirajana (34,000 inhabitants) in the Canary Islands, and in 1980 and 1982 in Marinaleda and Lebrija in Andalusia (Villasante 1995).

budgeting in 2005, a percentage far higher than in any other European country. The regional focal points were Catalonia, the south of the country and the area around Madrid. With its 700,000 inhabitants, Seville, the capital of Andalusia, was, after Cologne, the largest city in Europe to have implemented participatory budgeting.

Participatory budgeting emerged under José Maria Aznar's conservative government and most initiatives could be traced back to local politicians who wanted to differentiate themselves from the national government, rather than to local civil society. Activists from Izquierda Unida (IU), the neo-communist party, initially pushed hardest on the issue, before being joined by the socialists from the PSOE. Finally, these two left-wing parties had to work together before the procedure could really take off as the vast majority of local councils with participatory budgeting were run by coalitions. Later, politicians from other parties, including the Conservatives, also began to take an interest in participatory budgeting, a development that also took place in Italy. What was the background to this process?

### Community or Individual Participation (Albacete and Cordoba)?

Initially, Albacete and Cordoba symbolised two different approaches to Spanish participatory budgeting. The first, run by the PSOE, favoured the participation of local associations in a context in which they had exceptional levels of independence and vitality. The second, the largest Spanish city run by IU, was more directly inspired by Porto Alegre and based participation on voluntary individual citizens, thereby breaking with the Spanish tradition of association-based participation.

Albacete (152,000 inhabitants) is located in the Castilla-La-Mancha region, one-and-a-half hours south-east of Madrid by express train. The origins of the city go back to the Moorish occupation in the Middle Ages, when they colonised large swathes of Spain. Today, the town's main resource is the tertiary sector, with the industries gathered in the city's outlying areas providing a second, lesser source of income. The middle classes live in the city centre, which is clearly demarcated from a geographical point of view and encircled by the city's poorer neighbourhoods. Since the end of the dictatorship (1979), Albacete has always had a Socialist mayor, with the exception of the 1995–1999 term of office.[2] The city is characterised by a dense network of associations,

---

2 The Socialist Party had an absolute majority on the local council until 2007, followed by the Popular Party (PP, conservative). IU, a minority party, went into opposition in 2003 (coalitions in Spain generally occur only when the dominant party does not have an absolute majority) and only returned to the coalition during the 2007–2011 mandate. The PP won the 2011 elections.

with 23 socio-cultural centres. Neighbourhood committees have a particular status and are closely involved in the local participatory system. Above all – and contrary to the situation in many other communes – Albacete's associations and neighbourhood committees do not have a patron–client relationship with the government and are more active and representative than many other such committees in Spain.

Cordoba (319,000 inhabitants), formerly the capital of the last Islamic kingdom in the Iberian Peninsula, is the third-largest city in Andalusia, after Seville and Malaga. Its social situation was very different from that of Albacete. Unemployment (23 per cent) was over twice as high and, according to OECD criteria, 33 per cent of households lived in poverty. Between 2003 and 2007, IU had an absolute majority on the municipal council. The mayor, Rosa Aguilar, was a highly prominent national neo-Communist figure. The Socialists were only the third-largest political party, after the Conservatives. Cordoba was the first city in Spain to adopt a participatory system, back in 1979. The city had over 2,000 associations and neighbourhood committees, and there were a variety of mechanisms through which they could participate in the making of public policies. One aspect specific to Cordoba was the Citizens Movement Council. It coordinated local associations, particularly neighbourhood committees, and featured on the municipal administration's official organisation chart, for which it functioned as an advisory body. District councils included association representatives, who in fact held a majority.[3] Cordoba was also different from Albacete in that it managed to maintain a certain national and international prominence, particularly within the framework of the URB-AL programme, and it has organised several international conferences on participatory budgeting (Ganuza 2007).

Cordoba's participatory budget was established when the old participatory procedure, based on neighbourhood committees, was starting to show signs of fatigue: the committees' institutional privileges were being questioned by an increasingly diversified civil society and the procedures in existence involved only a limited number of citizens. When neighbourhood committee representatives attended a conference on participatory budgeting in 2000, they became favourable to the introduction of a procedure that they would later soundly criticise. Supported by advisors from Tomás Villasante's team, the municipal administration drew up a first participatory budget, under the banner of Porto Alegre. The selected method was in reality more an adaptation than a direct copy of the Brazilian participatory budget. While individual citizens were at the heart of the participatory process and its focus was the implementation of concrete projects, the administration also attempted to involve the local

---

3 The 2003 Law on Large Towns stipulated the establishment of districts but did not specify the composition of their councils.

associations. In addition, it was not the entire budget that became participatory, only certain parts of it. The procedure concerned investments and services and comprised a total sum of 9 million euros in 2003, a considerable amount (particularly considering that a very high proportion of investments were made through the participatory budget). While the municipal council retained all legal decision-making authority, it committed itself to following the decisions of participatory budget delegates. The first stage in the procedure took place at the neighbourhood level, where a vote was organised on the main proposals. Neighbourhood inhabitants selected delegates who then set out lists of priorities at the district and whole-town levels. As an adaption to Porto Alegre distribution criteria, Cordoba used criteria to rank citizens' proposals into a hierarchy. A support committee worked on the issue throughout the year, observing whether and how citizens' priorities were integrated into the draft budget and whether they later materialised. In order to take account of associations' interests, local government gave them a permanent seat on the participatory budget's district council and involved them in drawing up lists of priorities.

## A Meeting of Cordoba's Participatory Budget Delegates

At the beginning of October 2003 a meeting was held for participatory budget delegates in the Civic Centre. In the morning, the meeting was given over to prioritising requests, district by district, giving each project a certain number of points depending on the choices made by the participants and the distributive justice criteria decided upon at the start of the year (lack of equipment or services, wealthy or disadvantaged neighbourhood, population concerned). This complex system was a local adaptation of the procedures invented in Porto Alegre. The afternoon began, Spanish-style, just after 4 pm after a meal on the premises. The purpose of the afternoon was to set out an overall city-level list, going through the list by the number of points awarded, from lowest to highest, and refining it to ensure inter-district fairness. For infrastructure, each district had to receive between 150,000 and 480,000 euros and the number of projects could not exceed three. In total, 9 million of the 212 million-euro municipal budget had to be awarded through the process.

Around 30 people were present, of whom around seven were from the local council; the vast majority of the 28 delegates were therefore present. Most were men, aged between 45 and 65. This was in sharp contrast to the municipal team, which mainly comprised women, who were a great deal younger. As always, the proceedings were subject to lively discussion as they were highly significant in determining the outcome. Precise rules constrained delegates' decisions, whose position rested on a semi-imperative mandate and were therefore not traditional 'representatives'. One of the female participants distributed sweets, a gesture which placated those who were participating most intensely. The existence of a clear procedure and the points system further cooled discussions: it gave the feeling of a fairly objective and non-arbitrary discussion, based on the application of a rule that was considered fair.

Projects were adopted fairly rapidly – perhaps too rapidly for some of the participants. Nevertheless, they were all able to familiarise themselves with the proposals through bus visits to the locations concerned. In addition, most delegates were members of the volunteer groups that worked on the participatory budget throughout the year and were therefore well informed. Discussions on the nature of investments proposed were of reasonably high quality, despite the fact that figures sometimes appeared to be inaccurate. In general, discussions were oriented to the common good: each delegate had to convince the others of the advantages of the projects presented by his district. However, discussions dealt with one district-level investment at a time and did not focus on the overall city level. The only visible example of strategy was when the delegates from the El Higuerón district managed to carve up between themselves a project that was too costly and had to be spread over two years, without the others realising (they obtained the maximum sum of 480,000 euros for the first year). Formal voting was used only to clarify points of procedure or to decide between projects with the same number of points. Projects retained required fairly significant sums of money, ranging from a few dozen to hundreds of thousands of euros.

After two and a half hours of discussion, 25 infrastructure projects had been definitively adopted. After a break, discussions moved on to proposals regarding the other three service areas subject to the participatory budget: international cooperation, education and childhood, and citizenship. These projects did not have figures on them but it appeared that the amounts involved would be more modest and discussions were concluded more rapidly, particularly as any procedural uncertainties had already been dealt with. The meeting was adjourned at 7:40 pm in a good-humoured atmosphere.

In Albacete, implementation of the participatory budget resulted from a dynamic interactive process rather than a crisis. When the PSOE returned to power in 1999, following a participatory electoral campaign that involved large numbers of citizens, it organised an open meeting: 'We invited representatives from social movements and organised a kind of debate on the situation in the city', explained Manuel Perez Castell, Mayor of Albacete. 'However, discussions at the meeting did not lead too much in the way of results, which is why we started talking about the budget in 2002. The idea was not to have an incalculable number of suggestions, but to work out the best way to spend [our] 95 million euros'. The mayor, a philosophy graduate, was a firm believer in associative democracy. A participatory budget committee was therefore set up where, unlike in Cordoba, only representatives from organised civil society had the right to vote. Meetings to elect the participatory budget committee were held at the whole-city rather than neighbourhood level and all sectors (education, young people, trade unions, cooperation and development, women, immigrants and so on) had two representatives. The neighbourhood committees had a special status, being the only ones represented by three delegates. Selection criteria aiming to establish a hierarchy of proposals were used but they did not take account of inter-neighbourhood redistribution. The participatory budget essentially dealt with investments and municipal action programmes, with an occasional focus on general neighbourhood policy issues such as integrating migrants, price stability, the water supply or alcohol abuse by young people.

The strength of the Albacete experiment lied in the expertise of the groups set up. Discussions in the participatory budget committee were of excellent quality and the committee organised days dealing with specific issues: for example, the living conditions of immigrants. In particular, neighbourhood associations could call upon enough staff to draw up expert reports. The participatory budget did not have its own budget or direct decision-making powers, but nevertheless had considerable influence and authority. In 2005, the committee drew up conclusions that were used to guide municipal policy in micro-local investments. Some projects had effects in terms of social justice (Perez 2004): 'The municipal council had reservations, which were also political, with regard to the Traveller/Roma centre', explains an administration employee, 'but the [participatory budget committee] proposed the project, and the centre was established'. Measures implemented to help large families were another striking example: they enjoyed reduced fares on public transport and the commune built them council apartments of an appropriate size.

In Cordoba, after three years of participatory budgeting, open conflict broke out, following complaints from neighbourhood committees that feared losing their power to individual citizens. Their concerns were sufficient to convince the local council to suspend the mechanism, in spite of the positive changes that had taken place (a coordination committee had been set up to improve cross-cutting cooperation in the administration and the number of areas in which participatory budgeting was used had increased over the years). After long negotiations a new procedure was introduced that granted associations greater influence, but this agreement also came under fire. Then, the participatory budget went through a turbulent period, its legitimacy was called into question, and it slowly died as the municipal team started to lose ground, its management having become overly rigid.[4] In 2011, the PP won the elections and did not start again with a process that had been previously stopped. Some of its limitations appear obvious: selection criteria did not fully respond to expectations and the

---

4 In 2007, IU lost its absolute majority and the Left as a whole obtained only one seat more than the PP.

more heavily subsidised outlying neighbourhoods were not necessarily the least affluent. Even more worrying was the fact that, in spite of its radical nature, the system concerned only municipal resources in the strictest sense of the word, while at the same time the Communist town council multiplied the number of companies that were owned by the municipality but under private law, in order to tackle its financial crisis and improve services while getting around the inflexible nature of public service status. These municipal enterprises did not come within the remit of the participatory budgeting process.

The Albacete system also encountered difficulties. The Social Forum, a coalition of left-wing alter-globalisation groups, demanded the implementation of a participatory budget based on individual participation, as in Porto Alegre. Some neighbourhood associations dissented and entered into conflict with the Federation of Neighbourhood Committees, which threatened to exclude them from the participatory budgeting process. In addition, the mechanism did not really contribute to revitalising civil society and associations did not see increased attendance. The members of the participatory budgeting committee complained that it was always the same people that did all the work. Recognition should, however, be given to the fact that cooperation under the procedure improved the coordination of the groups that took part. They learnt more about their own objectives and were able to discuss joint actions. However, when the PP won the 2011 elections and decided to stop participatory budgeting, it could impose this decision without much opposition.

In both cities, the implementation of participatory structures was not simply a top-down process and civil society had considerable powers and independence. In Albacete, civil society drew up the procedural rules and its influence could be seen at press conferences, where it was citizens, rather than the mayor, who monopolised the microphone. In Cordoba, civil society was involved in designing the rules of the system and the neighbourhood committees were able to halt the procedure and renegotiate the entire framework. The adaptation of Porto Alegre to a European context certainly has meaning in Spain, even if there are obvious divergences from the system used in Rio Grande do Sul. Nevertheless, the two experiments are not easily transferable. The strength of Albacete rested on a highly specific associative structure, very different from the closed structures in other Spanish towns. The reproduction of the procedure in other contexts could produce a monopolisation of power by opaque intermediate organisations that are cut off from the grassroots or even working in accordance with a patron–client model. On the other hand, the path initially taken by Cordoba, which consisted largely of bypassing the neighbourhood committees, appeared strewn with obstacles and the unpredictable changes in its participatory budgeting process were a warning to other local councils that subsequently launched similar systems. In fact, those coming later learnt from these experiments and often implemented hybrid procedures that swing between two poles: on the one hand, the insertion – but limited role – of traditional forms of associational participation within an innovative procedure comprising a participatory budget adapted from the Porto Alegre experiment; on the other hand, the development of a participatory budget that essentially breaks with existing structures.

### Between Innovation and Integration (Seville, Puente Genil, Madrid)

Seville can be considered to have taken over the running from Cordoba. As we saw in the first part of this book, the capital of Andalusia also took inspiration from Porto Alegre. However, when the left-wing coalition initiated a participatory budget in 2004 it was careful not to repeat Cordoba's errors. Each neighbourhood had 'core driver groups' in which citizens, guided by external moderators, organised the process. They set the agenda for meetings, discussed awareness-raising campaigns and drew up the forms on which proposals were to be made. Civil society was able to influence the system as a whole through the criteria by which the proposals would be listed in order of priority. The system concerned the investments and programmes of certain administrations, with an increase in the number involved as the years passed. Associations were explicitly invited to join the 'core driver groups', but they had no special rights, unlike in Albacete. Their representatives participated simply as ordinary individuals (Talpin 2011). In this case, the neighbourhood committees did not turn against the participatory budgeting process. In fact, several of them appeared to see it as an opportunity to implement new projects. In a city traditionally marked by strong patron–client relationships, this development represented a genuine break with the past and those coordinating the structure aimed to use their strong political will and the size of the city to turn it into a model for the rest of the country. In 2006, there were around a dozen participatory budgets based on a more or less similar approach (Ganuza 2007; Ganuza and Frances 2012). However, the experiment stopped after the left lost the 2011 municipal elections.

In Puente Genil, a small Andalusian municipality (30,000 inhabitants), as well as in other experiments, the synthesis between the Cordoba and Albacete approaches was more developed: the rules of the participatory budgeting process had been set by a council half made up of civil society representatives and half of individual citizens. Puente Genil is located in the midst of a veritable ocean of olive trees. Its system was very specific in that it combined participation, administrative modernisation and the promotion of social justice in an extremely original manner. Participation and modernisation had not been carried out in tandem in any other European participatory budget. Traditionally Communist, in the early 2000s the local council broke with its previous management methods, which were becoming inflexible and running out of steam. Driven by a new leadership, it launched into an ambitious programme of investments and a complete overhaul of its administration, de-compartmentalising and regrouping sectors into relatively independent departments with their own budgets, boosting their cross-cutting nature, outsourcing some services and transforming some departments into municipal enterprises.

At the same time, citizens were urged to involve themselves in the everyday functioning of public activities, with the participatory budgeting process as the cornerstone of the system. This was not, like in Cordoba or Seville, restricted to certain areas, but covered all the municipality's areas of competence, including the municipal companies. A cross-cutting committee – including the municipal company directors – coordinated the implementation of projects adopted. A highly detailed system of social criteria, inspired by Porto Alegre, introduced rules regarding distributive justice and distinguished between investment and service-related proposals. While it would be too much to say that there have been wide-ranging social changes, the effects of this policy could be observed by stakeholders, at least in terms of proximity and the administration's responsiveness, particularly in the outlying villages of the town. Nevertheless, participation rates remained relatively low, involving mainly male leisure-oriented associations. In addition, the local council had taken on a significant level of debt by the beginning of its 2003 term of office. This has made municipal actions appear less than convincing and the 2007 election results were disappointing. IU lost its absolute majority and became a minority local government, supported by the Socialists. Participatory budgeting was interrupted from this year on. In spite of these problems, Puente Genil was a promising example of how a participatory budget, while staying true to the spirit of Porto Alegre in terms of social justice and devolving significant power to the citizens (at least at the procedural level), can be linked to administrative modernisation.

However, the experiment remained isolated. It was very different to those of around a dozen Spanish towns, often under Conservative administrations, that implemented participatory budgeting in 2006 in response to the need for administrative modernisation but provided citizens only with minimal levels of independence (Ganuza 2007; Ganuza and Frances 2012). Madrid local authority, run by the PP's Modernising wing, has integrated participation into its modernisation agenda and is also talking about implementing a participatory budget. A consultation exercise on the issue of finance has been undertaken in certain neighbourhoods, based on associating organised interests with the different sectors of the administration through municipal committees or neighbourhood councils whose functioning appears relatively opaque. This process has led to the almost total disappearance of the 'breaking with the past' element that appeared a fundamental part of participatory budgeting in Spain.

## 2. Italy: Is Another Town Possible?

An oscillation between breaking with the past and continuity was also a characteristic feature in Italy, where the Porto Alegre procedure also played a fundamental role (Allegretti 2005). Italy was the only country in Europe in which wide-ranging social movements called explicitly for participatory budgeting. At the turn of the century the alter-globalisation movement, very strong in Italy, included it in its vision of 'another world is possible', and *Nuovo Municipio*, a network comprising municipalities, academic institutions and intellectuals from the far left, took up the issue and made an active contribution to its spread (Magnaghi 2004). This was unprecedented in Europe, but did it produce experiments that were able to transform society?

The 1990s had brought significant changes to Italian local democracy. Operation *Mani pulite* (clean hands) sidelined a fairly substantial proportion of the political class, who had been involved in corruption scandals (the famous *tangentopoli*). However, the difference between the south and the rest of the country was only very partially reduced. While, over the long term, southern communes had great difficulties introducing a 'clean' process, many northern towns with right-wing mayors embarked resolutely on administrative modernisation with the aim of offering 'citizen-clients' high quality services. Left-wing communes, particularly in central Italy, had long represented a model of good local governance with a focus on high quality social services. However, they struggled to revitalise their former political system and the rampant crisis in this way of managing local affairs was highlighted by the loss of Bologna, which was governed by the Right for a single term of office. At the same time, Silvio Berlusconi's government introduced market criteria at all levels of public administration and carried out a form of politics that fluctuated between state centralism and unbridled neoliberalism. The reforms he imposed severely restricted local authorities' margins for action, due to an increasingly constrictive legal framework and a sharp decrease in the resources available to carry out their tasks. This recentralisation at the expense of the communes was in sharp contrast to developments in most other European countries (except the UK). It was experienced even more harshly because a reform of the local electoral system, with the direct election of the mayor and a bonus for the winning party's coalition, had resulted in majorities that could, politically speaking, act far more effectively.

In the 2000s, approaches aiming to involve citizens in decision-making and, more particularly, participatory budgeting, were progressively seen as tools with the potential to reinvigorate democracy (Bobbio 2003). As in Spain, it was left-wing, often Communist, mayors, or mayors with Communist deputies, who were the first to attempt these experiments, with the stated aim of differentiating themselves from the government's neoliberal policies. In addition, Italian delegates presented a charter for 'New Municipalities' at the World Social Forum in 2002, a call that was amplified when the first European Social Forum was held in Florence. The network that was set up at the Forum, *Nuovo Municipio*, proposed a programme that combined participation, social justice and sustainable development. It attempted to find responses to globalisation and considered that participatory budgeting was relevant to this end. The network comprised 80 local authorities that involved themselves in a variety of projects and working groups.

### Local Porto Alegres (Grottammare and Pieve Emanuele)

In the 1990s, the city of Grottammare, a tourist destination on the Adriatic coast, implemented an 'indigenous' participatory budget with almost no external influence and without explicitly using a term that was still unknown in Italy. With direct reference to Porto Alegre, Pieve Emanuele, located in the working-class suburbs of Milan, embarked upon an exemplary experiment in 2002. Around the new millennium, some large Italian cities introduced participatory budgeting. Sixteen examples existed in 2005; five years later there were over 250. But in 2012, the number massively decreased due to a right turn in local elections. How can these developments be explained?

In Grottammare, mass tourism had produced widespread speculation and corruption. In 1993, the municipal executive, heavily involved in *tangentopoli*, was swept away in operation 'Clean hands', with the town being placed under prefectural supervision. Young people from a variety of civil organisations and initiatives launched an independent list entitled 'Solidarity and Participation' and managed to win the 1994 election against a divided political Right. The alliance wanted to differentiate itself from the established parties, but also to substitute an effective administration for the one in place at the time, which was unwieldy and bureaucratic. Its cooperation with the Left enabled it to win the election and bring in a Communist mayor, a strong and highly independent personality. This was 'year zero' for the town, which found itself led by a participatory local government. Finances became public, with local council expenditure and investments discussed at neighbourhood meetings. Property speculation and construction on coastal greenfield land were blocked. Initially, discussions were taken into account in a selective manner, with the council summarising discussion outcomes as it saw fit. Starting in 2003, however, under the influence of national and international debates on participatory budgeting, the mechanism evolved. Following the example of the Porto Alegre system, citizens themselves could set the order of priorities. The participatory budget was now based on neighbourhood committees that implemented accepted projects and was part of a vast range of participatory tools centred on the weekly meetings of the 'Solidarity and Participation' list, which played an ambiguous role somewhere between political party and citizens' initiative.

This participatory approach was a big success: the citizens' list won the next three elections. People even voted against their national-level choices: they voted for left-wing lists in local elections but voted centre- and right-wing in parliamentary elections. Through various participatory tools the local government managed to establish trust between the citizens and the administration. Rather than getting tangled up in a labyrinth of bureaucracy, citizens' priorities were implemented rapidly and the method was used to comprehensively revise the urban development plan. The construction of enormous hotels and the destruction of ecological resources that had characterised previous years gave way to cautious development that preserved the town's cultural heritage and the ecological balance. In two working-class neighbourhoods, the participatory budgeting process produced a profound transformation of the social situation. As in Porto Alegre, the residents of the commuter towns of Ischia I and Ischia II, mainly disadvantaged people and immigrants, managed to make considerable improvements to their neighbourhood's quality of life through the participatory process, through which they produced public pressure that redirected public investments in their favour. Participatory approaches enabled Grottammare to completely reinvent its public and urban development policies. Corruption was beaten back and citizens exercised significant control over public affairs. Public opinion saw it as a major success.

Pieve Emanuele's experiment had many similarities. Speculation and corruption set in during the period of massive urban growth in the 1970s, during which the population grew from 3,000 to 15,000 (Amura 2003). At the beginning of the 1990s, the Communist mayor was publicly arrested for having sold the Berlusconi family a plot of building land located in a protected archaeological area. Following this scandal, the commune was placed under state supervision. A group of young politicians decided to attempt a fresh start: a left-wing coalition, led by Communists from the Communist Refoundation Party (PRC) which included Social Democrats from the DS (*Democratici di Sinistra*) and a group of independents won the 1994 elections and made residents' participation in the decision-making process one of its main concerns. One of the first measures was the adoption of a new municipal constitution giving citizen and association participation a more prominent place. A regular consultation process with associations was launched, while individual citizens' opinions were gathered on specific projects, such as schools. In 2003, there were no complaints when a participatory budgeting process based on individual participation, like the Porto Alegre procedure, was set up. It must be said that associations traditionally benefited from no formal privileges in the town, unlike in Cordoba or Albacete, and that the majority of them emerged from the local government's participatory policy. Citizens benefited from significant procedural independence in the system and were able to take direct decisions on a number of issues. This change in municipal policy not only affected the methodology: corruption appears to have been eradicated (the biggest success), several projects were modified or abandoned while others were set up, and the participatory approach had a distinct social impact. In particular, it led to the improved integration of disadvantaged groups.

### Increased Numbers and the Involvement of Large Cities (Rome)

Grottammare and Pieve Emanuele's participatory budgets were without doubt the European experiments with the widest-ranging effects in terms of social and political transformation, despite the fact that they differed in their long-term sustainability.[5] Both communes used participatory budgeting as a basis on which to end *tangentopoli*, make deep-rooted changes to their urban development and transform local social relations. A 'Porto Alegre in Europe' therefore does seem possible. The introduction of the Brazilian methodology certainly contributed to the success of these experiments, particularly in terms of strengthening civil society independence and avoiding or limiting the risks of the process being manipulated by the municipal executive. Nevertheless, the relatively exceptional circumstances that characterised these experiments and the small size of the communes involved urge caution: we need to consider whether these might merely be transient exceptions or developments that are likely to become more widespread.

In 2005, there were 16 participatory budgets in Italy. Most were located in the north or centre of the country, with no notable projects undertaken in the south. Two-thirds of these communes were governed by a centre-left coalition, with the remaining third run by independent lists. The network effect was an important factor in this spread, which affected mainly small or medium-sized towns. However, Rome and Venice, two major cities run by the Left, also embraced the experiment in some of their districts, which had just been established following the adoption of a national-level law on decentralisation.

In 2001, Rome XI, a middle- and working-class district, elected a left-wing coalition led by Massimilano Smeriglio, a Communist, a feat achieved through the support of social and alternative movements. Participatory budgeting was

---

5 Support for the Grottammare experience grew, to the point that the mayor was elected President of the Province in 2004. In Pieve Emanuele, on the other hand, the Left was divided in the 2007 elections and lost control of the local authority. As in Porto Alegre the relative success of the participatory policy did not fully revolutionise the institutional political system, whose legitimacy continued to be undermined by internal conflicts. While formally remaining on the municipal statutes, participatory budgeting was interrupted without eliciting any real protests.

introduced during his first year in office, accompanied by wide publicity. The initiators declared their inspiration to be the Porto Alegre system, with which they became familiar during the 2002 World Social Forum. One of the mayor's assistants was specifically allocated to the participatory budgeting process and the position was filled by an activist who was well known in alter-globalisation circles. The district joined the *Nuovo Municipio* network, which provided access to the approaches implemented by other member communes (D'Albergo 2005, Talpin 2011).

Taking inspiration from Grottammare and Pieve Emanuele, the procedure's cycle was established in the district's seven neighbourhoods. In January/ February, meetings were held to elect spokespersons, responsible in particular for running meetings with the help of external moderators. The intensive small-group work phase began in February/March. Concrete proposals were drawn up for investments, refuse collection, green areas, culture, services for young people and sport. These were then voted on at a further neighbourhood meeting in May. The municipal council then gave its opinion on the proposals: in December it had to provide information on project implementation. In 2004, participating citizens had an influence on 20 per cent of district investments (around 4 million euros). The district budget nevertheless had to be approved by the central mayor's office, which essentially held ultimate decision-making power in the city.

Like the Pieve Emanuele experiment, Rome XI's participatory budget had fostered the establishment and networking of new neighbourhood committees or associations, which focus on young people and the aged. The quality of discussions was particularly notable in the working groups that draw up the details of projects. While the procedure had a certain vagueness that made it similar to the proximity method, the strength of local civil society and the flexibility of its links with the system's key actors had resulted in a broader impact than was the case in the majority of French or German experiments we will analyse in the next chapters. Initially, non-elected citizens had only a slight, formal influence on the rules governing the procedures but their commitment and the vigour of the social movements that took ownership of the procedures led them to reflect on its rules. Without redistribution criteria to promote distributive justice, this increasing independence had no direct social impact, but it contributed to rebalancing the district's public policies in favour of outlying neighbourhoods. These were not the most disadvantaged, but had generally been neglected until that point. Based on improved communication between civil society and policy-makers, the mechanism faced two challenges. Individual participation decreased over the years, with the initial forum going down from 972 participants in 2003 to 714 in 2004 and 668 in 2005. The greatest problems remained poor cooperation with the administration, and the lack of a link between modernisation and participation and city–district relations. The district was still searching for its place in a commune that, after a major revival under the dynamic leadership of Mayor Walter Veltroni – who was also one of the main national leaders of the Left – moved to the right when he resigned in 2008. The participatory budgeting initiative stopped, due to internal rivalries within the Left and the opposition of the new right-wing mayor.

In Venice, the situation was even more precarious. The participatory budget was launched in 2004 following a decision by the central city council, which envisaged an experiment in three districts. The system varied slightly between districts but the respective administrations actively involved themselves in the working groups, unlike in Rome XI, and established internal committees to coordinate the proposed projects. Following a change in the internal balance of power of the Left, the mechanism was suspended after a year; the new process was again stopped after the 2005 elections when a new mayor came to power and removed the team that had set up the participatory budgeting project.

Was it the beginning of the end for Italian participatory budgeting? When in 2006 the centre-left coalition led by Romano Prodi came to power in Italy, creativity and the search for local-level alternatives tended to decrease because energies were taken up at the national level. When Berlusconi returned in 2008, local governments turned into centres of democratic innovation, and this was the most interesting period for Italian participatory budgeting. However, local elections at the end of the 2000s were difficult for the left and a number of experiments stopped. In addition, the financial crisis has restricted municipalities' margins for action and they are now highly dependent upon a central government that earmarks an ever-increasing share of communes' financial resources for predetermined purposes. Participatory budgets that were still in life were under threat of becoming a 'poor man's lottery'; this was even more the case given that they generally focus on investments and are therefore highly dependent on funding.

This development could have signalled an ebbing of the tide of participatory budgeting brought in at the turn of the twenty-first century were it not for another trend pulling in the opposite direction. Participatory budgeting was progressively 'contaminated' with other rapidly developing participatory mechanisms, losing part of its specific nature but gaining scope and becoming more deeply entrenched. By integrating it into urban development assistance programmes, local authorities managed again to finance more ambitious projects. Money sometimes came from European Union programmes or national government funds for experiments with e-governance and other innovative technologies. Some regions were interested in the idea and aimed to foster the implementation of participatory mechanisms in communes, as well as strengthening residents' involvement in regional decision-making. Tuscany implemented a model process in this regard, financing the development of participatory budgeting in small towns and adopting a new law on participation, following a wide-ranging consultation process. New participatory budgets in relatively large cities, such as Modena (176,000 inhabitants) and Bergamo (117,000), contributed to the fact that the numbers of citizens concerned by the procedure continued to increase (Laini and Andreozzi 2004). Lazio, the region of which Rome is the capital, adopted under a left government measures that strongly favoured the implementation of participatory budgeting, providing funds of 800,000 euros. Some dozen cases of this process were launched after 2007, mainly in small communes of various political hues.

The transformation of the *Nuovo Municipio* network revealed the developments taking place: while initially it put participatory budgeting at the heart of its concerns, later on it widened its scope to include techniques of social governance with an emphasis on the solidarity-based economy, for example. Was it trying to use this tool to promote those effects that participatory budgeting had not managed to produce? It is at least conceivable that the members of the network were aware that the system had not achieved the envisaged social transformation and that they had not lost sight of their original objectives, despite the fact that this pushed the Porto Alegre procedure into the background, where it had to compete with other forms of alternative governance. Italian participatory budgets are now part of multiple processes aimed at renewing local politics and modernising the administration, but the political exhaustion of the left reduces their scope.

## Conclusion: The Challenges of Reproducing Porto Alegre

In Italy and Spain, where participatory budgeting initially developed in a far more dynamic manner than in other European countries, attempts to import the Porto Alegre system were more faithful to the Brazilian procedure than elsewhere. As in Porto Alegre, in some of the experiments non-elected citizens were able to influence the rules of the game and benefited from real independence, sometimes due to procedural guarantees and sometimes as the outcome of the mobilisation of civil society. This did not take place without conflict between the various actors in the local political system, for example between the participatory system and the administration or between individual citizens working as volunteers and associations, although this latter tension was far less marked in Italy than in Spain, due to the two countries' different traditions. The adaptation of the Porto Alegre device, however, did manage to subvert the division of labour between politicians and citizens, either by breaking with previous forms of participation and management, by merging with them, or by triggering a wider participation process. On average, the quality of participatory budgeting procedures and debates was relatively high. In certain cases at least, use of the system produced far-reaching changes. The proximity paradigm played only a partial role, with other inspirations proving just as, if not more, important. In Puente Genil, municipal companies were included in the system, whereas in Pieve Emanuele and Grottammare private companies were strongly urged to become involved through public–private partnerships. In the wider context of privatisation, these innovations enabled the participatory policy to maintain its hold over developments in local society.

Nevertheless, one of the main dimensions of Porto Alegre – the link between participation and social justice – was only marginal in these experiments. Grottammare and Pieve Emanuele did demonstrate the potential of this link but they remained relatively isolated, with the results being less clear in large cities where deep-rooted changes, going beyond mere proximity, did not really emerge. While the criteria of distributive justice or mechanisms that foster minority integration can boost the social effects of participatory systems, to have a qualitative impact they must have a bearing on significant financial sums or on guiding public policy as a whole, which becomes more difficult when municipal enterprises are not involved in the process.

Locally, the Spanish and Italian experiments have faced enormous difficulties and some of them have fallen by the wayside. Those that have survived enabled radical innovations and during a decade, there was clearly an overall trend towards the strengthening and multiplication of participatory budgeting. From this point of view, importing the Brazilian experience was a success. However, the financial and economic crisis that has begun in 2008–2009 was fatal for the left at national level, with very hard repercussions at local level. The 2011 local elections turned into a disaster for participatory budgeting in Spain, as new conservative local governments decided to stop most of the experiments. Participatory budgeting, in this Porto Alegre style, was highly politicised and therefore very sensible to electoral changes. This was conversely confirmed by the Basque Country, where a number of new left-wing nationalist teams won elections and launched participatory budgeting initiatives.

In Italy the panorama also changed completely. After the initial experiments, the second wave of participatory budgeting was larger, but more influenced by proximity participation than by the Porto Alegre device. Important pilot projects were initiated by the governments of Lazio and Tuscany, while other reforms on the national level have detracted municipalities' financial capacities. And as in Spain, the victory of the right in local elections opened a third phase, of recession. In 2012, Italy only counted around 20 participatory budgets. Compared with the approximately 200 experiences three years before, this fall is impressive.

The next chapter turns to the development of participatory budgeting in France.

# 5

# 'PROXIMITY DEMOCRACY
# IS IN THE AIR'
## (France)

In 2001, during the National Assembly debate on the law on 'proximity democracy', a relatively small minority defended the idea of 'participatory democracy'. They shared the position of the *Motivés* (the 'motivated'), a group of young people involved in associations in Toulouse who compared these two terms by declaring that 'we should not confuse proximity democracy – which enables local elected representatives to keep their finger on the people's pulse … – with participatory democracy. This formula, which is more active in nature, aims to empower people to become actively involved in the decision-making process'.[1] This 'pro-participation' current was fairly close to the one which inspired approaches such as Cordoba or Grottammare. Bernard Birsinger, who was communist Deputy Mayor of Bobigny at the time, was particularly active in this debate. Three years later, the town, along with several others, committed itself to introducing a participatory budgeting process. However, an observer from Brazil would no doubt have felt lost if he or she had witnessed the 'scene of everyday participatory life' that took place in a public building near the Town Hall one November evening in 2004 and provides a good example of the proximity democracy model.

## The 'All-democratic Bobigny' Forum

In the four or five different forums organised at town level within the context of the 'Participatory Assizes' in 2004, the most active inhabitants demanded a session on participatory methods. The meeting started just after 8 pm. There was no podium facing the room, but rather tables set out in the manner of a huge restaurant. Some of them, reserved for distinguished guests, appeared to be more prestigious than others. As usual, the Communication Agency Campana-Eleb was in charge of organising the meeting, and the overall impression was one of a talk show. There was a good turnout: about 130 people showed up to take part in the discussion and to listen to the Mayor,

---

1 *Le Monde*, 23/03/01.

his staff and the many guests (elected representatives and members of NGOs from other towns, a university lecturer and so on). The participants were clearly working-class and represented a variety of ethnic origins. About one-third were women, and there were a few young people, too. People spoke up freely, and many 'ordinary' people, with little experience of public speaking, did not hesitate to express their ideas to the many people in the room. Was it the 'talk-show atmosphere' of the meeting which made them feel more at home, or because the journalist who moderated the discussion made sure that people got their chance to speak, or was it the result of hard-won trust, built up over the previous meetings? No doubt it was a mixture of all three, but it was a rare enough occurrence to be of note. From the outset, the Mayor announced that he had an open mind, and that he would take the outcomes of the discussion into account. He closed the discussion, which had lasted for over two and a half hours, with a general speech. He confirmed that the Town Hall wanted to introduce a participatory approach, and reminded the participants of the work already carried out, making general reference to the struggle against neoliberal globalisation. This conclusion did not sum up the discussion: in this meeting, dedicated to procedures, nothing had been planned with regard to deliberations leading to regulated decisions or specific recommendations. The inhabitants expressed their complaints and made their proposals, while the elected representatives listened and discussed things, and also announced some new proposals. They made the final decision about the proposals put forward during the debate and summarised the evening's discussions in a purely subjective manner.

What was at stake in the speeches of 2001 and the events of 2004? How did a forum like this point to developments that could reach beyond proximity democracy? What was the specific nature of French participatory budgeting that distinguished it from that of other European countries?

## 1. The Erosion of Republicanism

The law on proximity democracy, finally adopted in 2002, was introduced in a context of a crisis of legitimacy of the French political system, even though the population is highly politicised. From 1986 to 2002 all national elections – whether presidential or parliamentary – had led to the incumbent government being defeated and to a change of majority. In the first round of the presidential elections in 2002, Jacques Chirac, who was to have a run-off with Le Pen in the second, received only 19.9 per cent of the votes, compared with a 29.64 per cent vote for candidates with no parliamentary representation. Some years later, the referendum on the European Constitution, held on 29 May 2005, was again revealing: 92 per cent of the national representatives (both Parliament and Senate) voted in favour of a constitutional reform, which was rejected by 55 per cent of the electorate a mere three months later. There was a higher turnout for the presidential elections of 2007, with participation of 83 per cent, but the opinion polls showed a fundamental distrust of politicians; the parliamentary elections that followed did away with the illusion that a climate of trust had finally been created, as witnessed by the high rate of abstention. This panorama can be placed against a backdrop of increasing inequality, lack of economic growth and the undermining of the 'French model'.

Following discussions, the Jospin government introduced the law on 'proximity democracy' in 2002, which codified the proximity participation. Against a background of broad consensus, they introduced neighbourhood councils in all towns with a population of over 80,000 inhabitants. The differences during the Parliamentary debate concerned the manner of institutionalising dialogue between decision-makers and citizens. The Republican current, which is drawn from various right- and left-wing parties, had very little impact. They only barely accepted the principle of neighbourhood councils, which they believed might endanger local democracy in two ways: by weakening the legitimacy of elected representatives who would be threatened by the creation of new structures, and by creating parochial attitudes in neighbourhoods. This explains why parliamentarians of the Republican current extolled the virtues of the common good. According to them, this is a monopoly of elected representatives. The motto of the Republicans is 'good administration must be close to the ground', but 'good government is best carried out at a distance', because 'distance helps to avoid confusing the expression of individual interest with the common good and not giving in to short-term pressure'.[2]

The philosophy of this law could be situated halfway between the pro-participation perspective and classical French Republicanism. Most parliamentarians shared the idea that universal suffrage alone confers legitimacy with regard to defining the common good, and therefore making binding political decisions; citizens, however, should have the possibility to actively state their needs and specific interests and elected representatives should take this into consideration. From this perspective, a strict hierarchy needs to be respected: participation is merely a complementary function of representative democracy and, as such, should in no way compete with it. Within these limits, regular consultation with inhabitants, inasmuch as it enriches public debate, facilitates the representatives' capacity to listen to the needs of their electorate, and meets citizens' desire to participate in 'considering local decisions and the definition of projects that affect them on an everyday basis'.[3] According to

---

2 Jean Espilondo, Socialist Party deputy, minutes of the 2nd session on 14/06/01.
3 Daniel Vaillant (*Exposé des motifs*, document dated 29/05/01, n° 3089).

the actors, the step towards proximity democracy could be motivated by either genuine conviction, opportunism or strategic positioning in the political arena.

## 2. Redeveloping Political Links and Neighbourhood Management: Saint-Denis and Bobigny

The first French participatory budgets were born out of the discussions on proximity democracy. Among the dozen or so experiments that existed in 2005, those of Saint-Denis and Bobigny were among the most noteworthy at national and international level. These two towns, situated to the north of Paris, had Communist Party mayors heading left-wing coalitions, and were emblems of the old 'red belt'. Saint-Denis is of historical importance, because it is here in the basilica that the kings of France are buried. Bobigny is the county capital of Seine Saint-Denis, which at that time was one of the remaining two counties where the local government was Communist Party led. Both towns are rich, which is the result of economic activities based there, but they also have a poor working-class population, strongly affected by the processes of social, geographical and ethnic segregation.

Saint-Denis had a local population of around 94,000 inhabitants, which is quickly growing due to the economic development of the town, in which a major high tech zone is located. Many service sector companies have set up business here, and many companies are linked to the research sector or to new areas of economic activity. This has enabled the town to establish a positive financial balance, following a period of economic pressure. Moreover, it has a strong construction programme for council housing and created an intercity council with neighbouring towns, of which Saint Denis is the natural centre.

Bobigny, with a population of 45,000, is where the *Préfecture* is located, as well as being home to the headquarters of many civil services; it also benefits from being located between Paris and Charles de Gaulle airport. Whereas Saint-Denis is designed around the historical town centre, the physiognomy of the centre of Bobigny is characterised by high-rise buildings, reminiscent of parts of East Berlin. In 2005, the state of the town's finances and the per capita budget (200 euros) were similar to those of Saint-Denis. The social make-up of both towns was similar, with a high rate of unemployment (around 20 per cent, which was double the national average), an overwhelming working-class majority and a minority of middle-class inhabitants, working in the public sector. There were also many immigrants (the percentage of foreigners was 26 per cent in Saint-Denis and 23 per cent in Bobigny, which was about five times the national average), as well as a high percentage of council housing (around 55 per cent in Saint-Denis and 65 per cent in Bobigny). If we include people from French overseas territories and first, second or third generation immigrants (many of whom are French nationals) 'traditional' French people formed a small minority of the local population.

## From Neighbourhood Councils to Participatory Budgeting

Saint-Denis pioneered the introduction of neighbourhood councils. In the 1980s, the communist municipal authorities fell out with the orthodox line of the Party. The new mayor, Patrick Braouezec, had to cope with a major activist crisis, which fell as flat in Saint-Denis as it did elsewhere in France. The electoral results show an increasing lack of interest.[4] The right-wing party *Front National* progressed and regularly outdid the traditional right-wing parties, and the Town Hall team's results increasingly deteriorated. For the first time, in 1995 the left-wing alliance list was not re-elected on the first count. With the introduction of participatory processes, the new mayor tried to meet these challenges, to increase activist backing for the Town Hall, to promote a more localised delivery of public services and to overcome the pitfalls of management that had become excessively bureaucratic. It was also aimed at changing the mayor's and elected representatives' public image, as communist ideology and the traditional working class town had ceased to be things with which people identified. Although this strategy was initially criticised by the Communist Party apparatus, it aimed to re-establish a channel of communication with citizens that had traditionally been guaranteed by the Communist Party and its satellites. Although Saint-Denis has a rich layer of NGOs, the participatory process was clearly the result of a top-down approach.

Monthly neighbourhood meetings open to all and moderated by an elected representative were introduced in neighbourhoods targeted for the implementation of urban renewal policies in the mid-1980s. These were an informal version of the neighbourhood councils that appeared in dozens of other towns at this time. But this process seemed to be insufficient in the early 2000s. The limits of a purely consultative, micro-local procedure that involved little mobilisation were starting to be felt. Furthermore, there was a risk that Saint-Denis would lose its relatively advanced position if it did not take fresh

---

4 According to the 1999 census, there were 86,000 inhabitants in Saint-Denis. This included 63,000 French nationals, of whom 45,000 were adults, and therefore potential voters. A total of 32,000 people were on the electoral roll and 15,000 voted in the municipal elections in 2001, with just over half voting for the incumbents. The percentage of electoral mobilization – that is to say, the votes cast compared to the adult population in Saint-Denis as a whole – fell to the level of the 1870s, that is to say, before the workers movement took over the town. This is a recent phenomenon: in 1980 Saint-Denis still had an electoral roll of 45,000 for a population of almost the same number of people (Vidal 1995a, 1995b, Offerlé 1989).

initiatives. The encounter with Porto Alegre was to play a decisive role. Saint-Denis became actively involved from the outset in the World Social Forum, well before the national leaders of the French Communist Party. The town discovered the Brazilian experience and immediately thought of adapting it to France, officially launching a participatory budget initiative in 2001.

At the same time, at national level the Communist Party finally discovered the virtues of participation. Bobigny constitutes an emblematic example of this change. The French Communist Party had governed the town for over eight decades, and still considered it to be a model town. There were 1,200 card-carrying Communist Party members in Bobigny, which was an exceptionally high percentage of the population. The town had always been governed by 'orthodox' leaders, who vigorously fought the dissenting voices of neighbouring towns – particularly those of Saint-Denis, their sibling rival. But traditional Communist Party methods were visibly running out of steam. Average quality of services was declining and the very bureaucratic way of working, combined with cronyism, weighed heavily against them.

The political strategy based on supporting trade union struggles in local companies no longer worked, inasmuch as the companies moved away and the issue now was to attract new companies to set up locally. In addition, the Communist Party leaders had not succeeded in developing ties with the new post-colonial immigrant communities similar to those they had with previous waves of migrant workers from rural France and other European countries. These local factors were aggravated by the deepening national and international crises. As in the case of Saint-Denis, communist activism was in free fall in Bobigny. The percentage of votes cast in the first round of the municipal elections in favour of the left-wing coalition fell from 65 per cent to 51 per cent between 1989 and 1995. The new Mayor, Bernard Birsinger, was convinced that the only possible solution to save the town was to change direction. He initiated a new political approach, supported by the activities of local social movements and the emergence of the alter-globalist movement at national and international level. This renovation involved introducing new channels for participation, disconnected from party politics, similar to those introduced in Saint-Denis. In 1998, the town held a big municipal forum, the *Town Assizes*, which was to recur every two years. It also organised a *Consult'action*, which was an initiative partially linked to an opinion poll and partially a mass mobilisation. This enabled the inhabitants to express their opinions after years during which the expression of ideas had been strictly channelled by the party apparatus. From this point of view, the approach was a huge success: more inhabitants responded to the survey than had taken part in the elections, and the themes that emerged from the Assizes were innovative.

In both Bobigny and Saint-Denis, the emerging alter-globalisation movement was a boon. It appeared to open the door to a new political project after the fall of the Berlin Wall and the difficulties faced by French communism. Saint-Denis had monopolised the relationship with Porto Alegre, so Bobigny turned to the Brazilian town of Belém for inspiration. Participatory budgeting there was based on very strong popular mobilisation and also attached less importance to strict procedures. The idea of participatory budgeting was first discussed during the 3rd Assizes of the town in 2001, which was also the year of the first World Social Forum. In 2003, Bobigny hosted the second European Social Forum, along with Saint-Denis and Paris, which gave the town a certain international profile.

### Selective Listening (Cherry-picking)

A Brazilian or a Spanish observer would not have felt out of place in this context. The language used was partially the same as in Porto Alegre, with a marked Marxist vocabulary and critical references to neoliberal capitalism. However, not much of the procedural process of Brazilian participatory budgets, with their explicit rules and efficient decision-making mechanisms, was included. The procedural logic inherent in the Assizes meetings that we have just described was similar to that in most traditional participatory instruments. The spirit of participatory budgeting 'French style' of which Bobigny and Saint-Denis can be considered fairly representative, is based on proximity meetings in the neighbourhoods, leading to a discussion at town level. At the same time, it is left to the elected representatives and the town's civil service to summarise the discussion, that tends to range freely, by using a process that can be called 'cherry-picking' or 'selective listening'.

In concrete terms, the most important difference between the approaches of Saint-Denis and Bobigny was that, in the case of the latter, the participatory budget *per se* only lasted for a short time, and played a relatively marginal role. Over and above this, they shared many similarities. One key dimension was the direct contact between politicians, civil servants and citizens. This communication existed in the meetings that were organised once or twice a year in the neighbourhoods, during which the mayor met the local inhabitants in a very hands-on manner. These meetings provided an opportunity to deal with concrete micro-local issues and the mayor was asked to report back on the implementation of things to which he had previously committed himself. Other, more formal meetings were regularly organised in all the neighbourhoods. These meetings fell within the framework of the law on proximity democracy (Vaillant law), and were not formally limited, but open to all inhabitants who chose to volunteer. They were led by an elected representative and a neighbourhood manager, and were attended by municipal civil servants responsible for matters that were up for discussion.

Inhabitants had very little independence within this framework. Hardly any meetings bringing together residents from different areas were held. The themes under discussion, however, which previously had included only micro-local issues, now included issues that concerned the town as a whole. The idea behind these meetings was for elected representatives and those in charge within the civil services to develop closer ties with citizen-users. The goal was to make the town's public policies more visible, to develop closer ties with the most active inhabitants and thus develop greater political legitimacy, encouraging social contact through dialogue and impacting the management of daily affairs by developing greater responsiveness. The decentralisation of certain town services, with the opening of neighbourhood offices and an approach based on 'joined-up thinking' that was encouraged by the elected representative in charge of the brief, as well as by a neighbourhood manager, were designed to make public action more transparent and efficient at micro-local level.

Workshops and forums in the town helped to extend these contacts and to bring under consideration the town's budget. In Saint-Denis, a questionnaire on the budget was distributed to all local households, and the replies were summarised and analysed by the Town Hall, as well as in participatory workshops. Some budget workshops were dedicated to financial affairs. They were moderated by external facilitators and, in theory, brought together volunteers and delegates from the neighbourhood meetings. In reality, the distinction between the two was unclear, and the principle of delegation was rather lax. This partially accounts for the fact that the workshops never played the role of a genuine participatory budgeting council. When they were held, however, the representatives of the various departments did take part and hold discussions with the inhabitants. Policy documents presented in a didactic manner helped people to get involved in the budgetary discussions in a fairly precise way. Discussions covered a range of concrete issues, as well as the general lines of the town's budget. The outcome of these discussions was then conveyed to the respective departments by civil servants and elected representatives and incorporated into the budget, voted on by the town council. The outcomes of the participatory approach were also communicated by Internet on the town's website, and sent to all local inhabitants' homes in brochure form. Finally, the participatory budget was also covered by a specific paragraph in the general budgeting process, which took up three pages every year in the local weekly newspaper, *Le Journal de Saint-Denis*.

### An Uncertain Development

All in all, the procedure used in Bobigny and Saint-Denis was fairly close to the ideal-type of proximity democracy. In both towns, the approach remains informal and strictly consultative. Participation was based on a variety of different tools, but these were only loosely connected. These mechanisms were at any rate top-down and, unlike Porto Alegre, had not been appropriated by the working class in a process of social mobilisation. The results, in terms of participation, were variable. In Saint-Denis the process was weak: in most neighbourhoods and workshops participation varied between a few and a couple of dozen citizens. Most local inhabitants were not even aware that a participatory budget existed. In addition, young people and those of immigrant origin were not generally involved in the process. Although the objective of showing solidarity with the poorest communities was clearly stated, a policy of social justice founded on the use of direct participation had never been developed. As the 'outsiders' were generally absent from the participatory meetings, it was highly unlikely that any unforeseen pressure might be brought to bear within the existing processes. Women's participation was roughly speaking on an equal footing with that of men, but the idea of gender mainstreaming did not exist. The local Town Hall rejected the very idea of social justice based on an explicit body of rules such as those of the Porto Alegre matrix, and transparency did not extend as far as the question of sharing of investments between the various neighbourhoods. Saint-Denis participatory budgeting had characteristics similar to other participatory approaches in France.

The Bobigny experiment was far from promoting distributive justice or transforming the gender balance. It was singular only inasmuch as it had managed to gather many working class people together in meetings that were organised at municipal level. People were no doubt motivated at least partially by the festive nature of the events, although the process was not at all self-organised, any more than that in Saint-Denis. For the most part the rules were decided top-down, and the participants were not allowed to change them. Even the supervisory committee in charge of monitoring implementation, whose job was to evaluate the state of implementation of projects that had been adopted as a result of the participatory approach, was not in a position to modify things.

In 2004, the vote on the budget took place in a joint meeting of the Saint-Denis town council, the delegates of the participatory workshops and the volunteer inhabitants. Some associations mobilised to have their point of view taken into account, as it had not been possible to include all the inhabitants' proposals in the budget. The experiment of a joint session of the town council and the participatory process delegates, one of the most original aspects of the Saint-Denis process, was not repeated out of fear that there would be too much lobbying and because it was likely to encourage the emergence of a countervailing power. Without social mobilisation or decision-making impact, however, this approach illustrated the logic of cherry-picking that satisfied some people, but seriously disappointed the most active.

Yet, in the civil service offices the language was different and many employees explained that they had made very significant changes to the way they worked.

At this level, the declared objectives had been partly met. Neighbourhood management had been introduced and the communication channels set up in recent years enabled users' concerns to be included upstream. In the most far-reaching cases, a common diagnosis and project developed by citizens in cooperation with policy-makers resulted from such an approach.

Even if it was only partially perceived by the inhabitants, the increased communication also influenced political and administrative procedures at town level. The way in which the budget was designed had undeniably changed. It was more open to the needs expressed through the participatory instruments. The amounts of money involved went beyond the 700,000 euros officially dedicated to the participatory budget initiative in Saint-Denis:

We draw up the budget and hope it isn't out of synch with the local inhabitants. ... In the thematic workshops we get a feeling for some of their concerns, and we check to make sure that what we have budgeted corresponds to these needs. ... Generally speaking, we prepare our budget according to our political priorities, and by taking into account what comes out of the year-round participatory process.[5]

Paradoxically, the progress in terms of transparency that a participatory process often involves represented perhaps a greater advantage for elected representatives than citizens. They could use it to lean on the civil services, with whom there were sometimes rather strained relations. The need to present the budget in a clear manner had clearly supported the positions of the town counsellors, who previously had found it difficult to cope with a complex and difficult budget document. One of the main obstacles to proximity management in Bobigny and Saint-Denis was the fact that the administrative machine changed only slightly and that the budgetary accounting methods remained essentially unchanged. Overall, responsiveness was still insufficient, and certain municipal or para-municipal departments continued to work in a Kafkaesque way. The legitimacy of the participatory process also depends on its capacity to improve the little things that 'can make life impossible' or, on the contrary, by improving things on a day-to-day basis. If the town council's staff, who has daily contact with the local inhabitants, is unable to involve the rest of the administrative machine, however, the impact of the participatory process must remain limited. One regular participant in the neighbourhood process in Saint-Denis complained that 'this approach allows them to gauge the feeling ...', but then nothing is done to solve the problems'; this is echoed in the remark of a civil servant who said: 'The discussions are taken into account, but it's seriously difficult to respond in time. The inhabitants' time-frame is different from that of the town'.

---

5 Interview with the town counsellor in charge of the participatory budget.

The dialogue had, however, helped the town council teams to keep their heads above water and to regain a certain credibility among the most active inhabitants. At the same time, in both Bobigny and Saint-Denis, the participatory budget has failed to impact abstention (Rey 2005). The citizens who have become involved in the procedure were those who were already actively involved in the electoral process. The participatory process seemed to have gained the support of some of the most active sectors of the local inhabitants by providing a structure that enabled dialogue in the neighbourhoods and, to a lesser extent, at town level. In 2001, the left-wing alliance list showed considerable gains in both towns and was elected in the first round (up from 51 per cent to 65 per cent in Bobigny, and from 46 per cent to 53 per cent in Saint-Denis); it is highly probable that the participatory process was a strong contributory factor. Seven years later, however, the majority was so divided that they presented two separate competitive lists in Saint-Denis, and this happened again in 2014. The Bobigny team's majority dropped to 54 per cent in 2007 and the new mayor, less charismatic than the former one, had to accept the victory of the right in 2014. In the meantime, the specific role of the participatory budget as opposed to other participatory instruments was in no way guaranteed. Whereas Bobigny suspended the participatory budget in 2004 and did not really reactivate it afterwards, Saint-Denis progressed during a first period by introducing a ranking system for priorities but the importance of participatory budgeting tended to decrease at the end of the 2000s.

Neither of the two local authorities seems to have gone through a cumulative learning experience, and the issue of the sustainability of a process that requires so much energy and that has a relatively low impact remains a genuine question mark. For these reasons, it is necessary to look elsewhere to understand how a renewal might open up new perspectives.

## 3. The Challenge of a Regional Participatory Budget

As the years went by, participatory budgets had multiplied and diversified in France. In 2001, there were just two experiments, but over a dozen in 2005. The city of Bobigny contributed to this development. It regularly organised meetings on the topic, inspired other suburban communist town halls to follow suit. Groups such as ADELS, the main French NGO that worked on the theme of local democracy, also regularly contributed to the diffusion of participatory budgeting. Although a very minority concept, the theme was no longer the exclusive domain of communist mayors in the Paris suburbs. Socialist teams took up the idea in the 20th district of Paris, in the Council Housing department of the town of Poitiers, and even more so in the Poitou-Charentes regional council. In a more propagandist manner, some Greens also expressed an interest in the idea. *Le Monde Diplomatique*, a journal that was one of the originators of the World Social Forum, initially played an important role; they later dropped their interest in the subject. Over and above these activist networks, whether or not they were allied to parties, consultancies and communication agencies that were often of more or less distant activist origin played a considerable role in the design of participatory budgeting.

A new scale was introduced with the Poitou-Charentes experiment, in which the regional scale comes to the fore (Sintomer, Röcke and Talpin 2013). The approach received considerable political coverage in France, as the regional president is Ségolène Royal, who was the Socialist Party's candidate in the presidential elections in 2007. This procedure, which involves very considerable sums of money, entails the devolution of decision-making powers to participants by a vote that enables the ranking of projects. These two aspects are reminiscent of the Porto Alegre procedure.

Poitou-Charentes has a population of only 1,600,000 inhabitants, which makes it one of the least populated and most rural French regions. With a traditional right-wing political orientation, it swung to the left in the 2004 elections and remained so in 2010. The new leaders had placed the 'participatory democracy' issue at the forefront of their campaign. What it was going to include in concrete terms was fairly vague, even if a participatory budget and citizens' juries were explicitly mentioned. This did not stop the straightforward implementation of an original experiment, which proved within a few months to be one of the most promising initiatives in France.

There were several contributory factors. Ségolène Royal understood that participatory democracy was a winning idea in the national context of the political system's crisis of legitimacy. Furthermore, the project matched her profile, based on distancing herself from the political establishment. In 2002, she travelled to Porto Alegre for the World Social Forum. She gathered support in the regional administration from two long-standing supporters of participatory democracy, who brought broad political and managerial skills to the process. These were also the people responsible for the day-to-day running of the process. This team mobilised external experts who contributed to the credibility of the approach and its orientation.

In June 2004, shortly after winning the regional elections, which allowed her to become President of the Poitou-Charentes region, Ségolène Royal launched her participatory project in regional high schools.[6] This choice reflected reasons of visibility: high schools cover a large geographical area and involve different sectors of the population. This choice was also based on questions of feasibility, as high schools depend on only one administrative

---

6 High schools in France represent the major legal responsibility of regions.

department (Education). The allocated sum was 10 million euros, out of a total budget line of 110 million euros dedicated to high schools at regional level. The money could only be used for small investments and projects of up to 150,000 euros, and did not include major investments, such as building or complete renovation of schools. The commitment of the region was to respect the choices made by participants, on condition that the projects fall within their sphere of legal competence. Two meetings were held in each of the 93 high schools. They were open to all students, teachers, administrative and technical staff and parents. External facilitators provided moderation, and representatives of the regional executive and administrative services were always present.

An initial meeting in each school was held to present the participatory budget. Working groups then met to discuss projects that would improve the school. In order to encourage free discussion, the regional representatives and Head did not take part. The working groups presented a summary of their ideas to a general assembly. In the following weeks, technical services examined the proposals, evaluated whether they come within the regional sphere of competence and if so, estimated the costs involved. If it was deemed necessary to clarify something, it had become the norm to hold an additional meeting with the regional engineer and a group of volunteers from the school. In the second meeting, a document that summarised the projects that had been considered was presented. Following a debate, the participants voted to rank their preferences. Everyone could cast ten votes, and the ranking was based on the total number of votes each project received. All documents were available online on the participatory budget website and students were informed of the results of the regional council debate by notices pinned up on school noticeboards. Participants systematically completed an evaluation form (people generally expressed a high level of satisfaction with the approach). There was also an annual audit.

This process appeared to break with the proximity democracy model that characterises the vast majority of French experiments. This was due to the decision-making power, the relatively large sums of money involved and the clarity of the procedures.

Several key questions remained unanswered, however. The first concerned participation. In 2009–2010, around 23,000 people (including 19,000 pupils) took part in both meetings – more than twice as many as during the first year (2005–2006: 10,702 participants, including 7,018 pupils). These numbers clearly placed the process in the upper bracket of attendance of participatory instruments, comparable to attendance at neighbourhood assemblies in Porto Alegre. It was far higher than in most other European experiments. This figure was nevertheless limited, given the fact that the meetings took place within the schools, the logistics and human resources deployed, and the way in which students were encouraged – in some cases almost obliged – to attend, which obviously distorted the results.[7]

What these figures do show is that the participatory process has not involved a strong bottom-up mobilisation; nor has it generated a social movement among the young people in question – even though high school students had mobilised in strength in the region against the 'First Job Contract' in spring 2006.[8] The high school participatory budget initially had to overcome the scepticism and hostility of certain elected members on both sides of the regional parliament, as well as the national rector (who has the main authority in the schools), the trade unions and heads of schools, as well as some of the regional staff responsible for the schools brief. Ségolène Royal's strong political determination and that of her entourage were the decisive factor that allowed the project to commence.

The question of power, even though clearly posed, was yet to be defined. All participants had equal voting rights. The trade unions, associations, elected members of student organisations (administrative board and council), teachers and heads had no specific rights. Likewise the partial opening up of a historically relatively closed institution was in itself a considerable evolution. These characteristics differed from the way high schools traditionally operate. From this perspective, the process clearly constituted a democratisation of this institution. Traditional representative bodies of elected representatives within schools that function in a highly formal and bureaucratic way had been challenged and largely circumvented by the participatory budgeting process. Particularly in the beginning, the state tried to hinder a process that had been initiated by a region representing the political opposition. This was done by forbidding all schools to communicate the lists of students' names or parents' details to the regional executive: so that they were not able to contact them directly in the matter of participatory budgeting.

Overall, the procedure bestowed considerable independence on participants: they could vote on the hierarchy of projects, which the region was then committed to implementing. It was no easy task to achieve this. Ségolène Royal herself was initially reluctant to accept the idea of a vote; it was her team and the concrete dynamics of the project that finally convinced her (Röcke 2014). Nevertheless, the regional executive continued to be responsible for defining the participatory rules without directly involving the participants in this undertaking. A step

7 There was uneven participation according to category: although there was an overall increase of 20 per cent among students, parents' and teachers' participation went down and that of technical staff slightly up.

8 The 'First Job Contract', a draft law of the right-wing government led by Dominique de Villepin, aimed at modifying contracts for young people in their first job by providing fewer contractual guarantees. This led to a huge wave of student protests and the law was not implemented.

forward was made in 2008. This took the form of citizens' juries that brought together representatives of all the members of the educational community to jointly evaluate how the project was working, as well as the regional policies on high school education.[9] This went forward after the 2010 elections, when annual participatory budgeting assemblies at regional level focussed on the rules.

Meetings had also remained almost entirely organised by the regional executive and outside consultants hired for the purpose. If 'follow-up' groups of volunteers working were created, this would have provided a landmark improvement to the deliberative quality of the participatory process. It would have greatly improved the quality of the preparatory work carried out on the projects presented, as well as the preparation of the meetings. This seemed to be the approach adopted by the region in 2007, during a one-day training session of the cultural moderators that prepared the meetings within the high schools.

A third question concerned the modernisation of the regional civil services. It would appear that the strongest impact of the process was on how the civil service operates.

## Progress and Problems of Participatory Modernisation

Even more than in other French experiments, participatory budgeting in Poitou-Charentes encouraged better management at local level (as opposed to a reform of public services in general), based on actors' local knowledge. This limited the wastage resulting from decision-making by technicians who are not in touch with people's real needs. The vast majority of the civil servants in charge of managing the process were pleased with the progress that has been achieved. One member of the high school daily affairs department was convinced: 'It's a way of consulting grass-roots, and that's important. They may not always be right, but it's thanks to them that things move forward. I feel that at certain times the grass-roots' perception of problems is clearer … Because grass-roots represent great diversity, and because we need to avoid taking decisions based on only one current of thought'. This is echoed in the idea expressed by an operations' manager: 'It brings a lot of things to the surface; we discover the existence of problems. For example … when I went past the lavatories, they looked really clean to me …'. The management had heard about small problems but … nobody was (really) aware of them. And then suddenly, with the introduction of the high school participatory budget, we discovered that the students were complaining because water from the showers on the floor above leaked down on them'.

9 Citizens' juries selected at random also evaluated several aspects of regional public policy that same year.

All actors – from the most enthusiastic to the most critical – agreed that participation represents more than lip service, and that a real impact had been made on the delivery of the public services involved. The requests sent to technical departments in order to estimate the project costs have shown that technicians did not always have the relevant accounting tools or the skills to do this work in a fast and accurate manner. The introduction of participatory budgeting has strongly encouraged the modernisation of regional public administration. This is not always an easy task, however, and reorganising public services has proven to be a long-haul job. It also involved hiring new staff who were convinced of the usefulness of the process and who had sufficient know-how. As an education officer (*conseiller principal d'éducation*) of one of the high schools explained, the machine was still far from working under full steam: 'There weren't many people involved this year, because things hadn't started working yet. There would have been a huge number of people involved if the question of the sports' ground had been brought up …'. When the head welcomed the parents here in the autumn, there was talk of the participatory budget. But if nothing happens, things go quiet'. The problem is all the trickier, as it was initially difficult to carry out an inventory of the projects that had been effectively implemented.

Administrative responsiveness was problematic, inasmuch as the pace in no way corresponded to that of the participatory process, which is much faster. And while the latter emphasises the 'sluggishness' of the traditional administrative process, it also creates new challenges. The high school participatory budget initially implied a double administrative track, and many departments found it difficult to manage their traditional workload as well as a participatory process that worked at an entirely different pace. It also meant an increased workload, and caused some regional civil servants to complain.* Furthermore, some of them were shocked by the fact that decisions involving very considerable sums, but dedicated to 'superfluous' projects (such as a diving trip to the Red Sea, trips to Euro Disney), could be taken in a matter of hours. These projects were unrelated to real needs.

Nevertheless, such projects were few in number and the region has tried to overcome these obstacles by reinforcing and gradually improving the process. Estimating the costs involved in certain types of projects has been internalised in the high school participatory budget department. The regional staff has been able to use their experience to perform a better, faster evaluation of needs, based on the experience of previous years (projects tended to be recurrent from one year to the next). It has also been improved by holding a systematic intermediate meeting between the two public assemblies, which helps to define the projects more clearly. At the end of the day, by exerting pressure on the civil servants and encouraging their reorganisation, the participatory budget has meant that users' needs are taken into consideration much more quickly, and often at lower cost. Both coordination between departments and

---

*Note:* According to information gathered during interviews, the additional workload would appear to be around 20 per cent.

the degree of real assimilation of participation in the daily workings of administration are crucial questions. They contribute to avoiding the upsetting of the administrative logic on a 'political' whim, and to achieving greater quality of *modus operandi*. In the case of the Poitou-Charentes experiment, the entire regional administration responsible for schools was reorganised in spring 2008. This was the direct outcome of the participatory budgeting process and proof that participatory democracy can contribute to the modernisation of public services.

The final question was that of scale and, by extension, of the social impact of a participatory instrument. A procedural modification that has begun in 2010–11 was of prime importance in this regard. The initial project – a wave of meetings that brings delegates of every school together in order to move beyond the school-by-school level of discussion and establish genuine distributive equity between schools – was eventually agreed on. In 2005, the year of the beginning of the process, the regional executive felt that the priority was to stabilise the new device against opposition from the heads (and other actors). The latter perceived the new process as a creation that would interfere with the independence of their schools and their own power and many of them strongly opposed it.

After six years of the process, the organisers recognised the need for an important procedural modification. Not only did they want to counteract the merely strategic use of the process, which for some members of the high school community consisted simply of a tool for acquiring as much money as possible from the region, but the lack of inter-school discussion in recent years clearly limited the quality of discussions and the kinds of choice that participants were able to make. The method used meant that each school determined the hierarchy of projects, rather than sharing a predetermined sum school by school. The regional executive had turned down the latter possibility, on the grounds that it would merely represent a transfer of 'community funds' to schools, and would resemble a traditional grant system ('We spent what we have, irrespective of our real needs') rather than a needs-based logic ('What are our needs, and to what extent can we satisfy them?'). However, the selected approach hindered a balanced evaluation on the part of the project participants in terms of cost/benefit analysis: in many cases, it would have been preferable, for instance, to select six small projects rather than three big ones. If each school had had a variable budget established on a participatory basis at regional level, it would have made it possible to combine the logic of meeting needs and redistribution to the most disadvantaged schools.

As a consequence, during Royal's first term in Poitou-Charentes (2004–2010), the most disadvantaged schools did not receive more than others, but some of the most well equipped institutions did (Mazeaud 2011: 29). However, the Executive had taken upon itself to directly manage the redistributive process. They did this by including an additional series of projects that met regional priorities, over and above those accepted by the schools' votes. As one project manager said,

> The participatory budget has helped us to do a real audit of the state of the schools in the region. … We realize now that some schools have been totally neglected. The high school participatory budget has enabled us to speak up, and tell some heads that, in view of what they have already received and the state of the school, they are not at the top of the list for whatever it is that they are requesting.

As such, the participatory process already cut down on the 'secret diplomacy' of the past that tended to determine the choice of investments – but it was only an indirect tool of social justice, and partly produced effects contrary to the political and social goals.

Supported by the further victory of Royal at the 2010 regional elections and the overall very positive feedback the process was enjoying, the organisers eventually decided to introduce a second participation level – through which the process became a participatory budget in the sense we give it here, that is beyond the micro-local level.

Concretely, the new procedure was organised for the first time on 16 February 2011 (Mazeaud 2011). 900 people, selected from all regional high schools, met during one day. Groups of ten people coming from different high schools discussed the inequalities between different schools and spending criteria for a more just allocation of funds. External facilitators supported the discussions. Tables were equipped with a computer in order to write down the most important aspects, which were then directly summarised and publicised. At the end of the day, the participants selected three out of five allocation criteria put forward by the official organisers (people had the ability to propose new ones). These criteria clearly demonstrate the 'redistributory vocation' (Mazeaud 2011: 29) of the new process: quality of buildings and equipment; geographic localisation (in order of favor those institutions in rural areas with much fewer cultural activities); social background of pupils (in order to favor those institutions with a higher number of pupils from lower social strata). Every school received a certain number of points for these criteria, which were also accessible on the internet. Then, three groups were established: the 20 institutions with the highest and lowest needs received a sum of 150,000 and 30,000 euros respectively, and the remaining ones 66,000 euros. In the following months the voting meetings within single high schools took place as previously. An important step had been taken towards a much more political project, and the modification represented a move away from proximity democracy in the direction of participatory democracy. However, it was not repeated in 2012 because of the Presidential and legislative elections and the national career of Ségolène Royal and the fusion of Poitou-Charentes with a nearby region implied the end of this interesting experiment.

## Conclusion: A Paradoxical Situation

One of the original aspects of participatory budgeting as defined here, in contrast to neighbourhood councils or local community funds, is that it can reach beyond the micro-local level. It is by their way of functioning at the neighbourhood and city-wide levels that potentially enables them to overcome Nimbyism. In the declarations made by the initiators in Poitou-Charentes and elsewhere, it was supposed to serve as support for the introduction of participatory democracy, and to be distinguished from proximity democracy. As we have just seen, the procedural reform in Poitou-Charentes did indeed point in this direction. Most other French examples of participatory budgeting, however, have only marginally overcome the logic of proximity, in the dual sense of the term: proximity management (geographical) and proximity communication (political). The micro-local level remains the predominant one, and the one at which concrete impacts can be most clearly felt. Moreover, cherry-picking, which is based on establishing a regular dialogue, but with vague procedures, is typical of the proximity democracy approach.

The proximity democracy model does show severe limitations. Although it enables considerable improvement of local management and provides regular channels for communication between the local political-administrative system and the most active citizens, it remains a variation on classical representative government. Furthermore, proximity democracy is dogged by unsolved internal tensions: on the one hand, it affirms that matters of the common good are the monopoly of the elected representatives, and on the other, it emphasises the importance of public discussion with local inhabitants. It may help to improve the legitimacy of local public policies, but is rarely capable of achieving large-scale mobilisation such as that witnessed in Porto Alegre: it is highly unlikely that people will put a great deal of energy into projects that have no real decision-making consequences and whose concrete effects are limited.

The future of participatory budgeting in France remains an open question. At municipal level, the number of experiments got down and included in 2012 less than ten cases. However, participatory budgeting has become fashionable again in the 2014 municipal elections and the city of Paris has decided to launch an experiment, with 70 million euro a year, in a two track process based both at district and city level, in which participants can directly decide which projects will be selected. This new participatory budget benefits from the political support of the new Mayor, Ms. Hidalgo, and a very competent team; the success of its first edition has even forced the political opposition to endorse the process; 5000 projects were proposed by citizens in the second year edition, imposing local civil servants to work directly for their customers more than ever in the history of the city. This seems to emulate other experiments. At regional level, Poitou-Charentes had inspired other governments to instigate a similar process.[10] Even though many participatory projects in France today show very modest outcomes, the theme of citizen participation is still on the political agenda and projects show great inventiveness; the idea of devoting more importance to deliberative quality is gaining ground. The introduction of genuine decision-making power is clearly posed, as well as the creation of independent monitoring structures that would be able to carry out a genuine evaluation of the processes.

Proximity democracy is most clearly represented in neighbourhood councils, and France is the European champion in this respect. Perhaps their widespread diffusion is just the beginning of a more general political change. Is it possible that participatory budgeting in France is part of this process, and might even be one of the key aspects? For the moment, it is hard to give a clear-cut answer to this question.

---

10 So far, however, attempts to set up a similar process have lagged far behind the process in Poitou-Charentes in terms of overall impact.

# 6

# PROXIMITY: SPRINGBOARD
# OR TRAP?

## (Belgium, Portugal, Netherlands)

Proximity democracy is far from being limited to France. On the contrary, it is without doubt currently the most widespread participatory dynamic in Europe, in very different legal and political contexts. A wide variety of terms are used: '*neighbourhood democracy*' in the United Kingdom, '*bürgernahe Verwaltung*' ('citizen-oriented administration') in Germany, '*pieni demokratia*' ('small democracy') in Finland, '*wijkaanpak*' (neighbourhood approach) in the Netherlands and so on. Proximity is based on various procedures and, in particular, on neighbourhood-level management, committees and funding. Very often, urban regeneration policies have been test beds for experiments that promote citizen participation and participatory mechanisms have often been developed initially in disadvantaged neighbourhoods. Everywhere, or almost everywhere, the micro-local level is fruitful ground for participatory experiments. Generally, participation is also seen as synonymous with a more intense level of communication between decision-makers and citizens. Why has this approach been so successful? To what extent does it affect participatory budgeting experiments and how do the latter affect proximity democracy? Is France a typical case or an exception in the matter? To answer these questions without going into a detailed description of all the proximity participation procedures in existence, which would exceed our remit, we will satisfy ourselves with briefly describing three experiments, all of which are categorised as proximity-related: Mons in Belgium, Utrecht in the Netherlands and Palmela in Portugal.[1]

## 1. Mons (Belgium): Urban Regeneration Policy and Citizen Participation

Belgium has a complex political system which is both federal (Delperée 1999) and consociationist. A neo-corporatist system based on three pillars (Christian,

---

1 The first experience is labelled a participatory budgeting by local actors but, according to our criteria, is not one; the second lays no claim to be participatory budgeting and is not one, despite certain similarities: only Palmela is both labelled a participatory budgeting and corresponds to our definition.

Liberal Secular and Socialist Secular) has developed in certain sectors of public policy. These pillars are groups of organisations gathered around specific values, which organize individuals' social lives and benefit from institutional recognition. At the end of the 1990s, when the system entered a crisis, new sectors turned towards other actors than the members of the traditional pillars (trade unions, mutual insurance systems, women's and young people's associations and so on). The desire to open up to citizens and 'revitalize democracy' existed at federal and regional levels, as well as in various towns in the Walloon area, among others. This development, based on high levels of association, was due on the one hand to a crisis of confidence with regard to political institutions (Elchardus 2004), which was even greater in Belgium than in most of its neighbouring countries, but also, without doubt, to inter-party competition: the breakthrough made by the Belgian Green Party in 1999, strongly linked to participatory issues and the idea of 'doing politics differently', led to the Socialist Party, under its new leader Elio Di Rupo, appropriating the issue (Wynants 2004).

The town of Mons (91,000 inhabitants) is the capital of Hainaut, in the west of the Walloon region. It is divided into a hinterland, including the two old communes of Flénu and Jemappes, clearly identified as part of industrial Borinage,[2] and the town itself, with its heritage, tertiary sector, middle class and regional influence. Mons is the Socialist Party's flagship commune: when participatory budgeting was introduced, its mayor was none other than Elio di Rupo, the head of the Francophone Socialist Party (PS), who became later Minister-President of the Walloon region, and was nominated Prime Minister of Belgium in 2011. For him the town of Mons was emblematic. The PS received 61.4 per cent of the vote in the 2000 local elections and leaded a coalition with the Liberal Party (a practice that is not uncommon in Belgium). In 2002, the executive decided to focus on the Jemappes and Flénu neighbourhoods (15,000 inhabitants), which had historically been independent, were sociologically very different from Mons and had been severely affected by the decline in the mining industry from which, forty years later, they had still not recovered. Taking advantage of federal funds, a participatory budgeting experiment, initially envisaged as to be extended to the whole town, was implemented. The local council unanimously approved the project.

In attempting to achieve multiple objectives which in the end were barely implemented, the clearly top-down approach produced relatively confused expectations (Damay and Schaut 2007). The idea was to bring local politicians and government closer to citizens and it was to this so-called proximity that

---

2 Borinage was one of Belgium's mining and industrial heartlands until the early 1960s. Since then, in spite of significant public investment, the region has been in decline.

## The Link between Porto Alegre and Urban Regeneration Policies

The mayor of Mons, Elio di Rupo, had often expressed his interest in Porto Alegre. After a trip to the city in 2001, he wrote, 'At home, even though our levels of development and standards of living are different, … there are still pockets of precariousness, faith in our institutions is weak, to say the least, and the desire to see the 'human face of globalisation' and 'shared progress' is becoming more and more clearly expressed. The local level, the level par excellence at which policies are coordinated, can be an area in which to try out new responses to these challenges … . I am convinced that we can regain part of our citizens' faith by adapting the Porto Alegre experiment to our own realities. Several Belgian communes could take inspiration from Porto Alegre, particularly with regard to their investment budget' (Di Rupo 2001).

At the same time, from 2001 the federal government allocated Mons grants under a programme of urban renewal, aiming to revitalise certain neighbourhoods by fostering residents' participation (in 2004 this amounted to 2.2 million euros). All investments were planned for Jemappes and Flénu, the areas where the 'participatory budgeting' was to be implemented. The latter therefore benefited from part of the urban renewal fund, but did not receive the money directly and had no monitoring role over the projects being carried out. This led to a certain amount of confusion, with projects sometimes being presented as the outcome of participatory budgeting despite not corresponding to residents' actual demands. The participatory approach had not really become a central part of the urban renewal programme, due to insufficient planning with regard to the way in which the two would be combined.

participatory democracy was essentially reduced. As in the majority of French cases of proximity democracy, the final decisions remained in the hands of politicians. At the same time, there was a desire to renew public management, particularly through administrative branches in neighbourhoods and the affirmation of a project-based culture, with expectations that were not far away from those guiding the participatory approach. Nevertheless, the two processes were linked neither through discourse nor in everyday activities, despite occasional meetings between those running them. Finally, the participatory dynamic was supposed to contribute to affirmative action in disadvantaged areas that, among other things, manifested itself in a reinvigoration of society and local development.

When adopted, the project envisaged a participatory pyramid focusing on a specific geographical area and issues, with a structure similar to the Porto Alegre procedure. In 2003, several sets of meetings were held in the Jemappes-Flénu district, focusing on the six neighbourhood councils. However, the process stalled: no feedback was given to residents, several projects were not subjected to a feasibility study and, while some projects did come to fruition, this was because they were already due to be implemented as part of another programme. Citizens' area of intervention was reduced to investments, and even here no amounts were set, on the pretext of not imposing budgetary constraints. The procedure therefore provided no way of responding to the large numbers of complaints received. Out of an initial budget of 520,000 euros for suggestions emerging from the 2003 approach, only 132,000 were actually spent in 2004, that is, around 1.5 per cent of the town's investment budget, with even this being used for projects that did not necessarily emerge from residents' proposals. In 2004, there was a distinct decrease in citizens' interest in the project and politician and administrator involvement diminished. Participation levels dried up. In 2005, political leaders envisaged launching a process that would be less ambitious in terms of design, but more serious in terms of project implementation: the 2006 elections were fast approaching and politicians wanted to see concrete outcomes. Politicians involved themselves once more in an issue that they had initially largely left in the hands of the administration – a move that may well have boosted the process, but also risked turning citizens' visits to the mayor or government officials into mere 'photo opportunities'. In spite of this, the new process established in 2006 appeared to produce concrete projects that responded to the needs expressed by residents' delegates. Feasibility studies were carried out by a research agency. As for the local council, it seemed keen to implement the projects and provide feedback to local residents (Damay 2010).

The quality of formal consultation was low in local neighbourhoods, where residents' requests and complaints were not given due consideration because they did not accord with the administration's expectations. Problems highlighted were often individual and related to refuse collection, pavements, traffic, lighting, illegal parking, security and cleanliness; issues that could not be tackled because they were not part of the remit of the participatory budget designed by the local authority. From the town's point of view, it would have been preferable to promote more collective projects, such as developing green areas. In addition, meetings often started discussions from scratch and there was no cumulative process. The administration was in full control: the citizens barely interacted among themselves outside the administration's presence and had very little influence on working methods. In delegate meetings, discussions were of a higher quality, dealing with what a town should provide its inhabitants and covering the reasons for certain projects, even if there was no reflection on the priorities that should be highlighted to benefit less wealthy neighbourhoods. While participants made criticisms and proposals and worked to draw up a participatory budget charter, they did not set the agenda of meetings and had virtually no influence on the process as a whole.

In any event, even though more projects were implemented, the participatory procedure itself (whose existence depended on the urban renewal programme), did not in itself produce any redistribution effects. Few other outcomes stood out. A feeling of frustration was prevalent among residents because the work carried out was barely taken into consideration, with politicians not even always providing a justification for their decisions.[3]

The limitations of this particular experiment with 'participatory budgeting' are obvious, despite the existence of a genuine political will to increase participation and the multiplication of efforts to establish more communication with citizens. The approach was new and a process has been set in motion (Damay 2010). However, several questions remained at the end of the 2000s. Could the project last? Based on what kind of procedure? Using what resources? Its functioning required a relatively significant investment by the administration, for minor outcomes: in this light, was it realistic to widen the project to include all of Mons? While the reference to Porto Alegre fostered the awareness that another relationship between decision-makers and citizens was possible, it nevertheless produced a process that did not have a great deal in common with the original procedure and, even more than in Saint-Denis or Bobigny, became merely a paradigm of proximity. From this point of view, limiting the experiment to a specific district appears extremely negative. The difficulties and constraints that emerged in the implementation of the initial programme were identified and the town attempted to reconsider the programme, making the point that it took Porto Alegre more than ten years to properly establish its own programme. The comparison with the Brazilian experiment is, at the end of the day, a heavy burden. In the Mons case, the ideological reference to participatory budgeting perhaps served to make it more difficult to benefit from the potential advantages of proximity, because it did not focus attention on the link between participation and administrative modernisation and contributed to turning genuine integration of participation in urban regeneration policies into a problematic issue.

## 2. Utrecht (Netherlands): Neighbourhood Funds and Neighbourhood Management

In a context not dissimilar to that of Mons, Utrecht's participatory system seems to be more serious and more interesting, although it makes no reference to Porto Alegre. The procedure is a good example of proximity democracy. Utrecht is

---

3 New local elections took place on 8 October 2006. The Socialist Party suffered a considerable decline, receiving 'only' 51.55 per cent of the votes. With 8.37 per cent of votes cast and three local councillors, the National Front achieved a resounding success. The coalition between the Socialist Party and the Liberals was maintained.

the fourth-largest city in the Netherlands, with more than 316,000 inhabitants (2012). Dynamic, with a rapidly expanding population, it has nevertheless been affected by ethnic and social segregation. The unemployed (who make up only 6 per cent of the city's inhabitants in 2005) and foreigners (31 per cent of the commune's population) have been concentrated in certain neighbourhoods, in a context in which the city has bared significant social responsibilities (40 per cent of housing is social housing).

Like in Belgium, the Dutch political system was traditionally based on several pillars; a structure that began to fall apart from the 1960s. Religious divides eased and new parties were established (such as D66, a liberal party, and the Green Left). The political system had to face a new challenge at the turn of the millennium with the emergence of Pim Fortuyn's populist extreme right, which aggressively criticised the multicultural model and traditional parties, describing them as cut off from the people. Fortuyn's murder in 2002 and the overwhelming rejection of the European Constitution during the 2005 referendum (although the Treaty was supported by the vast majority of politicians) were two highly significant moments in an increasing crisis of legitimacy. This was of even more concern given that the Netherlands had a strong tradition of association and volunteer work. There was a low turnout[4] in the major cities (Amsterdam, Rotterdam, The Hague and Utrecht), which were particularly affected by a social crisis that was mainly concentrated in 'problem neighbourhoods'. In 1995, they launched an appeal for assistance that pushed the national government to establish a special programme of urban regeneration. The aim was to reverse the trend and develop the possibility for individual and collective action. This led to a three-pronged process comprising neighbourhood management, urban regeneration policy and citizen participation, with neighbourhood management[5] the link between the three dimensions.

With the benefit of a national-level framework providing increasing encouragement (Swinnen 2005, Ketelaar 2005), Utrecht became part of a trend of which it represents one of the most advanced examples. Progressively, starting in 1984, the commune devolved its administration and ten districts (with no legal political independence) were created, each with its own manager. From the end of the 1990s participation became an important element of

---

4 In the 2001–2002 local elections, turnout was 44 per cent in Utrecht and The Hague, 47.8 per cent in Amsterdam and 55 per cent in Rotterdam (compared to a national average of 58 per cent).

5 The reorganisation of municipal public action was facilitated by the significant functional independence of Dutch local councils which, like their Scandinavian counterparts, have considerable resources at their disposal (Utrecht's municipal budget per inhabitant was around 5,120 euros in 2005). In addition, they are much freer to decide how the money is to be spent than local councils in neighbouring countries.

this neighbourhood management. While the theme was the object of a fairly wide consensus, the populist 'Leefbar Utrecht' Party made it a central issue in the 2001 local elections, which probably contributed to its electoral success (it suddenly became the town's leading party, with 28 per cent of the vote). As part of the coalition that came to power following the election, under a Social Democrat mayor, the party made a major contribution to developing the mechanism. In 2002, participatory councils were established in each district, comprising between 9 and 25 people appointed from among volunteer residents by a district manager. These committees met once a month or every two months. In addition, the manager controlled fairly sizeable district funds (in 2011 700,000 euros per district) that enabled the administration to set up projects proposed by residents in a rapid and non-bureaucratic manner, as well as responding to their complaints. Other funding was also available, such as the 'Initiative Right' that enabled residents to come together (there had to be at least 25 residents) to request funding for a self-managed project based in their neighbourhood, up to a maximum of 30,000 euros per project (almost 500,000 euros were disbursed under this mechanism in 2004).

## A Participatory Cycle (2005)

Since the participatory approach began to focus on neighbourhoods, a veritable cycle of participation was established in Utrecht. Were the approach not limited to the neighbourhood and district levels, the cycle could evoke participatory budgets functioning in the manner of Porto Alegre. Nevertheless, the idea was not to provide the inhabitants with direct co-decision-making power, but to establish a regular information and consultation process fostered by a proximity administration capable of integrating the knowledge and requests of citizen-users.

The cycle comprises a regular series of stages for citizen participation, administrative expertise and decision-making by local politicians. District managers play a central role because they act as the contact points for the three types of actors. Between January and March the district's participatory committee works on an annual action programme, the criteria governing the allocation of the funds available under the district funds framework and sometimes on concrete projects for which funding is to be requested. To this end it is noteworthy that the committee gathers residents' opinions (through meetings, questionnaires, interviews or group discussions), for which it is able to provide 15,000 euros (out of its 22,500 euro operational budget). On this basis, in April each manager was asked (in cooperation with those responsible for municipal services in each district) to draw up a 'district plan', including both concrete projects financed by district funds and more general short- or medium-term objectives (long-term goals are set out in a document called 'Vision of the District', produced every four years). This plan is the cornerstone of the procedure. It is discussed with the participatory council before being presented to the Municipal Executive, while the municipal committee is involved through committees set up in each district. In May–June the executive compares these proposals, explains to the participatory committee why some projects have been agreed to and others not and transmits the project to the municipal council that has to validate it and vote on the municipal budget (October–November). In December, the appropriate district politician provides feedback on the decisions taken to the members of the participatory council and the administration implements the decisions, with the manager coordinating local-level service activities. External assessments bestow a certain transparency on the process as a whole. A new cycle can then begin.

As has already been seen, Utrecht remained and intended to remain within the paradigm of proximity. However, this does not mean that the experiment should be disregarded. Utrecht represented one of the most dynamic European experiments in proximity democracy and studying it provides increased awareness of the procedure's potential and limitations. A complex procedure comprising a wide range of innovative tools such as that used in Utrecht enabled the administration, at district level, to be far more receptive to the requirements expressed by residents, as well as giving them a certain power to initiate micro-projects. As the administration restructured its functioning at this devolved level, the procedure had certain effects that were very different from the Mons procedure and also superior to most of the French participatory budgeting experiments. The link between relatively significant funding levels used to respond rapidly to residents' requests, a participatory committee involved in multiple activities, an annual district plan drawn up through a dialog with citizen and associations, and a manager benefiting from recognised authority seems to be a particularly effective element. It is also remarkable that an issue that was particularly promoted by a political trend regarded as populist was so deeply integrated into the community's everyday administrative practices. This development probably contributed to a certain re-legitimisation of the local political system: in the 2006 municipal elections participation increased by 10 per cent, significantly more than in the three other major cities (where the increase was between 3 and 6 per cent), at a time when the national trend was slightly negative.[6] Nevertheless, the procedure was mainly managerial and there was only fairly limited participation (around 200 people were involved in the district committees and a few hundred in the 'Right to Initiate'). While

---

6 In addition, following a national trend, 'Leefbar Utrecht' collapsed and the Social Democrats gained ground (once again becoming the main local party).

the mobilisation of participants drove the local council to commit itself to providing specific feedback on how it followed up citizens' proposals, the effects of empowering residents in the process were generally limited and the 'Right to Initiate' produced only small-scale projects. The almost exclusive focus on districts significantly limited the scope of the participatory mechanism, both with regard to its effects on the modernisation of the municipal administration and its social achievements: what are 3 million euros of funding provided for residents' projects when compared with a municipal budget that in 2004 consisted of over 1.2 billion euros?

## 3. Palmela (Portugal): Taking Proximity Seriously?

We should not be too hasty in concluding that European participatory approaches should either restrict themselves to proximity democracy (implemented seriously) or risk being disconnected from local concerns if they deal with more general issues. The experiments assessed so far are still quite new and have probably not yet shown their full potential. In addition, while remaining within the realm of proximity democracy, some approaches have aimed to turn this into a springboard rather than a trap. This is particularly the case with regard to Portuguese participatory budgeting. The first significant experiment there took place in Palmela. This rapidly growing semi-rural medium-sized town of 58,000 inhabitants is known for its wines and its cheeses, but also for its car industry, which produces certain affluence in terms of municipal finances.[7] Located in the Setubal region, the 'red belt' to the south of Lisbon, it has historically been run by the Portuguese Communist Party, the leading member in a Front that holds 15 of the 26 seats in the Municipal Assembly and gathers around 50 per cent of the vote (the left as a whole receives over two-thirds). The local strength of the Communist Party was in stark contrast to national-level developments where it had lost a great deal of its sway and now finds itself competing with an active far left. The PCP had partly opened up after having long been one of the most Stalinist in Western Europe. Like for the French towns or Mons, Porto Alegre, which many mayors visited, had a direct influence, but this combined with a local tradition whose roots stretch back into the various self-management, association and participation experiments of the revolutionary years (1974–1975). The Portuguese national context differs greatly from that of the Benelux countries, less because of absolute wealth levels (Portugal first experienced strong economic growth since it joined the European Union, before to crash with the economic crisis of 2008–2009) than because of its political-

---

7 The municipal budget per inhabitant, at around 780 euros in 2005, remained, however, significantly below that of a city such as Utrecht.

institutional structure and the issues tackled under the participatory framework. Democracy is far younger and the Carnation Revolution of April 1974, after the turbulence of the early years, produced a relatively weak civil society; the welfare state remained one of the least developed in Europe. In addition, the authoritarian traditions that previously marked the country continued to have an influence. In spite of its recent beginnings, for the most part post-2006, participatory budgeting is today (2012) very widespread, with the percentage of communes involved by far the highest in Europe.

The 1976 Constitution, currently in force, paved the way for the establishment of independent local powers: while the regional level is non-existent and the equivalents of French departments have limited power, communes are run by elected bodies and have progressively benefited from wider ranging powers, even if these remain modest in comparison with the European average.[8] Just three decades after the fall of Salazar's dictatorship, Portuguese democracy was already marked by the political disillusionment that affected most European countries. There was a low turnout (around 61 per cent for the municipal and legislative elections of 2001–2002 and less than 50 per cent for the presidential elections of 2001)[9], a decrease in party and trade union activism and a lack of faith in the political system.

In 2002, Palmela was the first Portuguese commune to implement a participatory budget. The procedure used was an original combination of some of the Porto Alegre ideas and a proximity-based decentralisation of which the participatory budget was more a component than a driver. Palmela's participatory cycle was different from that implemented in Utrecht. Initially, the municipal executive drew up a draft investment budget together with the service providers concerned. The financial documents were then simplified and rewritten in layman's terms, and the initial draft was presented at a public local council meeting and discussed in the twelve urban neighbourhoods and rural villages that make up the commune (generally in October). Participation was on an individual basis and associations had no formal privileges. Between 3 and 4 per cent of the adult population participated in the meetings; 40 per cent of participants were women (a figure that is constantly increasing) and a large majority working class. At the same time, a questionnaire was distributed to enable the various projects under discussion to be placed in order of priority.

---

8 Communes are governed via a dual system, with the mayor and the executive on one side, and the Municipal Assembly on the other, both directly elected in separate elections. Portugal's unique feature is that the executive seats to be filled are distributed in a proportional manner between political parties, with the opposition therefore also having a share.

9 Turnout remained at 61 per cent for the 2005 local elections but raised to 63 per cent for the 2006 presidential elections.

Information gathered during the public meetings and through the questionnaires was looked at by the municipal services, which modified their initial draft to include the requests made by the citizens (in 2004 between 60 and 70 of the 250 projects proposed were included). The final draft was presented and discussed publicly at town level, after which it was adopted by the executive and then the Municipal Assembly. Implementation was controlled by local participatory committees made up of elected neighbourhood and village delegates working closely with the inter-service technical group that was responsible for following up on the participatory budget. One of the procedure's original features was that it included specific meetings to gather the contributions of council employees that prioritise measures to improve the municipal administration's internal organisation.

Palmela's experiment represented another side of the proximity paradigm. It was structured at town level as a whole and was a genuine participatory budget as defined here, unlike Mons or Utrecht. While the mechanism favoured close communication between politicians or administrators and citizens, its outputs in terms of geographical proximity were more ambiguous because it initially

---

### The Difficulty in Combining Different Levels of Representation and Participation

One of the specific features of Portuguese local democracy is the institutionalisation of a decentralised structure within the country's 308 communes. The 4,259 *freguesias* are a kind of mini-districts that receive a part of their resources directly from central government, while another part is provided by the municipalities in exchange for the delegation of a small part of their competences. They have a directly elected council and a President, who is also a member of the Municipal Assembly. Palmela has five *freguesias*, four of which were run by the Communist Party and its allies and one by the Socialist Party. For several years, Palmela had been decentralising its competences to the *freguesias* in order to foster neighbourhood management. Nevertheless, the participatory budget was implemented in parallel and, while it did produce direct dialogue between the executive and the citizens, it did not directly involve elected residents in the *freguesias'* committees. Initially this provision was partly a way of respecting the *freguesias'* independence, but this was soon no longer the case and some *freguesias* contested the outcomes of the participatory budgeting, obliging the commune to engage in more discussions with them. Talks took place to attempt to resolve the problem. It was decided that presidents of the *freguesias* should be present at participatory budget meetings and the municipality envisaged a participatory committee at town level, which would gather delegates appointed at open meetings, residents selected by lottery and representatives of local communities.

functioned in parallel to rather than in conjunction with the *freguesias*, the main neighbourhood-level administrative structures. An URBAL network study highlighted the fact that there was a certain impact on administrative modernisation at town level. In spite of significant participation by the working class, it did not seem to produce major effects in terms of social justice or the integration of immigrants, and even less in terms of gender. It remained clearly advisory, but the listing of priorities in order of importance, the implementation of a monitoring mechanism through local participatory committees and very good feedback with regard to follow-up on the process showed that there was some adequate methodology to produce selective attention to community priorities.

In any case, participatory budgeting has been producing increasing interest in the country, particularly in the south where left-wing parties are more powerful than elsewhere. Palmela's example made a major contribution: the town set up a network around it and provided advice and technical assistance to those implementing the process, before the Federation of Portuguese municipalities became active in popularising the concept.[10] Palmela's procedural method was used as a blueprint for the majority of Portuguese experiments until 2006. The biggest difference of Portuguese experiments with Saint-Denis or Bobigny is that citizen participation has been less ideological. There was much less claim to reproduce Porto Alegre in Europe. Instead, proximity has been taken very seriously, and has been converted in a flag of the renewal of politics and policies at local level. This has proved to be sustainable: the economic crisis has put an end to several experiments but others have begun, including the whole political spectrum: Among the 24 experiments that have been going on in 2011, only one was organised by the communists, the majority (17) was taking place in towns or cities governed by socialists, and 6 by the right – among them, Cascais, the most dynamic at the middle of the 2010 decade. A dynamic NGO, In Loco, plays a major role as a consultant in this process, and Portugal was in 2012 the European country in which the highest percentage of people lived in cities with participatory budgeting. This innovation is talked about in the national press and the number of experiments is still taking off.

## Conclusion: The Challenge of Neighbourhood Management

At this stage, what can be concluded with regard to the proximity democracy model that we initially assessed through the French examples? One obvious

---

10 An important role in this awareness-raising was played by a university institution in Coimbra, the *Centro de Estudos Sociais* [Centre for Social Studies] run by Boaventura de Sousa Santos, one of the most prominent international participatory democracy theorists (Santos 2005).

point is that there are two main reasons why the idea of proximity democracy is so successful in its communicational and geographical dimensions. Firstly, for local leaders it appears an excellent way of restoring contact with citizens at a time when the traditional political framework is being increasingly called into question. To describe it in more political terms, when neo-corporatist entities and mass parties can no longer play their roles, institutional participation comes to the rescue, establishing a more open and less hierarchical structure than traditional forms of organisation without producing the risk of an alternative political power. The other advantage of proximity democracy is that it makes a significant contribution to improving public action by encouraging management to take place as close to user level as possible. From this point of view, the more the administration reorganises its structures and activities in accordance with the procedure, the more the effects of participation appear positive. None of the experiments looked at in these two chapters exactly resemble one another and all have experienced difficulties and limitations. Nevertheless, on each occasion the development of systems of participatory proximity has had the benefit of highlighting the issue of Modernising micro-local public action and producing discussion on some of the challenges faced by traditional representative democracy.

The examples of Mons, Utrecht and Palmela show that participatory budgeting is not automatically the most effective tool for the proximity paradigm, understood in a geographical sense. Out of the various participatory experiments assessed in these two chapters, Utrecht's district managers seem best placed to foster effective micro-local management because they have a great deal of influence and are highly integrated into the everyday functioning of the administration. Nevertheless, there is nothing to prevent the others learning from their experiences and adopting the Dutch procedure. Above all, participatory budgeting's potential can best be seen outside the neighbourhood in that it targets the general budget and through that the functioning of the entire administrative machine, as well as the local council's major policy choices. On this point, the proximity-based systems that have spread throughout Europe, like neighbourhood committees and funding, would appear insufficient. This important lesson is confirmed by the Portuguese case: most of the participatory budgeting experiments that were only consultative were stopped after some years, and those who lasted were decisional. The reason may be simple: when citizens have the feeling that 'it is just talk', their interest declines, and with it the legitimacy of the devices. Politicians themselves do not have any interest in going on with a fake process – and they turn their energy in other directions. When something more concrete is at stake, with some decision-making power, a virtuous circle is –at least potentially– possible.

Thus, when they remain within a paradigm of proximity, participatory budgeting can be interesting but does not appear to fulfil the promise that emerged from the Porto Alegre experiment. Of course, the citizens involved can better see the results of their activities and make direct use of their knowledge. The administration shows itself to be more flexible and politicians must hold more discussions prior to summarising what has been said. These are important outcomes. There is still, however, a division of labour that continues to reserve a power monopoly for politicians. Participatory processes remain top-down and their overall effects in terms of social justice or administrative modernisation are limited: they do not allow any independence or power to be given to civil society actors, particularly those that are most disadvantaged, and they seem to have only a marginal effect on the most important decisions. Are European participatory budgets condemned to fail to respond to the expectations that attend them? The answer is not so clear-cut. We have already seen that the most audacious experiments in Spain and (to a more limited degree) in Italy, as some of the most recent experiments in Portugal, go beyond the proximity paradigm. It is now time to consider how other countries have adopted the Brazilian process.

# 7

# PARTICIPATORY MODERNISATION
## (Germany and Finland)

In the countries looked at so far, the link with administrative reform was not central to participatory budgeting, with the small Andalusian town of Puente Genil and (as an unexpected result) the French Region Poitou-Charentes exceptions to the rule. The question arose in an entirely different manner in Germany, where between 50 and 70 participatory budgets were going on in 2012. In Germany, the inspiration came from the New Zealand town of Christchurch rather than Porto Alegre. In addition, the German term *Bürgerhaushalt*, literally 'citizen budget', is not a literal translation of *orçamento participativo* (participatory budget). It is doubtless due to these specific origins that the link between participation and Modernising the public administration was more pronounced than elsewhere. Using a description of German participatory budgets as a starting point, this chapter aims to assess whether this unique situation gave rise to different outcomes from those encountered in the countries presented so far. Moreover, it allows us to gain insight into the empirical reality of the participatory ideal-type, and addresses the question of whether it is possible to establish a close link between state modernisation and a participatory approach. Finally, we ask whether it is really democratic to use the participation of citizens, above all addressed as users (and not as joint decision-makers), to produce administrative modernisation. To broaden the range of the discussion we will compare the German experiments with those of the Finnish town of Hämeenlinna. Without implementing participatory budgeting (the device was implemented late in this country), Hämeenlinna engaged in an exemplary process of administrative modernisation that was linked to participatory procedures, with the goal of establishing 'small democracy'.

## 1. The Beginnings of the *Bürgerhaushalt*

Participatory budgeting could have passed Germany by completely were it not for a financial crisis affecting local authorities, which increased in severity in the 1990s. The reasons were structural: towns were not receiving adequate funding from the state or *Länder* to cover the growing number of tasks for which they were responsible, while tax reforms and the difficult economic situation reduced local business tax revenues. This led several municipalities to seek innovative solutions to help improve the effectiveness of their administration while reinforcing their legitimacy. A second favourable factor was the development of the local political system. During the 1990s, the direct election of mayors and an increase in their powers became the norm across practically the entire country, together with the increased popularity of local referendums (Wollmann 1999). At the same time, consultative forms of participation such as round tables, citizens' juries and local Agenda 21 mushroomed. These developments drew sustenance from an administrative reform and the implementation of a new model of local democracy, the 'citizens' municipality' (*Bürgerkommune*) (Banner 1999). The 'New Steering Model' *(Neues Steuerungsmodell)*, a major 1990s reform project, recommended applying some private sector management criteria to administration with the aim of improving public services by increasing their competitiveness. This new model was a Social Democratic version of international New Public Management theories and was different from the purely market-oriented model of modernisation, which essentially relied on privatisation, increasing competition in services and introducing profitability-related criteria. The *Bürgerkommune* took the New Steering Model a step further, affirming that citizens are not merely users and should contribute to the production of public services on a voluntary basis. In exchange, citizens would receive new opportunities in terms of consultation. The vast urban regeneration programme 'Social City' launched by the Schröder government at the end of the 1990s, however, had barely any effect on the development of German participatory budgeting, despite the fact that it aimed to promote close cooperation between public sector actors, economic actors and civil society in disadvantaged neighbourhoods.

In an intermediate assessment of the New Steering model, Reichard (1997) observed that progress had been made on internal administrative reform and opening up to competition, but communes had done little to work with citizens. The establishment of the 'Municipalities of the Future' network (1998–2002) can be seen as an effort to react to this situation. The Bertelsmann and Hans Böckler Foundations launched a project with the KGSt[1] to design effective administrative tools for citizen participation. Participatory budgeting was part of the project, but when at its launch ceremony the network looked for local governments to pilot the experiment only Gerhard Dietz came forward. In spite of his colleagues' scepticism Dietz, the young mayor of the small town of Mönchweiler in the Black Forest (2,500 inhabitants) was brave enough

---

1 The *Kommunale Gemeinschaftsstelle für Verwaltungsmanagement* is the research and advisory institute for the Assembly of German Municipalities. Its analyses and the practices that it recommends strongly influence municipal administrations.

to implement the new procedure. To understand the process undertaken in Germany it is necessary to remember that the New Zealand experiments it was based on did not emerge from political reflections on participatory democracy but promoted a citizen-based modernisation through the participation of citizen-users.

## The Establishment of Participatory Budgeting: Hilden and Emsdetten

Mönchweiler was the first commune in Germany to set up a participatory budget in 1998, but others soon followed. Gerhard Dietz was elected mayor of Rheinstetten (near the city of Karlsruhe) in 2000 and made it the first commune with over 20,000 inhabitants to discuss its budget with its citizens. Certain distinguishing features of German participatory budgets – the combination of the elements 'consultation, involvement and accountability' – were already appearing: for example, discussions centred on the administration's services and not, like in Porto Alegre, investments and the redistribution of public resources between neighbourhoods in the name of social justice. Also, politically independent actors played an important role, particularly institutions involved in Modernising the administration, which took the 'citizens' municipality' as a model.

Two years after the 'Municipalities of the Future' network was launched, the Bertelsmann Foundation and the regional government of North Rhine-Westphalia launched another pilot project, the 'Participatory Municipal Budget' (2000–2004). Among the six communes that took part, Hilden and Emsdetten were particularly interesting cases and their systems are examples of the two main types of German-style participatory budgeting. Both were influenced by the participatory modernisation model, but the first focused on optimising public services and the other aimed first to balance the municipal budget. In addition, the two towns were distinguished by the fact that they did not face an imminent financial crisis, unlike most local authorities in North Rhine-Westphalia. Emsdetten (35,000 inhabitants, mayor of the conservative party CDU) was a reference of good management and very rapidly applied various elements of the model of New Public Management. The strength of the city of Hilden (56,000 inhabitants, mayor of the Social Democratic Party SPD) laid in its proximity to its citizens.

Hilden kept its residents informed on participatory budgeting through brochures and the media, and based its procedure on a central citizens' forum. There municipal employees presented the public services and institutions and answered citizens' questions at information desks. Most participants were drawn at random from the civil registry, but anyone interested could become involved. It was possible to record suggestions on special forms and anyone who made a proposal received a personal letter informing them of the local council's decision. Where appropriate, other letters followed at the project's launch and termination. In Emsdetten, participatory budgeting was introduced in 2002. There the local council also organised a citizens' forum with information stands during the consultation phase. Together with a group of randomly selected citizens, invitations were sent to citizens who participated in previous editions of participatory budgeting as well as to active citizens. However, the aim was not to assess public services but to come up with proposals to rebalance the budget (in 2002 the deficit reached 2.8 million euros, out of a municipal budget of 63 million). This could take the form of staff cuts, reduced public expenditure, decreased optional spending (culture, sport, leisure activities and so on), or tax rises. Each participant came up with a personal suggestion by combining the various possibilities. Views were gathered in a questionnaire and quantified, with their sum total representing the citizens' forum's overall vote. The whole council then announced its decisions, after a period of deliberation, and provided feedback to the participants.

## Mixed Outcomes

A strong point of Hilden and Emsdetten's participatory budgeting was budgetary transparency; this is particularly notable when compared to the majority of the initiatives to be found elsewhere in Europe. Nevertheless, citizens learned little about expenditure on large flagship projects, which emerged more from public opinion than through participatory budgeting. They also had no real control over the process itself, and while their knowledge was used to produce concrete improvements in services and infrastructure, these consisted mainly of secondary projects, such as putting a roof on an underground car park or lengthening a cycle path, rather than central issues.

German participatory budgets have had few social effects, with the Emsdetten citizens' forum the only one to have issued a recommendation with wide-ranging social relevance: citizens believed it was better to balance the budget by increasing local business taxes rather than by cutting services. The local council partially followed the recommendation, which produced an additional 610,000 euros in tax receipts. A comparison between this sum and neighbourhood funds in use in other countries does not diminish the influence of the citizens of Emsdetten. However, it should be pointed out that following the recommendation was also to the local council's benefit, as its tax rate was lower than the level recommended by the *Land*. In the medium term, the town would have seen some subsidies withheld if it had not increased its rate.

People who participated in the consultative processes were generally middle class; two-thirds were over 40, less than 5 per cent of participants were young people and there were almost no foreigners. Women represented only a third of those involved: withdrawals meant that the random selection system (used particularly frequently by German participatory budgets) did not automatically produce a representative group of residents. Adherents of this process maintain, however, that potentially it boosts participation and limits the influence of lobbies.

Participatory budgeting is often expected to play a part in countering the mistrust of politics that is as much a feature in Germany as in the rest of Europe, but statistics show that in the average, it neither improved the electoral results of incumbents nor increased the turnout. Most surprising is the fact that, despite all the talk of participatory modernisation, the effects in terms of administrative reform have remained meagre and have concerned mainly on improvements in transparency and certain marginal issues. From this point of view, the lack of in-depth discussion was a major limitation on making use of citizens' knowledge. Unlike in Porto Alegre there was a lack of regular meetings at which small groups analysed problems and drew up proposals.

## 2. Berlin-Lichtenberg: The Renaissance of a People's Republic?

There were nonetheless developments in German participatory budgeting after the first World Social Forum, held in Porto Alegre in 2001. The first German study on the Brazilian town's participatory budget was published that same year (Herzberg 2001), the *Bundeszentrale für politische Bildung*[2] began to be interested in the development of the system and local citizens' initiatives multiplied following two delegates' visit from Porto Alegre. Discussions were further boosted when the new government of Berlin, elected in 2002, adopted a series of measures aimed at Modernising the city-*Land*'s administration. The post-Communist PDS (today the party is unified with another leftist party under the name 'Die Linke' [The Left]) persuaded its Social Democrat coalition partners to undertake a participatory budgeting experiment at the district level. With the project no longer producing a consensus in Mitte, two districts in the east of the city were chosen. Marzahn-Hellersdorf then began a process that comprised high-quality consultation and partly linked it to urban regeneration policies. However, the experiment encountered many problems and was abandoned following a change of mayor in 2007. Lichtenberg (252,000 inhabitants) turned out to be more committed. The district, home to one of the largest agglomerations of high-rise housing in eastern Germany, had a reputation as reform-friendly. It implemented a series of modernisation measures but appeared torn between innovation and tradition. A PDS stronghold, where the party achieved its best results, and home to the greatest concentration of party members in the

---

2 The Federal Institute for Political Education is a federal government body tasked with improving citizens' knowledge of democracy and the German political system.

entire country, the district's reputation suffered as a result of extreme right-wing violence. The non-partisan objective of participatory budgeting was to contribute to firmly entrenching democracy and improving the district's image. In addition, the PDS's aspiration was to turn Lichtenberg into a showpiece for its political approach.

When Berlin-Lichtenberg solemnly inaugurated its participatory budget in September 2005, some activists compared Lichtenberg with Porto Alegre. Berlin's alternative newspaper *Die Tageszeitung* announced in a humoristic tone that Lichtenberg had got a 'People's Republic'. This provocative expression was an allusion to the local prominence of former Communists and the high expectations that the participatory system produced. Lichtenberg concluded numerous cooperation agreements with external service providers for publicity, mobilising citizens, the Internet, moderating the process and its evaluation. With 125,000 euros a year, it spent more on its participatory budget than all the other German examples put together. Was the money well spent?

Despite some scepticism with regard to the implementation of participatory budgeting in a large city, Lichtenberg found an appropriate methodology by using a procedure specifically designed for a large city and drawn up under the *Bundeszentrale für politische Bildung*. The method was slightly different from the previously described procedures. Participants were not limited to discussing the projects to be carried out, but put their priorities in order of importance through a voting system in which each participant was given five votes to distribute among the various proposals. Proposals could be made and put in order of priority during neighbourhood meetings, on Internet forums or through questionnaires sent by the administration to randomly selected people. This was a break from most previous participatory budgets in Germany, which were marked by politicians' cherry-picking participants' views. Lichtenberg also ran a major communication campaign to mobilise citizens. Mini-meetings were held to persuade immigrants and other 'hard-to-reach' groups to participate.

Despite these specific features, the new procedure was generally in line with previous German experiments. The process was top-down, but monitored by a committee composed of around 15 people (civil society representatives, civil servants and politicians). The central issue was administrative modernisation: the procedure focused on forty 'products'[3] on which the district had a direct influence (libraries, green areas, sports equipment and so on). In 2006, the

---

3 The term 'product' *(Produkt)* officially used in Berlin is derived from the concept of New Public Management. It goes along with budget reform. Lichtenberg like many other local authorities transformed the conventional bureaucratic budget plan into an enterprise budget format called '*Doppik*'. This budget is supposed to be more transparent, but still not as clear as some programme-based budgets in Brazil and North America.

majority of the 38 validated proposals were financed with no additional costs due to budgetary transfers from one product or product group to another. The idea was to evaluate public services in a participatory manner by offering citizens a wider area in which to use their expertise than in other German experiments, but there was no intention of adding a social dimension to the debate. The 'Social City' policy and its participatory structures were managed by the city government and had no real link with participatory budgeting in this district which, moreover, was not related to the previously-established citizens' juries.

Did this new methodology produce a new pace of development? In Lichtenberg, budget transparency became comparable to that in Emsdetten, Hilden and Rheinstetten, with information available in brochures and on the Internet. The greatest change resulted from placing proposals in order of priority. However, proposals often contain only two or three lines. This may seem a little brief to fully integrate citizens' knowledge, and discussion, which may have produced more information, was sorely lacking. In theory, the Internet discussion forums did offer this possibility, but these focused on micro-local or

---

## A Neighbourhood Meeting in North Hohenschönhausen

The second decentralised neighbourhood meeting of the year 2006 took place in a school. Around 100 residents from the nearby area were present. The majority were aged between 40 and 50, but there were also some young people and pensioners. Those present sat in a large circle. The mayor opened the meeting by welcoming the participants and presented the participatory budget project. The moderator, from a communication company, then took the floor and reminded those present of the different ways in which it was possible to participate: the Internet, written forms and meetings. She explained that three-quarters of the budget corresponded to fixed expenditure that could not be changed. The district council did, however, have a direct influence over 30 million euros. These 'manageable' funds had been arranged into products that could be changed through the participatory budget. A catalogue describing the services was distributed. The moderator explained that the purpose of the session was to gather proposals with a view to their adoption or rejection. When she wanted to elect an editing team to work on the proposals, nobody volunteered. The meeting therefore focused on discussing existing proposals and making new suggestions. The administration had set up information stands to this effect and each service had its own information chart. At the 'construction and traffic' stand, participants discussed matters with civil servants of the respective administrative department. They then used the appropriate form to recommend improving the connection between the school and the cycle path. A group of young people wanted the skate park to be repaired and another one enlarged. After some time, one of the organisers announced that the meeting would be closing in ten minutes. The noise in the different corners of the room showed that participation was active, but nothing had been proposed with regard to health care. On the other hand, this time the editing team was elected first time around, and included a member of the skateboarding group. During the voting that followed the young people's proposals showed that they had garnered considerable support and came first, followed by maintenance of a commemorative monument.

secondary issues and the result was highly segmented discussion that made it difficult to get an overall view.

Quantitatively speaking, participation in Lichtenberg was relatively limited given the efforts made to mobilise people, because it was comparable to that in Hilden and Emsdetten. It is true that there was a greater proportion of young people and young adults involved than anywhere else in Germany, but it was still a far cry from being a 'People's Republic'. The influence of civil society, apart from the capacity to rank proposals in order of importance, remained weak.

With regard to political communication, however, Berlin-Lichtenberg's participatory budgeting initially had highly significant effects. The support of the *Bundeszentrale für politische Bildung* provided the district with unprecedented local and national media coverage and Lichtenberg certainly contributed to stimulating discussion on participatory budgeting in Germany. The Berlin experiment also produced some linkage between overall commune (here district)-level discussions and micro-local neighbourhood-level meetings, a feature that was lacking in previous German participatory budgets. Despite this prestigious initiative, the PDS recorded important losses during the 2006 municipal elections in Lichtenberg and lost its overall majority. Electoral participation was among the lowest in all Berlin; moreover, the district was one of the rare places where the NPD, an extreme right-wing party, has had local councillors elected. With these contrasting outcomes, there is no German 'left-wing' participatory budgeting that would be closer in spirit to Southern European experiments.

Outside Berlin, there are few actors with the kind of national-level stature required to push participatory budgeting. In addition, the number of experiments is increasing only at a medium pace, because the establishment of new experiments is being countered by the halting or suspension of other processes. This is perhaps not surprising given the modest nature of the achievements with regard to modernisation.

In the 2010s, we can observe a split in the landscape of participatory budgeting in Germany. The first trend reduces the idea of modernisation to the discussion of budget cuts. Some municipalities such as Essen or Solingen have invited their inhabitants to discuss the question of how public spending could be reduced. In this way, these experiences give continuation to the approach introduced by Emsdetten. In contrast to the pioneering experience, however, options of tax increases are no longer topical. On the contrary, participatory budgeting on costs reductions is exclusively organised on the internet, without citizen meetings. The administration still has much stronger control over the discussion issues. These participatory budgets are often accused of giving legitimacy to policy that has been decided before.

The other tendency seeks to extend proximity democracy procedure. In Lichtenberg, for instance, the process has been slightly reformed in this direction.

---

## Internet Participatory Budgeting on Costs Reduction in the German City of Essen

Many German cities constantly spend more money than they receive. In order to prevent uncontrollable fiscal stress, local governments are obligated by law to elaborate plans on costs reductions if structural deficits reach a certain level. This has been the case in the city of Essen, situated in the Ruhr: the former industrial coal region of Germany. In this situation, the local council did not want to decide alone and submitted government's proposals on cost reductions to citizens' debate. For this reason, an internet platform was created in 2010. In all, 78 proposals representing €381 million were exposed to the public. Here, people were able to make comments on these proposals and cast their votes (more than 3,700 people registered for this process). In this way, the local government wanted to find out which measures were supported and which were not. Furthermore, citizens could also make their own proposals for budget reductions or additional income. In this process, participants supported budget cuts of €117 million. This was nearly half of the amount under discussion. People tended to avoid budget cuts foremost in social areas and education (support rate: 11 per cent), while the acceptance was higher in cases concerning politicians or public administration (support rate: 85 per cent). However, the people's preferences were not respected. Local councilors received the participatory budgeting proposals just in the moment in which they had to vote on the budget plan. For that reason, local councilors approved the full amount of cost reductions, representing €500,000 in all. In the following year, the procedure was repeated, but participation was 10 per cent lower. Essen's government has decided not to continue with participatory budgeting, as the city is now free from the burden of financial stress. Citizens are now invited to participate in other topics (Stadt Essen 2010, 2012a, 2012b).

The number of decentralised neighbourhood meetings has been increased. The district has also introduced special neighbourhood funds for their participatory budget regions in 2011. But the limits of these changes are obvious: 5,000 euros are allotted to each participatory budget region, totalling 65,000 euros for the whole borough. Interestingly, the other famous German experiment of participatory budgeting, in the city of Cologne (1 million inhabitants), moves in the same direction. The city has won various UN and international prizes for good governance for its internet-based process. Participatory budgeting has become a city-wide discussion topic, and a lot of inhabitants participate in the online forums. Some of the outcomes are fascinating, but all things considered, is this really an adequate tool through which to achieve participatory modernisation?

## 3. Hämeenlinna (Finland): Small Democracy

Analysing Hämeenlinna's 'small democracy' may help us to answer this question. Porto Alegre had no notable influence in Finland; and the Christchurch experiment, which was known about, did not, like in Germany, inspire the launch of participatory budgeting.[4] There were, on the other hand, numerous administrative procedures aiming to involve citizens in the 'land of the 1000 lakes'. Hämeenlinna's 'small democracy' was one of the best-known examples and brought the town to worldwide prominence when, as in the case of Christchurch, the Bertelsmann Foundation highlighted it as a noteworthy example, publicised it in Germany and included it in the Cities of Tomorrow network. 'Small democracy' was not dissimilar to German participatory budgeting in that there was no social movement campaigning for more direct participation and because the approach was less related to political and social issues and had more to do with administrative modernisation.

As we saw in Part I, the Scandinavian model is one of functioning municipal independence par excellence, and Finland is no exception. Finnish towns finance most of their expenditure through their own taxes and, boosted by the absence of an intermediate level of government between themselves and central government, fulfil most public functions. New Public Management, the introduction of market-based criteria and privatisation, had long been on the agenda, but the structure of independent municipal government is still intact (Rose and Stahlberg 2005). The 'free communes' experiment was fundamental in this regard.

This reform process produced deep-seated administrative modernisation but the outcomes in terms of local democracy and participation were far

---

4 The first participatory budgeting process in Finland was launched in public libraries in Helsinki in November 2012.

## The Free Communes

'Free communes' originated in Sweden in the 1980s and became established in Denmark, Norway and Finland during subsequent years (Baldersheim and Stahlberg 1994, Rose 1990). Between 1989 and 1996, the Finnish government gave communes the authority to modify their administrative political structure, upon their own initiative. Fifty-six towns piloted the experiment, the objective of which was to streamline political decision-making structures, strengthen municipal self-governance, increase the quality and effectiveness of services, increase the involvement of citizen-users and reinforce local democracy. In Finland, the free communes experiment focused particularly on administrative reform and produced an enormous decrease in the numbers of committees of all kinds, eliminated hierarchies through the delegation of powers, promoted inter-service cooperation and introduced general budgets. Changes eventually went much further than those that took place in the pilot towns during the specified period of time. The vast majority of local council decisions no longer required central government approval, communes were given a greater margin of action with regard to public finances and their overall position was greatly strengthened

removed from initial expectations. A series of growing problems, in particular a decrease in electoral participation, led the central government to launch several programmes to consolidate local democracy, starting in the 1990s. Traditional forms of Finnish municipal participation were based on associations, interest groups and voluntary work, and these are still the most widespread today. Neighbourhood committees, citizens' juries and other institutionalised forms of participation are rare (Kettunen 2003). For a long time, Hämeenlinna was no exception. This small to middle-sized Finnish town (67,200 inhabitants (2011), located 100 km north-west of the Finnish capital) is part of a conurbation between Helsinki and Turku that is experiencing strong economic development. In spite of high unemployment (12.5 per cent compared with 8.8 per cent nationally in 2004[5]), its economic situation was relatively stable; the number of immigrants was very low (1.7 per cent). There was a clear majority on the municipal council, due to a coalition between the Social Democrat and Conservative parties.

The free communes experiment, in which Hämeenlinna took part, profoundly changed its administrative structure. The experiment established new relations with citizens. According to the terminology used by local administrators and politicians, 'small democracy' was designed to complement 'large' – that is,

---

5 The situation was broadly similar in 2012.

representative – democracy and generate improved communication between politicians, the administration and citizens. 'Small democracy' did not, however, start out with the aim of increasing participation: its goal was an effective and proximity administration, as well as high-quality outputs for citizen-users. Those who came up with the 'small democracy' concept came from all corners of the administrative and political spectrum. Civil society actors, as in the first German participatory budgets, did not play a decisive role.

The idea of 'small democracy' developed slowly. Initial interest focused, here as elsewhere, on reforming administrative structures in accordance with the New Public Management model. However, despite the changes in the administrative structure, participation in local elections continued to fall and progressively fewer citizens appeared interested in municipal matters. The town's political-administrative management therefore came up with a double-edged development strategy. On the one hand, wider-ranging participatory rights had to be given to citizens, and on the other, the administration needed a better presence in the neighbourhoods and to genuinely take citizens' requests and complaints into account. This link between participation and improved service quality (Naschold 1999) was the distinguishing feature of the 'Hämeenlinna system' and the one for which it became well-known. While this has been introduced later in other Finnish communes, Hämeenlinna was a pioneer in this area during the second half of the 1990s.

The quality of public services, a political priority, was permanently monitored through a complex charting system. It specified precise delivery deadlines and contents for services, compared the quality of local authority provision with that of other towns and elicited on-going feedback from residents through customer satisfaction surveys. In addition, the municipal administration sent administration contact persons into each neighbourhood; set up an information centre in the main square; and implemented a complaints management system that worked through feedback forms, to which a response was provided within a month. Since the 1990s, Hämeenlinna's political leadership has also established a series of specific participatory mechanisms, in particular various meetings that have enabled discussion between the administration, politicians and civil society. Civil servants and members of sporting associations, for example, meet several times a year at the 'Parliament of Associations' to discuss relevant problems.

Starting in the 1990s, Hämeenlinna residents have also been able to participate in urban development, which is run on a cooperative basis between politicians, the administration and citizens. The main objective was to inform the citizens of upcoming projects in as timely a manner as possible and to establish a permanent exchange of ideas throughout the planning process. Another participatory procedure worth mentioning was one specifically aimed at teenagers and young adults (13–20 years old), the *Vaikuttamo* ('the place where one has influence'). The *raison d'être* of this approach, which since 2005 has been integrated in the town's youth work department, was the low voting turnout of people under 25 years of age. The aim was to spark young people's interest in their environment through various projects, strengthen local e-democracy by providing it with a new public sphere and use innovative techniques to increase the attraction of education. The website, whose content was provided mainly by the young people themselves, played a central role. Young people could chat with politicians, teachers and pupils and find information on many of the themes taught on school curricula. A weekly interview carried out by pupils provided information on a subject in the news at the time. In addition, young people had been given the opportunity to elaborate project proposals, seen as an intermediate step before an official plan's submission to the local authority. This system produced funding for a school's skateboard park, for example. *Vaikuttamo* was part of a new way of looking at local government administration. The trend was clearly to better coordinate the modernisation of public-sector action with citizen participation, to continue to develop existing mechanisms and to complement them with experiments from elsewhere, all carried out in a pragmatic manner that equated to the idea of 'small democracy'.

## Conclusion: Conditions for Participatory Modernisation

'Small democracy' has engaged in participatory modernisation – that is, a high quality administration comprising consultative participation in the largest number of sectors possible – but has left political structures unchanged. It has not called 'large' representative democracy into question. Formally, citizens have had only an advisory role. Unlike in Porto Alegre, the approach has not been bottom-up and citizens have not had real monitoring mechanisms apart from regular meetings with decision-makers. The process has been dominated by politicians and civil servants and it has been more about modernisation than increasing democracy.

However, this modernisation has been based on widespread consultation and multiple forms of advisory participation that also enable participants to actively influence public policy design. At some meetings, members of local associations have even been able to influence the procedural rules of participation adopted and central town planning-related issues have been included in the approach. During the past twenty or thirty years a culture of transparency and concerted planning has emerged that has significantly affected the ways in which the administration and local government act. Direct contact with citizens and regular consultation are now part of the everyday life of local government. To quote the first assistant to the town's mayor,[6] Juha Isosuo:

> The most important thing is attitude. The democratic structure, elections every four years and so on ... all that has barely changed. However, life is completely different: the Internet, consultations, civil society organisations ... Citizens participate as a matter of course. They can call me or send me an email. There is far less distance between representatives and those they represent.

At the end of the day, why do the outcomes of 'small democracy' probably seem more significant than those of most German participatory budgets, which have not had the envisaged impact in terms of administrative modernisation? Is German participatory budgeting, which comes close to the participatory modernisation model, an appropriate way of bringing about administrative modernisation? Comparing the ways in which users' complaints are handled is highly revealing. Except for the presentation of the budget, the feedback system in Hämeenlinna appears to work like Hilden's participatory budgeting: citizens write their criticisms and suggestions on forms and receive a personal reply. Feedback forms, however, cost almost nothing and can be made available throughout the year, not only during specific events. It is true that this system does not provide citizens with any information on the budget. If consultation on the budget is, however, limited to discussing secondary issues, such as lengthening a cycle path, and if there is no general discussion on overall budgetary policy, the good day-to-day management of user complaints is more than sufficient. The last developments in German participatory budgeting have tried to counterbalance the problem of efficiency by the introduction of online procedures. The experiment of Cologne and others are mainly internet-based, but with the introduction of mere online procedures, the influence of citizens might be even further weakened compared to the previous situation.

However, the potential scope of participatory budgeting is greater than merely a modernised neighbourhood-based form of management with no discussion of long-term policy objectives or complex issues. Participatory budgeting can enable discussion on fundamental strategic issues such as balancing the budget, policies in areas such as culture, sport or youth, or enable improvements in service provision and outputs to be listed in order of importance. The German

---

6 There are no (or not yet) mayors in Finland in the strict sense of the word. Rather, there are 'municipal directors': government employees who are not members of the municipal council but are appointed by it. Their political leanings therefore play a role but they do not exercise any political function. Legally, they represent the town and head the administration.

experiments demonstrated several dimensions of this but the procedures used have until now been too restrictive to produce a qualitative leap when compared to other participatory instruments.

The specific contribution of German participatory budgeting and Finnish 'small democracy' is mainly programmatic in nature: in other words, the attempt to link participation and modernisation. This approach is rooted in a specific orientation, the New Public Management or the New Steering Model rather than Porto Alegre. Outside their respective limitations, these approaches raise an essential question for the future of public services in general: their added value compared to privatisation policies lies in the benefits for the wider public, but how can this be ensured if citizens have no say in how they work?

# 8

# BETWEEN COMMUNITY DEVELOPMENT
# AND PUBLIC–PRIVATE PARTNERSHIPS
## (United Kingdom, Poland)

We believe that the time has come to disperse power more widely in Britain today; to recognise that we will only make progress if we help people to come together to make life better … The Government believes that we need to throw open the doors of public bodies to enable the public to hold politicians to account … The Government believes that it is time for a fundamental shift of power. We will promote decentralisation and democratic engagement, and we will end the era of top-down government by giving new powers to local councils, communities, neighbourhoods and individuals.

This citation from the 2010 Conservative and Liberal Democrat coalition manifesto cuts to the heart of the debate about citizen participation in the United Kingdom. It has been characterised, since roughly the second mandate of the previous New Labour government, by an increasing emphasis on a more 'localist' agenda that involves citizens and communities in the making of (local) public policies, as well as a shift to a more user-oriented delivery of public services.

On the one hand, the citizen has become the 'customer who is always right'; a new force within society to drive innovation and efficiency in public services. Choice for these new consumer-citizens is exercised individually or within a close 'nuclear' family. Wealth is linked with opportunity and with social mobility, not just income, which is in turn linked to your individual ability to exercise choice. Choice means you can select between receiving treatment within a state-run or a privately-managed hospital; or that you have the choice of becoming a property owner through your right to buy your council house from the state (and at a subsidised price). After becoming a property owner, through trading in your place of residence, you should be able to choose a more successful education for your children based on reading the newly available school league tables. Choice represents the shift from the state supplying all your services, to citizens demanding their entitlements. Public service, in theory, becomes demand-led.

On the other hand, in the UK the past decade has seen increasing recognition of the role of community activism and of community cohesion in curbing social conflict and reducing entrenched inequality. It has become generally accepted that community development protects the weakest, and an active civil society leads to better and more democratic governance. The UK governments since the late 1990s has been seeking mechanisms that stimulate more community- and neighbourhood-based activism, particularly in areas experiencing multiple social deprivation. The accepted model is that a partnership between empowered civil society organisations, private interests and local government can improve the caring functions of the state, sensitively targeting tax-payers money in difficult social contexts in the most effective way. In this multi-stakeholders world, participatory budgeting supposedly allows the demands of well-informed local citizens to penetrate the new partnership-based commissioners of public services.

This double perspective characterises the tension that underlies participatory budgeting in the UK. Is support for participatory budgeting simply part of the choice agenda, followed by both the previous New Labour, Conservative-liberal and current Conservative governments under the auspices of the New Public Management? Or is participatory budgeting's main added value a greater empowerment of local communities and the re-building of a local accountability that strengthens democracy from the bottom up? How does participatory budgeting respond coherently to both a very centralist managerial – that is, 'New Labour' – political culture that seeks to engineer social change, and small-state, entrepreneurial (liberal conservative) concepts like 'the Big Society' espoused by David Cameron and the 2010 coalition[1] (but which after 2013 has not been used any more in government statements)? To what extent is the participation agenda being influenced by neoliberal policies, and what is the interplay of private enterprise and social responsibility in this field?

These questions are not restricted to the UK, but also, at least partly, related to policy developments in Poland. Both countries are characterised by their neoliberal economic policies. The approach to participatory budgeting in Great Britain and Poland differs quite clearly from those we have been describing in the previous chapters. In relation to the ideal types described in Part I,

---

1 A 2010 policy manifesto published by the Cabinet Office lists five main priorities for the development of a 'Big Society': 1. More powers to communities (for example, a reform of the planning system; communities receive the right to bid to take over local state-run services); 2. Encourage people to take an active role in their communities (measures that encourage volunteering and involvement in social action); 3. Devolution of power and greater financial autonomy for local authorities; 4. Support of coops, mutuals, charities and social enterprises; 5. Publication of government data (see: http://www.cabinetoffice.gov.uk/news/building-big-society).

the British and Polish cases are in between the multi-stakeholder participation model (especially the Polish ones) and the community development model (especially the British ones). Put differently, this means that they are situated between the ideas of community development/empowerment, aimed at giving civil society organisations more power and means of action, and that of a policy agenda that creates diverse public–private management structures outside democratic control. How do participatory budget institutions function in this context? What are their political, social and administrative impacts? Can they contribute to the strengthening of local democracy or do they accentuate the trend towards 'participatory decentralisation' (Baierle 2006), characterised by the outsourcing of previously state-managed competences to various civil society and business groups, which inevitably weakens the influence of local councillors and local democratic structures?

## 1. From the Grassroots to the National Policy Agenda

Originally introduced to the UK in 2000 by a small number of NGOs interested in its redistributive power, participatory budgeting has been accepted inside the mainstream UK debate on community empowerment. The United Kingdom (mainly England, but increasingly also Wales and Scotland) is the only European country with Poland where participatory budgeting has achieved such a national political echo and degree of institutionalisation. Participatory budgeting in the UK is no longer promoted as an exotic idea imported from overseas but as a home-grown phenomenon. Although no accurate data exist, by the middle of 2010 upward of 100 local authorities had declared they had launched some form of participatory budgeting. This represents a marked increase from a couple of years earlier when there were fewer than 10 examples. In 2005, only one or two local authorities might have said they used or were at all familiar with participatory budgeting. In the UK debate on participatory budgeting, it is no longer a requirement to acknowledge the influence of Porto Alegre, the Workers' Party and the World Social Forums. Participatory budgeting is most often seen as a process that, within a specific area, 'directly involves local people in making decisions on the spending priorities for a defined public budget' (PB Unit 2010:1). It has been estimated that so far in excess of 20 million pounds has been spent through participatory budgeting. Little evidence exists, however, about how effective many of these experiments are, also because only a minority of cases involves the second, city-wide participation level that turns a local community funding approach into participatory budgeting in the sense developed. Moreover, it is not clear whether participatory budgeting is yet embedded inside the democratic culture of England, not least given the speed with which it has been adopted. Finally, it is important to acknowledge the overall political context that is marked by the creation of various public–private partnerships or even the simple outsourcing to private companies of previously publicly managed services.

How can we explain the rapid development of participatory budgeting in the UK? How does it relate to the overall policy development of recent years?[2] What have been the outcomes of participatory budgeting so far?

Understanding the stakes and the issues of participatory budgeting in the UK implies paying particular attention to the domains of citizen participation and local service delivery, as well as understanding the relations between central government and local authorities. The fiscal, institutional and political power of municipalities was radically changed by the Conservative governments of the 1980s and 1990s. The Thatcher government, elected in 1979, drastically reduced the financial independence of local authorities and began the shift towards privatised public services. It was able to do so despite considerable local resistance from Labour-dominated councils and public sector trade unions. This had a considerable impact on local authorities which is still being felt today.

After New Labour came to office in May 1997, it drove forward a broad reform programme of local public services and institutions, while refusing to undo some of the significant centralising policies of the Thatcher years or to reverse the neoliberal allocation of an important role to the private sector in driving public sector modernisation. However, New Labour didn't abandon all its principles and did promote many policies aimed at improving social justice, such as its pledge to abolish child poverty and a new legal minimum wage. Blair's government significantly increased the funding available for health, social care and education – a policy priority not followed by the newly elected government, in a context of radical budgetary cuts.

In 1997, local governments were facing a difficult situation as their powers had been significantly weakened over many years. From a legal standpoint, local government has historically been much weaker in the UK than in most other European countries: the *ultra vires* doctrine restricts their scope to explicitly mentioned fields of action and forbids their involvement in other areas. There isn't a single codified document called the English Constitution which delimits the activities of government or enshrines local autonomy. In effect, sovereignty ultimately belongs to Parliament and the concept of particular inalienable local rights, privileges or rules does not exist.

Under the Thatcher government, the powers of local authorities were reduced significantly. Overall, the 'Iron Lady' pursued two major objectives in her conservative reforms. First, that of implementing a neoliberal policy aimed

---

2 At the margins, the following presentation also includes the changes that have occurred, or are likely to occur, since the election of a conservative-liberal coalition in May 2010.

at developing a 'minimal state' and second, liberalising markets and services by promoting privatisation and competition. This had a considerable impact on local authorities. They had been part of the foundation of the welfare state and had an effective monopoly on large areas of local service provision. In the drive towards a more market-oriented economic policy they became obvious candidates for introducing competition. The limitations on local authority spending had a devastating effect on poorer communities across the UK at a time of very high unemployment. The working class and the poor depend on the effective and comprehensive provision of local services more than the rich or middle classes. Particularly hard hit were the post-industrial northern cities which remain the heartland of the Labour Party's support.

Margaret Thatcher also tried to close down opportunities for social and political opposition to her neoliberal policy of freeing up the UK labour market from trade union restrictive practices and local authority monopoly over service provision. She weakened the hold of Labour politicians and the old left on local councils through new policies such as the selling off of council housing. Another example of the convergence between private interests and the Thatcher government was the way national newspapers, owned by unaccountable press barons, championed the neoliberal rhetoric of the Conservatives. At the same time, private owners were profiting from new laws that limited the power of trade unions in the newspaper industry.

A similar coalition of the right led to a direct challenge to the trade unions which were strong in local authority workplaces. New legislation introduced private sector competition which drove down wages and led to a new non-unionised workforce operating alongside public employees who had previously enjoyed better pensions and better employment conditions. Through outsourcing, redundancies and competitive tendering, acceptance of a shared 'public service ethos' that operated between staff and managers broke down. Mainstream media stories continued to challenge public perceptions about the value of old-style public service and its cosy but inefficient values. Media reports and television dramas in the 1980s continually parodied public officials. Local councils and public servants were characterised as ineffective, corrupt or outmoded, while the Conservatives were praising the achievements of private entrepreneurs. As we have seen in the previous chapters, this was quite the opposite of the European trend of the 1980s and 1990s, which tended to enlarge and reinforce the powers of local councils.

One of Margaret Thatcher's first initiatives was to implement a vast privatisation of local services by outsourcing public sector delivery in key areas such as public housing, social care, waste collection and cleaning services. She used 'Compulsory Competitive Tendering' to achieve this, thereby obliging local services to go out to open tender, which created a new de facto competition between public and private sectors. An increasing number of local government responsibilities were given to private enterprises, with lower wages and less democratic control. Citizens increasingly came to be seen as customers. It became normal for private companies to profit from consultancies and contracts with the government. Local economic development in particular became influenced by private business leaders who were co-opted onto new urban planning bodies and regeneration agencies. Public money that had previously been spent through local authorities was now routed through agencies increasingly modelled along the lines of private companies. Efficiency and small government was achieved by holding down wages in the public sector, and by bringing in a new competitive culture, with senior management adopting the more aggressive language of private business. Executive boards with non-executive directors, rather than formal committees of elected councillors, became the preferred procedure for managing public contracts.

Another of Mrs Thatcher's priorities not reversed under 10 years of New Labour was to create a lot of new semi-public institutions, controlled by central government regulation, but operating outside clear democratic control. Since the 1980s these 'Quangos' (quasi-autonomous non-governmental organisations) have gained influence over fundamental public sector responsibilities such as regional policy, local economic development, energy policy, transport policy, physical regeneration and strategic planning frameworks. By the turn of the twenty-first century there were about 5,000 of them, employing 60,000 people. These are not elected bodies, but are generally nominated by the government (Wilson and Game 2002). This process of 'quangoisation' further reduced the power of local authorities and considerably reduced their functional independence. Increasing the number of regulators, Quangos and statutory agencies with which they have to engage adds extra complications to the work of local councils when delivering their remaining activities.

The Thatcher government additionally limited the possibilities for local councils to increase local taxation. In 1984, she introduced 'capping' (a legally binding upper limit on the amount of tax that could be levied by local councils, under pain of personal sanction of local political representatives). Much local expenditure was now also being constrained by budgetary 'ring fencing' (housing, environmental works and public education, for example, had to respect priorities dictated at national level) and budget freedoms were limited by centralising the collection and redistribution of local business rates. Furthermore, the considerable income generated by the sale of council housing was not available to councils to rebuild their stock. Instead, it was often handed on to new housing associations, nominally non-profit public businesses, in reality modelled in their operations along the lines of private companies with limited local accountability. These measures all reduced local democratic control over municipal budgets to a point where local councils almost became an operational arm of central government and local councillors were left powerless, whatever their local mandate. For an illustration of how power was shifting to the centre, in the major northern city of Manchester in the early 1980s around 75 per cent of the council's expenditure was raised and spent under the direction of local politicians. By 1995 this was down to around 25 per cent, with even this expenditure constrained in the numerous ways explained above.

Furthermore, any undue raising of council taxes is always politically dangerous. The local council earns its local tax income from a very visible and often inequitable tax on property, not on income. It is the largest individual bill local electors are likely to receive from any source, and thus unlike national income tax, which is taken directly from wage packets and relatively invisible. In the age of the 'small state', higher council tax is never described as the action of a caring local council keen to deliver important services, but is always a sign of inefficiency, poor management and waste.

Finally, Margaret Thatcher delivered another blow to the reputations of local councils through her ill-conceived Community Charge or poll tax. This was an attempt to replace the established local property tax known as 'the rates' with a new tax on each individual resident, not property owner. Irrespective of income, and varying widely for little apparent reason, the poll tax was seen as deeply unfair. Continuing public protest throughout the 1980s finally led to the abolition of the poll tax policy after 1990 when John Major replaced Thatcher and bought in the current system of the Council Tax, based again on property valuations; but not before creating great resistance to paying local taxes even among those who traditionally supported bigger local government. In some areas up to 30 per cent of taxpayers defaulted during the 1980s. Councils were forced to chase large numbers of these new tax avoiders, often for many years, with little benefit to the public purse. Trust in politicians and local politics was on the slide.

The privatisation of the public sector, the increasing financial dependency of local authorities and the fragmentation of service delivery under various public–private partnership boards and Quangos has had negative consequences for local democracy. In 1997, which was the year of a massive electoral swing back to the Labour Party, the Council of Europe's Congress and regional authorities of Europe underlined that local democracy in the UK was facing 'major problems', comparing it in this respect with the situation in Bulgaria, Latvia, Moldavia and Ukraine (Wilson and Game 2002). This acute situation in the UK came on top of a more structural problem of legitimacy within local democracy, to which we turn below in greater detail. Compared with other European countries, the electoral turnout is extremely low in the UK (Power Inquiry 2006, Steward 2003): in certain constituencies no more than 15 per cent or 20 per cent turn out to vote in local elections, and over the longer term the fall in voting rates has become obvious both nationally and locally. The rolling system of Local Council elections – which are based on a 30 per cent annual renewal of elected members – is another important contributory factor. Having to repeat local elections every year seriously complicates long-term planning and the allocation of responsibilities in decision-making. Repeated elections tend to weaken rather than strengthen the ability of local authorities to work effectively and be trusted by their electorate.

Tony Blair won the 1997 elections partly on a promise to fight the catastrophic situation that had developed within local councils. By promising to save public services from the mismanagement of the Conservative government, and by offering new investments in health services, education and housing, Blair convinced the electorate they would see improved social outcomes for all. Significant and ambitious electoral pledges included an end to child poverty, something that could be delivered only by organisations operating at the local level. However, his initiatives have also led to a complex and confused policy landscape, with as many similarities as differences to the previous government.

Blair's political programme was not a simple copy of Margaret Thatcher's. The Third Way that falls between the 'old social democracy' and the 'new right' (Blair 1998a) is supposed to be less neoliberal than social-liberal. The market is not controlled, but there is a social 'shock-absorber' to cushion the most negative effects of private enterprise on wages or jobs. Further central targets are the modernisation of public services, a new recognition of citizens' participation and new investments, particularly in education, to support the social opportunities of a post-Conservative world. The market rhetoric of opportunity through increased 'choice' nevertheless remained at the heart of the Blair agenda, and this included, for example, encouraging wherever possible a number of different service providers, or increasing NHS patients' choice of treatment providers through promoting foundation hospitals, and the power to opt 'failing' schools out of local authority control into becoming privately sponsored 'academies', nominally run by local boards of parents and business leaders.

Even if local councillors no longer felt the same risk of being penalised in the courts instead of reversing fiscal policies that enfeebled local councils, Tony Blair and Gordon Brown maintained tight control. Labour's election manifesto had promised an end to 'crude and universal' rate-capping, but Blair reserved the right to use capping in individual cases, and in 2003 capping was still being threatened by John Prescott, then the minister responsible for local government. Local autonomy further became circumscribed by rigorous performance management regimes and continuous restructuring and reform. And as under Mrs Thatcher independent-minded local decision-makers that risked creating a significant challenge to New Labour were still generally resisted, even when coming from inside the Labour tradition or enjoying a healthy mandate.

For example, Blair tried to block Ken Livingstone's election as the Mayor of London, partly because Livingstone consistently refused to buy into the rhetoric of the 'third way'. Thatcher had originally got rid of the highly popular but politically troublesome Livingstone when in 1986 she abolished the Greater London Council (GLC) of which he was then leader. At that time Livingstone was labelled by right-wing newspapers 'Red Ken' and linked with other politically unsavoury left-wing council leaders such as Derek Hatton in Liverpool. When in 2000, under New Labour, Livingstone stood for and won the position of Mayor of London he was strongly opposed by 'Blairites' and even temporarily suspended from the Labour Party for standing against the official Labour candidate. This move was later reversed when his public appeal and individual political influence became too strong to deny. However, the newly formed London Assembly and the Mayor never enjoyed the sort of powers enjoyed by the old GLC.

Under Blair the range of ring-fenced local expenditures and the number of Quangos increased compared with the Thatcher years (Stewart 2002). Nor did Blair end the policy of privatisation, and New Labour introduced a broad range of Private Finance Initiatives (PFI). PFI largely replaced more traditional means of financing the major public capital programmes that build new schools, hospitals and roads and make possible economic and urban development. Under PFI, the government does not borrow from the private sector through government bonds to finance construction projects that it then operates autonomously. The private sector borrows the capital needed to build new public infrastructure on private money markets and also provides some or all of the services linked to the project under separate contracts. In return, the government pays for the services over a certain period of time and leases the capital assets, including the costs and compensation of risk linked to the capital investment (Stewart 2003: 145). Although adherents of these partnerships aim at a better quality of service at a lower cost, the reality is that they often significantly increase the costs of service provision and are indirectly responsible for the substantial debts of local authorities.

Many commentators feel that a short-term need to show that PFI is working has simply meant that private business has been given a very good deal. After all, if sufficient profits were not to be made, accompanied by low risk, private investors would not have come forward with the money. The poor return to the taxpayer from private finance deals of course may simply be because public officials are not trained to negotiate complex contracts with the private sector. Increasingly, private finance agreements have been constructed by private sector consultants employed by the state just for this purpose. These consultants are generally employed by public officials, often at a national or regional level, so not under the close control of local politicians. Furthermore, there is little democratic control over how the services are then being offered and often a considerable reduction in the quality of services provided occurs (Marlière 2001). The increased citing of commercial confidentiality as a mechanism to resist calls for transparency further obscures how public money is being used and makes it nearly impossible to calculate the actual waste of tax receipts, or to report poor social outcomes from PFI. It is likely that PFI and private sector delivery will grow under the market-oriented Conservative/Liberal coalition. Significant public expenditure will therefore remain hidden behind confidentiality clauses that protect private competition, with public bodies left tied up in complex contractual agreements with private companies that are beyond citizen accountability or local political scrutiny.

Another similarity between New Labour and the Conservative governments of the 1980s and 1990s was their belief in centralised regulation when implementing public policies – although Blair did not resort to simple brute force as Thatcher had done in the 1980s. Instead, he implemented the tactic of 'carrot and stick' – although he undoubtedly favoured waving the stick, at least during his first term. Blair clearly underlined this when addressing local authorities and admonishing them to cooperate in the face of the challenge of modernisation:

> If you accept this challenge, you will not find us wanting. You can look forward to an enhanced role and new powers. Your contribution will be recognised. Your status enhanced. If you are unwilling or unable to work to the modern agenda then the government will have to look to other partners to take on your role. (Blair 1998b)

In Modernising the working of local authorities, the Labour government constructed its programme around four main pillars. They included the strengthening of the discretionary powers of local authorities; measures to modernise local political institutions; the introduction of measures aiming to improve the quality of service delivery; and the involvement of users, citizens and communities.

Without going as far as the abolition of the *ultra vires* rules, Blair's government introduced measures aimed at improving the legal situation of local authorities. For instance, the so-called 'Well Being Power' was introduced in 2000 to increase local authorities' ability to act on behalf of their areas outside the straightjacket of the *ultra vires* rules. It allowed principal local authorities in England and Wales to do anything they considered likely to promote the economic, social and environmental well-being of their area unless explicitly prohibited elsewhere in legislation. These powers, however, could not be used to raise new money. In addition, the government introduced Local Area Agreements (DCLG 2007). They considerably reduced the number of centrally fixed targets for local authorities and gave them more possibilities for establishing local priorities. Set up by Local Strategic Partnerships (LSP)[3] and agreed between the local

---

3 Created in 2000, LSPs have the task of bringing together local plans, partnerships and initiatives to provide a common forum for public service providers in order to match

area (local authority and LSP) and central government, they functioned on a three-year cycle, with an annual review process supposed to be open to the influence of local people. This programme seemed still on the political agenda of the coalition government. At least in a policy manifesto about the 'Big Society' published on the website of the Cabinet Office, one could read that the Conservative–Liberal Democrat coalition intends to 'promote the radical devolution of power and greater financial autonomy to local government, including a full review of local government finance'; moreover, it would 'give councils a general power of competence'.[4]

Still under New Labour, the creation of new partnership boards between public agencies, private companies, community groups and voluntary organisations – for instance Local Strategic Partnerships – became a central focus of central government in regulating the delivery of services, particularly at the local level. These powerful but unelected partnerships place obligations on local authorities which are mandated to support and lead them. Local councils, for instance, must ensure that there is public consultation on combined service strategies. Moreover, they have to lead on commissioning services from a variety of potential suppliers, sometimes pooling budgets, and also to report back to government on the use of public expenditure according to investment plans developed through partnership work and by broad consensus.

Second, New Labour also introduced institutional measures in order to modernise the local political system. For example, it experimented with new electoral arrangements, such as postal voting, electronic voting and early voting in order to increase the electoral turnout. Moreover, it introduced clearer political management structures with separation between the making, scrutiny and execution of council decisions. This has led to the setting up of cabinet-style local government executives that mirror the national parliamentary cabinet, with backbench councillors becoming an oversight body for the scrutiny of executive decisions. The new system largely replaced the previous committee-based system. Furthermore, the government introduced the possibility of directly electing the mayor (after approval by authority-wide referendum), although this reform has so far not led to many local initiatives of this kind.[5]

---

local needs and priorities. Since 2007, LSPs have become a mandatory requirement for all local authority areas; they have the duty to develop and monitor local action plans; that is, Local Area Agreements.

4 'Building the Big Society' (publication date 18/5/2010, see: http://www.cabinetoffice.gov.uk/news/building-big-society).

5 Councils in England and Wales (except shire districts with populations of less than 85,000) were required to select one of the following arrangements after consultation with the population: Mayor and cabinet executive; Leader and cabinet executive; Mayor and council manager; or alternative arrangements (Wilson and Game 2002: 103).

Third, the blind policy of privatisation by always selecting on lowest price was moderated early on by a new appreciation of service quality, as witnessed by the move from Compulsory Competitive Tendering towards the Best Value regime. However, it turned out to be 'every bit as centrally prescriptive and potentially even more interventionist' than the CCT (Wilson 2005: 165). This is why some took the view that it constitutes simply a new label for an approach still highly impregnated by the ethos of CCT. In the absence of reliable ways to value non-financial social benefits, and under tight legal constraints from the fair competition rules that control public procurement, commissioning through Best Value remained highly technical and bureaucratic. Ultimately, it became a process undertaken only by trained professionals that are becoming used to interfacing with private businesses, and not open to much influence by ordinary councillors or citizens.

Finally, there was a shift in the orientation of Labour government policy in relation to the topic of citizen participation – a trend that seems to have continued under the coalition government and its emphasis on the 'Big Society', aimed at fostering citizen participation and volunteerism. From the outset, New Labour instituted a vast new array of consultations of users, citizens and local communities. Various forms of one-way interaction with service users (such as satisfaction surveys or random sampling mechanisms) had already existed prior to New Labour and continued to grow. The Labour Party took up these actions, and systemised and embellished them with other forms of participation (including forms of local community empowerment such as participatory budgeting). Citizens' Juries[6] were used in the early Blair years as a way of developing national policy. Customer service panels, more parent governors, community champions, children's boards, parish councils, the New Deal for Communities and Neighbourhood Management all presented opportunities for more active citizenship, becoming ways of bolstering and legitimising a weak political mandate and providing much needed local intelligence. In the last years of the Labour government, participatory budgeting was introduced onto this participation and empowerment agenda.

## 2. Consumer-orientation or Community Empowerment?

During its first term of office, the Labour government was mostly oriented towards the participation of citizens in the role of *consumers* of local services.

---

6 The Institute for Public Policy Research has promoted this process since 1994 and set up a first series of experiments in 1996. After the election of the Labour government, the number grew considerably, with more than 200 examples initiated (Sintomer 2011a: 166).

'Innovations in citizenship or democratic engagement were relatively neglected', although the organisation of citizens' juries or of local referendums constituted noticeable exceptions (Wilson and Game 2002: 359). In the last years of the New Labour project, the focus continuously shifted from a consumer-orientation towards the greater involvement, engagement and empowerment of citizens and communities (for example, Cabinet Office 2007; DCLG 2006, 2007, 2008, Ministry of Justice 2008). Already before this point the topics of participation and empowerment were part of the neighbourhood renewal agenda (for example, Social Exclusion Unit, Cabinet Office 2001). Thereafter, the language of empowerment spread to other policy domains, such as the police (Home Office 2008), health (National Health Service Act 2006) and justice (Ministry of Justice 2008). One reason for this shift was probably linked to the growing practical and academic evidence of the potentially positive outcomes of local participatory practices.[7] Another reason was related to a legitimacy crisis that had engulfed representative democracy:

> [A total of] 61 per cent of citizens feel that they have no influence over decisions affecting their local areas; only 42 per cent of people are satisfied with the performance of their local council; only around a third of the population vote in local elections, and of those who do not vote 41per cent claim that it is because they do not think it will make a difference; and residents in the most deprived areas have the highest level of alienation from the political system. (DCLG 2006: 30–31)

Further signs of this democratic 'crisis' have been losses in party membership for the Labour and Conservative Parties, while extreme right parties expand their influence (albeit quite slowly and without breaking through at the parliamentary level).[8] During the 2009 local elections, which took place in the shadow of a strong internal Labour Party power conflict, a deepening economic recession and the scandal about MP expense claims, the Labour Party even lagged behind the Liberal Democrats. This called into question the traditional two-party system, a trend that was confirmed with the election of the first national coalition government of Liberal Democrats and Conservatives in May 2010.

The emphasis of the previous Labour government on citizen participation ('We want all councils to focus more on their citizens and communities', DCLG

---

7 The Department for Communities and Local Government itself published research reports that underline the positive outcomes of participatory budgeting and of other participatory instruments (DCLG 2009, 2011).

8 UKIP has become much more influent than the British National Party that had won 2 seats in the 2009 European elections, but lost them in 2014. UKIP instead received 27.5 per cent in the 2014 European elections.

2006: 7) has definitely led to a spread of participatory practices in the United Kingdom. Today, the great majority of local councils have established some form of citizen involvement, be it user- or citizen-oriented. Probably never before have citizens in the UK had so many institutionalised possibilities for becoming involved.

The development and empowerment of local communities have become a policy priority since around 2000, alongside the earlier, dominant focus on mere 'user participation'. In terms of guiding ideas and concepts, however, 'community' was already part of the underlying values of the Third Way (Blair 1998a: 3). The idea of community was 'discursively central' to the New Labour project, because it allowed for the establishment of a distinction from both New Right and Old Labour ideas (Levitas 2000: 188). Generally speaking, the notion of community became 'the central collective abstraction for New Labour, in a discourse whose organising concepts are: community, opportunity, responsibility, employability, and inclusion' (Levitas 2000: 191). Under New Labour, the concept of community experienced a strong revival, which was partly linked to the Third Way project, partly an expression of the urban renewal policies initiated by the government. Although previous governments had dealt with these issues, too, the newly elected Blair government put a strong focus on them and launched two major urban social regeneration programmes: the New Deal for Communities, and the National Strategy for Neighbourhood Renewal.[9] At the same time, the idea of 'community' was not new, having become the centre of attention during the 1960s within the framework of a strategy to fight urban poverty. The creation of bottom-up managed community projects was also pursued by left-alternative movements, which found an intellectual platform in the New Left Review founded in 1960s.

Later on, the Labour government linked the idea of community, which also occupied a central position in the 'Big Society' initiative of the coalition government, to a more participatory approach to politics. 'We want to shift power, influence and responsibility away from existing centres of power into the hands of communities and individual citizens. ... A vibrant participatory democracy should strengthen our representative democracy' (DCLG 2007b: 1). This type of programme is close to academic discourses and analyses,

---

9 The total cost of the 10-year programme New Deal for Communities was about 2 billion pounds; in each area the regeneration plans attracted around 50 million pounds of funding. This included 39 areas (on a very small scale: for example, a neighbourhood or community area) which were among the most deprived in the country. Apart from one, they were all located within the areas of the 86 authorities part of the National Strategy for Neighbourhood Renewal. These authorities were also eligible for the Neighbourhood Renewal Fund, at least if they accept certain conditions, such as the setting up of local partnership boards.

which regularly aim for 'reforms that move beyond the traditional forms of representative democracy' (Dalton 2004: 204; Smith 2009).[10] At least at the discursive level, there was a shift from a focus on user participation and consultation, characteristic of the first years of the Labour government, to a more political approach to citizen participation, which found expression in terms such as 'shift of power', 'participatory democracy' and 'empowerment' (Röcke 2014).

'Empowerment', like 'community', has been defined in different ways (Biewener and Bacqué 2013). In the most conflict-oriented interpretations, empowerment is seen as a means for the emancipation of suppressed groups and their access to power. In more consensual interpretations, it is rather defined as a top-down approach through which a government agency helps the members of certain groups to develop a greater sense of pride in themselves and to be able to 'manage' their lives, but without altering existing power hierarchies. The previous government – or at least the Department for Communities and Local Government – followed a rather consensual and extremely broad orientation, which subsumed under the notion of empowerment any kind of participatory practice, from websites to petitioning and citizens' juries (DCLG 2008: 21). It is probable that the coalition government continues to employ the term in this way. Moreover, it will probably also maintain the position of the previous Labour government, which highlighted the importance of devolution and local empowerment, but was unwilling to cede its own power. Citizens and communities were called on to participate at the local level (and local councillors were called on to devolve their power to the citizens), but the overall institutional framework was not subject to modification: 'The Government believes that representative democracy – and therefore Parliament – must remain at the heart of the governance of this country' (Ministry of Justice 2008: 3). This is one of a number of reasons why some observers characterised the emphasis on community participation and empowerment as a 'rather conservative reform strategy', unlikely to really empower local people and to tackle the 'crisis' of representative government (Smith 2009). Probably, this combination of the devolution of single decision-making competences to the local level, together with the protection of the 'core decision-making responsibilities of national and local representative institutions' (Hay, Stoker and Williamson 2008: 4) will continue to exist, in a context of strongly increased budgetary constraints and even greater emphasis on private investment.

---

10 It is noteworthy in this regard that the New Labour governments always had close links to centre-left think tanks working on participatory reforms, for instance the Institute for Public Policy Research (or Demos) that promoted, among other things, the idea of citizens' juries in the UK (Bevir 2005: 30).

In summary, the main ambivalent aspects of the recent policy approach to citizen participation in the UK are the following:

i.   The rhetoric around participation and community empowerment, while retaining practices such as the creation of more 'semi-public – semi-private' boards that operate outside democratic or community control.

ii.  The emphasis on local community empowerment, although the centres of power at local and national level remain outside the scope of participatory processes.

iii. The aim of strengthening the power of local authorities while, at the same time, imposing on local governments a series of new requirements under the name of the participation and empowerment agenda[11] (or, in relation to the coalition government, while introducing radical cuts in public expenditure).

## 3. Participatory Budgeting: A 'National Strategy' for Local Community Empowerment

The beginnings of the story of participatory budgeting in the UK were, as in most countries, very modest. One of the first channels of diffusion was a 'learning exchange' between two English cities (Salford and Manchester) with two in Brazil (Recife and Porto Alegre). This exchange had been initiated by Community Pride Initiative (which later became the PB Unit and in 2012 the PB Network), a Manchester-based small organisation sponsored and supported by OXFAM, an international NGO. The Community Pride Initiative produced a number of discussion papers that attempted to match up the annual cycles in Porto Alegre and the idea of budget matrices for decision-making with the mechanism used in the UK for involving residents. Following a first 'pre-participatory budgeting' project in Salford organised partially under the auspices of Community Pride, other towns – including Bradford and Newcastle – ventured to try out forms of participatory budgeting. In recent years, alongside a few other cases, these exemplar cities have become the main mechanism for raising awareness about participatory budgeting in the UK. The spread of participatory budgeting has been significantly supported by the introduction of a 'national strategy' by the previous government for implementing participatory budgeting in all English local authorities by 2012 (DCLG 2008). Moreover,

---

11 These were, for example, the 'Duty to Involve' for local authorities (Part 7, section 138, of the Local Government and Public Involvement in Health Act 2007), 'Comprehensive Area Agreements' to monitor the effectiveness of Local Strategic Partnerships or indeed the national participatory budgeting strategy.

participatory budgeting had been among the recommendations of the 2004 Power Inquiry, a cross-party review of the state of democracy, funded by the Joseph Rowntree Foundation, a leading social justice research body in the UK.

### The First Years: A Few Cases of Participatory Grant-making

The first 'official' participatory budgeting in the United Kingdom was organised in the city of Bradford in 2004. Inspired by the Porto Alegre experiment, which had been presented in the book Reclaim the State by Hilary Wainwright (2003), leading members of the Local Strategic Partnership decided to launch such a procedure on the basis of the existing system of local community involvement. In the UK, the procedure adopted in Bradford is labelled 'participatory grant-making' or 'community grants' and has been very influential. Today, probably most examples in the UK are similar to this approach. In this process, public money is handed over to be spent for a particular area (usually one or several local areas or neighbourhoods) or theme (for example, children and young people). It involves generally third sector organisations and community-based associations and allows them to undertake small-scale projects to improve the local community. The mechanism used for deciding expenditure is a public voting day, when short presentations are made by applicants and the community uses paper or electronic balloting. Generally, there is limited deliberation, but commonly many of the participants will be part of an existing group in which discussions have taken place beforehand. Most of the projects funded in this way are short-term and small-scale and do not bring an expectation of repeat funding to maintain the new initiatives.

A fairly typical example of such a procedure organised in just one city area (and which, following our criteria, we do not consider as a 'full' case of participatory budgeting) is the process in Manton, a small and deprived neighbourhood with very low levels of political participation in the district council area of Bassetlaw, Nottinghamshire. The process is organised by Manton Community Alliance (MCA), the local neighbourhood management. Using around £50,000 of their own funds to leverage support from other partners – including the local NHS, police and local authorities – MCA have developed a highly participatory process which they have been using since 2007. The process starts with local residents identifying the local priorities for the year. They then vote for their top ten priorities, the five with the highest scores are then selected. Using ballot boxes, residents decide how much money should be allocated to each priority. Organisers then ask voluntary, community and public organisations to come up with projects that meet the priorities. Residents learn about each of the projects through a short video clip, which is displayed online and in local meeting places. Residents then vote on which projects they want to see funded by postal and ballot box voting and those with the most votes are funded. The successful projects are then delivered throughout the remainder of the year, with regular feedback to residents.

This procedure was inspired by the initiatives started in Bradford that were diffused via a growing national network and the activities of the PB Unit. Since 2004, several other such 'participatory grant-making' events have been organised in the city. This points to another characteristic of this 'British' approach to participatory budgeting, which again does not fully correspond to the criteria developed here: there is no annual process cycle – every process needs a new decision by the organisers, as well as a new pot of money to be spent. Finally, there is hardly any link to the local political system because the participants (mainly community and third sector organisations) decide on a specific budget that does not relate to the overall spending priorities of the local council. This could lead to the creation of a participatory space that is separate from the existing institutional life. Moreover, Local Strategic Partnerships or neighbourhood management structures often launch such a procedure, but not the council itself. This approach is completely different from the first procedures of participatory budgeting in Germany, as we saw in the previous chapter. Whereas the latter consist of a global budget consultation of all residents based on the transparency of municipal finance, the 'grant-making' approach aims to empower local communities or deprived areas through the devolution of decision-making powers over specific funds. As in most cases in the UK, there is a strong social orientation. The following description of the 2004 process in Bradford provides a good illustration of this.

Participatory budgeting in Bradford was from the outset based on allocating a strong role to the communities and the Local Strategic Partnership proved to be an appropriate basis on which to move community development forward from neighbourhood to city level, or at least to several areas of the city. Independent decision-making was the foundation of the project and, unlike what we have observed in the vast majority of participatory budget experiments in Europe, ethnic minorities were closely involved in the process. The projects needed to

---

Bradford (474,000 inhabitants, 2005) is situated in the North-West of England, the historic industrial area of Great Britain. Bradford council has swung from Conservative to Labour and back on several occasions over the past twenty years. The far right British National Party also gained seats in a context of violent clashes between the white majority and Pakistani minority of local inhabitants. Bradford is a post-industrial city, with social problems concentrated in the inner city. This is why these areas received national funding for social, economic and political development from the national programmes Neighbourhood Renewal and New Deal for Communities. Part of the funding from these urban renewal programmes was made available to the communities in the neighbourhoods in question. This was with a view to supporting local projects and contributing to the improvement of quality of life. This method enabled Neighbourhood Action Plans to be funded in the amount of £2.5 million in 2002–2003, as well as £1.2 million in specific areas (fighting crime, improving environment and health and so on). The board of the Local Strategic Partnership, called Bradford Vision, managed these sums. Neighbourhood Action Plans had to conform to the general criteria of the Neighbourhood Renewal programme and the priorities of Bradford Vision.

In Bradford, the 2004 participatory budget was an extension of local community development projects in certain neighbourhoods throughout the town (deprived areas receiving money from the Neighbourhood Renewal Fund). The idea was developed in 2004 by the Neighbourhood Renewal Team within Bradford Vision. They had already been involved for some years with development and coordinating the Neighbourhood Action Plans in certain parts of the city. They succeeded in convincing another of the Bradford Vision partners, the Environmental Partnership, to commit around £700,000 to a participatory budget, rather than redistributing it as usual to other partners. Participatory budgeting was organised in 2004 – and several times during the following years, each time with a new budget – involved local community groups, who proposed projects involving between £1,000 and £10,000. The organisers accepted the projects that met the criteria particularly well. A participatory budget forum was then held at city level to decide on the projects put forward. The process was restricted, as we saw in Part I, to members of the local community and representatives of Bradford Vision.

meet social criteria and were placed in order of rank by the participants. However, the experiment did show up certain limits of a participatory budget anchored in a community development process. The procedure was not open to the entire population, as only the members of community groups whose projects had been accepted had right of access. In the case of Bradford – and most other processes of participatory budgeting in the form of participatory grant-making – public meetings did not allow any real debates to occur: the advantages and disadvantages of projects presented were not discussed, and it was not even possible to request additional information; meetings concentrate on the voting procedure. Furthermore, the project was based on the commitment of a small group of people working in the local LSP and did not get a real institutional grounding. Relations with local politicians and city administration were weak; the approach was unlikely to have any impact on modernisation and could at best hope to have an indirect impact on the legitimacy of municipal policy.[12] Finally, the finances that fall within the scope of the participatory budget were

---

12 The rate of participation in local elections, which was 46 per cent in 2004, has not improved, however.

'funny money', drawn down from the national programme for urban renewal; this programme was limited in time and does not involve local government finance. Although the procedure was repeated several times up to 2010, there is no guarantee of further funds being made available.

## 4. A 'Fourth Way'?

The Bradford procedure has influenced other initiatives in the UK. Participatory budgeting in the city of Newcastle, for instance, has learned from the Bradford process, as well as from the European network 'Partecipando', which was part of the URBACT programme (Lavan 2007). Newcastle, where the council was led by a Liberal Democrat majority (and Labour), had a reference point for projects involving children and young people (2006), as well as the environment ('Liveability pilot' 2007). In both the 'U-Decide Children and Young People's pilot' and the 'Liveability pilot', the organisers (Local Strategic Partnership and council) used £75,000 from the Neighbourhood Renewal Fund over two years (£30,000 for year one). Whereas the first pilot targeted its funds citywide (the process was repeated in 2008[13]), the second involved three council wards.

### The Tower Hamlets Experiment

Moreover, other towns – such as the London borough of Tower Hamlets (process launched in 2009) – copied the U-Decide branding used in Newcastle. As one of the participatory budgeting project managers explains: 'We liked the

---

### U-Decide Liveability Pilot: The Process*

The U-decide pilots used funds allocated by the LSP but were delivered by the local council. Both U-decide pilots developed on the basis of a participatory grant-making procedure in which the funds were allocated either directly to community projects, or to groups who would work in partnership with the council and other service providers to deliver their ideas.

---

*Note:* 'This presentation is taken from Lavan (2007: 16).

---

13 A total of 139 young people took part in the process in May 2008. This time, they were allotted a 20 per cent share in the vote on the procurement of services for the city's £2.25m Children's Fund.

> The Liveability pilot took place in three wards in the outer west of Newcastle, an area often considered peripheral to the city which had received relatively less regeneration money than other areas. The priorities for the pilot were 'safer, cleaner and greener', and were the top two priorities of each of the three wards, based on extensive surveys that had been carried out across the city.
>
> The design of the pilot was decided mainly by a Working Group of local residents working with a community development officer from the council. This 40-strong group were responsible for decision-making about all aspects of the pilot from publicity and process, to venue and refreshments. A Learning Group of council officers, partner organisations and representatives from the local universities followed and occasionally advised on the process. Support was also given throughout the process by the PB Unit.
>
> Publicity and the strong branding of U-Decide were developed to inform both residents and other stakeholders about the process. Residents were invited to complete a very simple pro-forma with their ideas on how the money could be spent on one of the three themes. After being checked for their legality, a council officer worked with the groups to develop their ideas. An event was then held in which a representative from each project gave a short presentation to other proposers and residents about their idea. Support was offered beforehand to help with presentation skills. Participants in the event then scored each project with marks out of 10. The top 15 projects were then prioritised for funding. After the event, groups were given the money and support in delivering the project was provided by the council.

implication behind Newcastle's branding and copied it with a few small changes. … I think it's one of the simplest ways to express the quite complex nature of participatory budgeting'. The process was initiated by the Director of the Tower Hamlets Partnership and the Local Strategic Partnership. Tower Hamlets is a very urban borough in the East End of London with a Labour dominated council. Despite being only about five miles across, it has nearly 220,000 residents speaking 110 different languages. Nearly 50 per cent of the population is not 'white British'. The Borough is split into eight Local Area Partnerships (LAP) areas and it is these which formed the basis of the participatory project. The council provided £2.4 million of funds for the 2009 procedure and all residents above the age of eleven could take part in the voting. The money came from the Area Based Grant, a general grant allocated directly to local authorities as additional revenue. Over the course of eight events in the eight local areas or LAPs (of around 25,000 people) that were organised between January and April 2009, residents had the chance to vote for the services that should be 'bought' for their local area; there was no city-wide discussion, meetings took place in individual neighbourhoods. The money on offer in each area was roughly

£275,000. Residents were able to choose from a menu of 46 services (delivered by the council, Primary Care Trust or police), which were are all based on the Cabinet's five priorities for the year. The offers were put together by council officers (or, in the case of the Primary Care Trust or police, by representatives or officers from those organisations) and then shown to a group of residents and the Cabinet for amendment and approval before being offered to the public at large.

Over 800 people came to the meetings and the process was repeated in 2010. The money needs to be approved each year through the formal budget-setting process. There is a specific code within the budget for this project, which means that the council must consider how much money (if any) to allocate to the project every year.

---

### The 'U-Decide!' process in Tower Hamlets, London (2009)*

The events were split into three sections:

*Inform*: This took two parts. Initially, the co-chairs of the LAP Steering Group introduced the LAP priorities and why they were important for the local area. The service heads who would deliver the 33 services on the menu presented their services to the residents (As they were grouped under headings this meant that only three senior managers would present at each event). The idea was to give information about the level of the problem, what services were already provided and what difference the additional funding would make. At the end of each presentation there would be time for questions.

*Deliberate*: When the people arrived they were asked to sit at tables laid out around the room as in a café. Each table had a trained facilitator and during this part of the event the facilitator worked to encourage the residents to talk to each other about which services they favoured and why they considered them to be so important for their local area. While this took place they also had some food which helped add a degree of informality to the discussion.

*Decide*: They then moved to the voting stage. Each participant had a 'who wants to be a millionaire' style quizpad. In the first round of voting all participants were asked to vote for the service they considered to be most important. The item that received the most votes was purchased, the money for that item removed from the total and another round was opened. In each round, the item with the most votes was

---

*Note*: Description taken from webpage of PB Network: http://pbnetwork.org.uk/tower-hamlets-you-decide/

purchased and this continued until all the money was spent. All votes were displayed on the Big Screen as they happened (Chris Tarrant-style) and the items purchased were shown on another big screen alongside the remaining choices and the total budget. This made the process instantaneous and very open.

After the events had been completed we invited all of the LAP Steering Groups (although only resident and councillor members could attend) and all of the services to an evening event nicknamed 'service speed dating'. Each service was invited to bring along a rough outline of what they were planning to do with the money allocated to them (providing more detail than had been available at the events). The LAP Steering Groups could then negotiate with the services the sort of changes they would like to make. This led, at the end of the event, to the preparation of a rough blueprint between each Steering Group and the services purchased in that area, describing what was going to be delivered. Many of the services were changed quite considerably because of resident involvement and many of the Steering Group members welcomed this as a way of shaping services for their local area.

After this event the services had a mandate to deliver the services. Each month the services fill in a basic highlight report which is monitored by the central Strategy and Performance team. This is also sent to the Steering Groups who are invited to comment on the report/service and submit those comments to the central Strategy and Performance team. These reports are then passed to the Cabinet on a quarterly basis and reported on an exception basis.

Although the Tower Hamlets process does not involve a borough-wide discussion about overall spending priorities (and therefore does not correspond to a participatory budget in the sense developed in this book), it differs strongly from the participatory grant-making approach: it involves mainstream funds and concerns municipal services, not individual initiatives of single community groups. The amount of money allocated to the process goes beyond that of many other pilot projects, for instance in two wards of the city of Lewisham (£60,000 each) or in Salford (£100,000 for roadwork in one area). Tower Hamlets received a 'green flag' for its participatory budgeting, an award from the Audit Commission that represents an 'exceptional performance or innovation that others can learn from'. This example, next to other interesting initiatives, like the one in Norfolk (which also received a 'green flag' for its participatory process, a county-wide procedure using £200,000 from revenues accrued from council tax on second homes[14]) or in Newcastle, exhibits continuous experimentation and

---

14 For 2010, however, the organisers chose to organise seven local events throughout the area, where participants decide on projects for their area and not the whole county.

the development of more complex procedures – even though most examples remain very small-scale and involve very small sums.

## The Development of a National Agenda

This development has been strongly supported by the fact that participatory budgeting has entered the national policy debate on community empowerment. Put firmly on the national policy agenda in mid-2007 by Hazel Blears, then Secretary of State for Communities and Local Government, by September 2008 her Department had published its 'national strategy', which planed the introduction of participatory budgeting in all English local authorities by 2012 (DCLG 2008). Blears subsequently took much of the blame for some terrible election results for New Labour in the 2009 local government elections. However, participatory budgeting seems to have survived the fall of its most important political champion, as well as the end of the New Labour government. Possibly this is because this process has been institutionalised through its identification with a wider empowerment strategy developed over recent years by consecutive New Labour governments,[15] which apparently has also been taken up by the subsequent governments.

The integration of participatory budgeting to the national political agenda around citizen participation was the result of initiatives being carried locally and of an active network of supporters deliberately aiming to place the Brazilian process within the New Labour policy framework then developing around greater participation and the devolution of powers. Through a National Reference Group for participatory budgeting, under the auspices of a small grant from the previous national government, a useful conduit was created for the exchange of ideas between policymakers in the process of framing the national strategy for neighbourhood renewal and the relatively few practitioners experimenting at the grassroots with participatory budgeting. This close connection between advocates of participatory budgeting and empowerment professionals working at policy level was critical in situating this procedure squarely in the centre of the new national policies on empowerment (Röcke 2010).

In April 2006, delegates from 80 British local authorities took part in a conference specifically on participatory budgeting and decentralisation. The meeting was organised in London and sponsored by central government. Participatory budgeting was later explicitly mentioned in successive government White Papers about local participation and community empowerment (DCLG 2006, 2007, 2008). In July 2007, participatory budgeting made a real

---

15 Participatory budgeting was presented as being 'at the heart of the government's drive to pass more power to local communities and help re-invigorate local democracy' (DCLG 2008: 9).

breakthrough at national level with the promotion of Hazel Blears MP to Secretary of State for Communities and Local Government. Incidentally also MP for Salford, where the PB Unit undertook its first pilot projects, Blears, in her first significant policy speech, called for a national roll out of participatory budgeting.[16]

One of the more fruitful outcomes of the connection between policymakers and practitioners was to focus on how best to communicate and 'sell' participatory budgeting to local authorities. It was realised early on that local councillors may see this process as a threat. Focusing on the well-developed Latin American procedures, or on the emerging European experience was not considered as useful as promoting a home-grown participatory grant-making procedure. There was a strong attraction to local authorities in terms of resident satisfaction from the use of participatory budgeting to hand public resources over to community and not-for-profit organisations. This appeal was reflected in its – admittedly short-lived – branding in the UK of participatory budgeting as 'community kitties', a title that reflected the accessibility, human scale and very localised perspective of many initiatives in the UK. However, those advocating participatory budgeting were also aware that the Bradford grant-making procedure was not sufficiently empowering or comprehensive to bring about a real shift in power.

During 2007 the PB Unit began to promote the idea of varying 'levels' of participatory budgeting and to abandon the initial emphasis of the 'original' Porto Alegre procedure. Crudely, this was seen as a sequential approach to introducing this procedure. Offering a number of steps towards a mature process was felt to be more realistic than expecting a fully developed programme to emerge from generally cautious local authorities. Documenting some of the early participatory budgeting processes as fitting within this common framework allowed newly aware local authorities to see where they might fit this instrument into existing engagement work, and also where the process might eventually take them. Most important was not to rock the boat too early and antagonise local councillors.

In addition to the 'national strategy' that emerged as the centrepiece of a significant national conference, two documents have been published by the PB Unit: *Values, Principles and Standards* (2008) for participatory budgeting and a *Tool Kit* (2008) with practical advice on how to implement a participatory budgeting. These remain the main policy documents underpinning the growth of participatory budgeting in the UK. DCLG (2011) commissioned an independent evaluation of the impact of the Brazilian process and they collected important baseline data. The research evidence of the impact of participatory budgeting remains mostly qualitative, but there has been some

---

16 See http://politics.guardian.co.uk, 05 July 2007.

attempt to measure progress. Many organisers emphasise the supposedly positive outcomes of participatory budgeting on community involvement or even the empowerment of communities (also illustrated by the numerous video spots available online on the webpage of the PB Network), an agenda shared both by Labour politicians and, more recently, by Conservatives and Liberals. This is probably one reason why participatory budgeting has been introduced in as many local authorities ruled by Labour as by Conservative councils, with the Liberals becoming increasingly interested in the process.

### An Ambiguous Balance

In 2010, the New Labour project came to an end, but the verdict of the electorate was not clear-cut. The Conservatives were faced by the unwelcome necessity of forging an alliance with the previously marginal third party, the Liberal Democrats. This unexpected political coalition has brought about a huge policy upheaval, with civil servants and think tanks trying to marry Liberal Democrat professions of concern for social justice and progressive government with post-Thatcherite neo-conservatism keen on dismantling the apparatus of the 'big state'. And all this against a perception of unsustainable government spending that supposedly necessitates a slashing of public expenditure to shrink the size of the public debt. This means that the UK faces the wholesale abolition of regional government structures, Quangos and non-elected boards and partnerships, the ending of government targets and reining back New Labour pledges such as 'ending child poverty', with some radical public sector cuts. Only economic growth and volunteerism can compensate for the expected severe reduction in local government budgets in the coming years. Many councils are expecting their budgets to decrease by as much as 30–40 per cent over five years.

Participatory budgeting was a still new idea before the 2010 election, but was then integrated in official government papers. Participatory budgeting in the UK is usually seen as a means of engaging with and empowering local people – using urban renewal funds to benefit those living in deprived areas – and of creating more locally rooted and more user-oriented service provision. The introduction of this procedure to the national political agenda has led to a significant development of new experiments and its diffusion throughout the UK (DCLG 2011). Could the success story of this procedure indicate the development of a 'Fourth Way' that combines the modernisation of local administration and strong local authorities with the development of new participatory spaces for the empowerment of citizens, all three elements being held together by an overall agenda of social justice (or 'the fair society', as the 2010 coalition preferred to say)?

The results of 'participatory grant-making' or 'community grants' are ambivalent in this respect. They usually have a strong social emphasis because they aim at the empowerment of specific (possibly deprived) groups of the population through the transfer of decision-making competences and may involve several areas or the whole town. However, they have weak links to local institutions and are often based on specific, non-mainstream pots of money (so-called 'funny money'). Projects are usually small and run by single community groups (although the funds at stake can be considerable) and are not related to 'big' politics or the delivery of services, also because they lack a second, city-wide level of participation, as found in the ideal-type of community development. Taken together, these factors create the possibility of a participatory space emerging in parallel to that of municipal political structures and the greatest challenge consists in linking participatory with institutional politics. As to the projects that involve mainstream funds, one important challenge is reaching beyond micro-scale processes involving discussions within single neighbourhoods and rooting the procedure in the institutional structure. Even though processes like the one in Tower Hamlets involve a mainstream budget for the whole city area, discussions take place in single neighbourhoods and do not involve a deliberation about borough-wide priorities or matters affecting different neighbourhoods.

Overall, if participatory budgeting in continental Europe and Latin America is seen as a cyclical annual budgeting process, the UK approach has been very pragmatic. Local authorities were encouraged to identify with a procedure which best fitted their own context, and then learn by trying out participatory budgeting through to the end of a first pilot round. By setting up a local learning and evaluation group, hopefully with resident members and also local councillors, it was suggested that one could then go on to explore how to develop a participatory budgeting programme that was more meaningful, co-designed, widely accepted and also locally owned. It became normal and even acceptable that one could enter participatory budgeting at the easiest point possible, and only later need to refine the process.

A danger of this approach is of course that it becomes normal to allow a very limited version of the Brazilian process (in the form of a community fund initiative in a single area), and it is possible to question the transformative value, given the simple and small-scale nature of most UK participatory budgeting experiments so far. Although the growth in the diversity, number and scale of new experiments is still very positive, the relatively small sums involved in many of the initiatives claiming to be participatory budgeting and the limited scope of many of the projects, coupled with limited evidence of institutionalisation at the local level make it still uncertain whether participatory budgeting can make a meaningful difference to the power and influence available to ordinary citizens or even constitute a vector for a more just society. Participatory budgeting has

155

managed to remain attractive to politicians of all political persuasions, and has generally received strong acceptance by ordinary citizens where it has been tried. It taps into a recurring theme in the UK of more localism, individual choice over services used, devolution of powers and the loosening of some old ultra vires restrictions on local councils. It remains to be seen how far this trend will continue also in a context characterised by severe cuts in public budgets, and also how far participatory budgeting can really be at the centre of this development. There are promising examples, such as Newcastle or Tower Hamlets, but it is not sure whether they will be more influential than the much easier path via participatory grant-making.

## 5. Participatory Neoliberalism? The Case of Płock (Poland)

The challenge in Poland is somewhat different, because participation is even more influenced by the neoliberal context and public–private partnerships than in in the UK. In the context of Eastern Europe, which is scarcely fertile ground for alter-globalisation movements, the example of Porto Alegre has had no influence on any of the procedures introduced, which are instead inspired by the ideal-type multi-stakeholder participation that has progressively spread to civil society. What is the role of civil society groups and communities in this context? Is the issue really to reinforce citizens' participation and local democracy, or is the real motivation of towns with low financial resources to attract private capital?

The Polish context is marked by a breakdown of public trust in political institutions that is even more marked than in the UK or other Western European countries. Since the beginning of the transformation that started with the fall of the Communist regime, support for Parliament and the Senate fell from nearly 90 per cent in 1989 to a mere 31 per cent in 2003. A total of 77 per cent of people polled considered politicians were dishonest, 78 per cent considered them untrustworthy and 87 per cent thought that they put their own interests first as opposed to a mere 4 per cent who considered that they put Poland's interests first. According to the media, the rate of criminal activity is higher in parliamentary circles than in the rest of society (Ziemer 2003). There is serious lack of faith in the present way of working of representative democracy, even though this does not extend to the democratic system per se. This phenomenon is now spreading from the national to the municipal level, and electoral participation is very low, even compared to other Eastern European states.

This evolution is all the more remarkable given that Poland gave birth to Solidarność, one of the most powerful opposition movements in Central and Eastern Europe. The neoliberal stance taken by a considerable number of the members of this trade union, however, has blurred political divisions, particularly in terms of left and right. The transformation era was, moreover, characterised by massive privatisation and rapid expansion of social inequalities that have not disappeared with the economic upturn linked to joining the European Union in 2004. The instability of the political scene and the political system in general has been reinforced by the ideological conflicts between supporters of an ideologically neutral state and those who would like the Church to play a dominant role in affairs of government.

Since the change of regime almost everything has been transformed in the local government system. One of the priorities of the first post-communist government, constituted in September 1989, was to undertake local government reform. The centralist doctrine of the communist era had left no scope at all for local self-management, and town council elections did not exist. After the return of democracy, the system that was introduced included a relatively high degree of independence for town councils (Swianiewicz 2005). Since 1998, Poland has had a three-tier system, with town and cities, regions and the central state; all of them have an executive body and a democratically elected assembly. Unlike the UK, however, local governments are empowered to take action in the matters that concern them. These powers are supported by the principle of subsidiarity. Their missions include the local economy, primary schools, kindergartens and child day-care centres, social services and preventive medicine, libraries and other cultural institutions. Their financing is based on a combination of local taxation (council tax), a percentage of state tax revenues and sums transferred from central government. In 2002, a much wider reform introduced the direct election of mayors, who have considerable administrative powers. This innovation led to structural power struggles between town councils and the mayor, which were all the more intense if they represented different political parties (Raciborski 2005).

The first Polish experiment of participatory budgeting took place in Płock, a town of some 130,000 inhabitants whose history stretches back over a thousand years (Dakowska 2013). This town has the biggest petro-chemical complex in the whole of Poland, and is situated in the centre of the country, in the region that falls under the economic influence of the two major cities of Warsaw and Łodz. The economic strength of the town is largely due to the existence of PKN Orlen, the largest Polish oil company. In 2004, the town was economically stable and dynamic, and had the second highest per capita income in Poland. The local government's budget was approximately 112 million euros. The increase in unemployment that affected 20 per cent of the population in 2005 was problematic, however. The mayor was right-wing, and there was no clear majority in the town council.

The participatory budget goes back to 2002, when the 'Płock Forum' was created as a cooperation project between the town, PKN Orlen and the United

Nations Development Programme (UNDP). It was a public–private partnership aimed at improving living standards, as well as economic, ecological and social aspects of the town. In 2003, on the initiative of the United Nations, the project was extended, with the creation of a 'Grant Fund for Płock'. Members of this fund included members of the town council, local business leaders as well as civil society organisations. The heart of the procedure was the selection of projects put forward and implemented by local NGOs. In this sense, as in the case of the UK, we can talk about a form of community development. This innovation was probably introduced by the UNDP officials on the basis of their experience in developing countries.

This project was characterised by a combination of a relatively classical kind of public–private partnership with the rudiments of community development and an urban development strategy. According to the project's initiators, all the stakeholders should gain from this approach: the citizens, because there were more social projects in the town; the NGOs which had their activities financed; the private sponsors whose image improved and who could claim the added value of corporate social responsibility to get European Union funding (which in turn should simplify the sponsoring that they would have done in the first place); and finally the local authorities which were able to avail themselves of additional private funding, as well as of NGO and UNDP expertise in matters of urban development. The public image of the town was also enhanced as it is the first town to implement something of this kind. This was doubtless one of the reasons that explains why Płock went down this innovative road, which has already been copied by other towns, with yet others expressing an interest.[17] At a time when many towns were still trying to establish a democratic approach and public monies still tend to flow through obscure channels, Płock was a case of best practice.

However, with limited financial means, the limited impact of civil society on procedure, as well as their lack of access to discussions on strategic matters of town policy in the existing process, participatory budgeting in Płock was far from being a process of political transformation. There was no interconnection with local government departments, nor was there any link with the potential reform of administrative services. The social aspects of the procedure, the support of NGOs and the active involvement of civil society were undeniably positive dimensions, particularly in the current context in Poland, where Płock was pioneering the participative approach at national level. These aspects in no way undermined the preponderant role played by the traditional political actors and private business interests. This differed fundamentally from the procedure as implemented in Bradford, UK, where participatory budgeting was strongly

---

17 In 2007, the cities of Ostrów Wielkopolski, Wałbrzych and Tarnów introduced the model in some form.

anchored in a process of community development and closely linked to the idea of empowerment of local groups. In Płock, the NGOs could well be in a position to manage social services, but there was no question of their being granted more power in what remained a fundamentally top-down process. The limited role played by civil society and relative lack of a move towards democracy in the procedure meant that Płock was something of an outsider in the panorama of European participatory budgeting. Even the instigators of the process did not use the term, preferring to speak of a 'small grant fund' or 'public–private partnership'. Nevertheless, the fundamental structure of participatory budgeting as defined in the first part of this book did in fact exist, and British experience shows us that the democratic aspects of the procedure (reinforcing the part played by civil society) are indeed liable to improve with time. There are many signs that indicate that these kinds of public–private partnerships are liable to continue to spread, particularly in Eastern Europe and the Third World. They are one of the UN's designated priorities, and in Europe are sometimes a prerequisite for obtaining European funding. Does this manner of participatory budgeting represent a procedure that can enable poor towns to finance their urban development on the basis of private finance? The example of Płock does not validate this hypothesis. It is a rich town and can actually 'allow' such a process to be implemented (the town actually shoulders half the financial burden and pays someone to manage the procedure).

## Conclusion: Empowerment, Minimal State and 'Big' Politics

What conclusions can we draw from this presentation of British and Polish experiments? Unlike most of the participatory budgets in Europe, they have a strong social dimension, and one key aspect is that they are related to the idea of community development: local associations and community groups act in the role of joint-managers in that they often implement themselves the projects voted at the participatory budgeting event. In the UK, this approach is pursued above all within the framework of so-called participatory grant-making or community grants events (the example of Bradford), where third sector or community groups bid for projects which they then carry out in their local community. When this approach involves different areas or the whole town, it comes close to the community development model which includes procedures of community funds at the neighbourhood and town level. Public sector agencies are more often involved in the delivery of projects within the framework of procedures involving mainstream funds (examples of Tower Hamlets or Salford). They are usually directed towards all residents, whereas the first procedure usually involves only organised citizens. The empowerment of specific population groups, either across a town or in specific (deprived) neighbourhoods, lies at the heart of the first approach; the second focuses more on the delivery of services that meet local needs and expectations and involve citizens in defining local service priorities. The biggest challenge of the grant-making approach is the linkage of the sphere of institutional politics (otherwise a parallel participatory structure may emerge) with that of the local service-delivery model to go beyond the scale of single neighbourhoods. If procedures remain restricted to this level, they represent a neighbourhood fund process rather than a participatory budget as we have defined it in this volume (and as it is commonly known in Europe and Latin America).

Overall, the situation in the United Kingdom seemed to be far more dynamic than in Poland: the 'national strategy' of participatory budgeting initiated by Hazel Blears, as well as the global shift towards a more 'localist' style of politics, had clearly put the topic of citizen involvement high on the political agenda. A process of institutionalisation had taken place, supported by the development of an active national network and the experimentation with different approaches to participatory budgeting involving different funds (municipal, national, possibly private), scales (from micro-local to city-wide), publics (all residents, third sector, community organisations and specific groups, such as children) and organisational bodies (local councils, LSPs, police authorities, neighbourhood management structures and so on).

However, the situation has changed with a national law adopted in Poland in 2009 that strongly promotes participatory budgeting in rural municipalities (and with the financial crises that provoked a sudden end for many 'participatory budgeting' processes in the UK). Originally, the idea of participatory budgeting had been imported to Poland by international organisations and the instrument became a 'local' device only in the late 2000s, in the form of a part of money transfers from the state to local governments given to local community projects in rural areas (and to some experiments in urban municipalities). This evolution has made rural Polish participatory budgeting more similar to their British counterparts. Initially, participatory budgeting had involved a public–private fund and private companies steering the process, whereas the empowerment of local communities was very weak. The aim was to enable them to implementing certain social services, which in a liberal welfare state are no longer guaranteed by the government. To exaggerate somewhat, it would almost be possible to call this 'participatory neoliberalism', as the process served economic interests and contributed to abolishing the traditional social functions of the state. From a normative perspective, one might question whether such a process can still be labelled a 'participatory budget' in the Brazilian sense, but we have focussed here on the procedural dimension in order to compare a broad range of different experiments. Moreover, the Płock experiment has had some influence in other Central and East European countries, and the new wave of urban participatory budgeting that took place in the 2010s has been more influenced by international experiments than the first one.

In the UK, participatory budgeting constitutes a potential nucleus for the development of a 'Fourth Way', as it represents a concrete way of putting citizens at the heart of political processes and always involves the transfer of decision-making competences. Nevertheless, many challenges remain, starting with the need to enlarge the micro-local initiatives of participatory budgeting to a broader political agenda in order to reach 'big' politics. Moreover, the current context of severe cuts in public spending represents a completely new situation. The problem is simple and reminiscent in some ways of the situation that we saw in the German case: will the same people participate when the discussion is about priorities, not investments? With local councils facing cuts of 25 per cent in some services and seeking to close down whole areas of their discretionary services, such as youth services, how can local people really engage in difficult and politically contested decisions, such as which policeman to sack, which school to close or which private firm to contract to run services more cheaply? The jury is still out on whether the mainstream of participatory budgeting will follow the path of small grant processes that are part of an overall dismantling of the state – one may ask whether the 'big society' was anything other than a positively framed version of the 'minimal state' – or whether they will turn out to be an innovation that can usher in a new age of responsive, targeted and efficient public services and democratically active citizens.

# Conclusion of Part II:
# The 'Porto Alegre Effect'

We are now in a position to assess the 'Porto Alegre effect' that we initially proposed as a hypothesis. The link between the development of European participatory budgeting in the 2000s and the alter-globalisation former 'capital city' is clear and the transfers that took place through visits, networks and the diffusion of procedures or ideology were decisive factors. Without the Brazilian experience and its appropriation by the alter-globalisation movement and other actors, first among which were left-wing activists, Europe would not have experienced the set of procedures now labelled 'participatory budgeting'. Even in Germany, the Porto Alegre process has been imported in a second phase. However, its role in Poland or other 'new' countries (former Yugoslav countries, Sweden) seems less decisive. Since the 2010 period, there has been a great diversification of procedures and actors, making the Brazilian model one reference among others. In addition, the idea of an initial wave emanating from Porto Alegre should be put into context, given the significant differences between one participatory budgeting process and another. Many European countries have so far missed out on participatory budgeting altogether and even where the procedure exists, it varies greatly from one place to another. Furthermore, when one looks closely at the development of participation, as well as its administrative, social and political effects and challenges, one is forced to admit that these differences are not merely procedural in nature. Rather, they appear due to different local actor coalitions, who differ greatly between one town and another, even within countries. Sometimes, the situation can be significantly affected by a single individual. In addition to these micro-sociological interactions, case studies have shown greater contrasts that are due to the political culture and context of each of the countries analysed, as well as the ways in which administrative modernisation and participation are linked, and the extent to which participatory procedures are integrated into the overall political process.

By way of example, it is enough to mention the democratic constitutions that were copied, adapted and reinvented throughout Europe and the world after the French and American revolutions and at the end of the Second World War. These clearly show that it is necessary to differentiate between those situations in which the import/adaptation retains an essential part of the initial socio-political meaning and those where any similarity with the original is merely superficial. In general, are European participatory budgets an intelligent adaptation or a misrepresentation of the Brazilian model? The question cannot be brushed under the carpet by simply saying that the situations in Brazil and Europe are totally different. Europe is also riddled with differences and yet some European experiments are more similar to the Porto Alegre model than others. Europe has certainly not seen the emergence of 'one, two or several Porto Alegres'. The social dimension of Brazilian participatory budgeting has almost no equivalent and, in the majority of cases, the power given to civil society cannot be compared with that handed over in the capital of Rio Grande do Sul. Nevertheless, a number of ideas and procedures has spread from one continent to the other and then from region to region and town to town within Europe.

Even moving from a cognitive perspective to a more philosophical or political assessment leaves us unable to define an ideal model comprising the advantages of each of the developments that we have analysed, while avoiding their faults. Political experiments cannot be carried out in the laboratory and it is not possible to eliminate 'impure' factors, such as the effects of the location or path dependencies, which make it more difficult to adapt the procedure once it has been established. Hybrid combinations are the order of the day and this is a trend that is increasing over time. A lack of comparative studies, flaws in previous assessments and a lack of systematic cross-cutting criteria that would enable those involved to make clear choices in accordance with their margins for manoeuvre, political objectives and lessons learned from past experiences negatively affect this development. Nevertheless, the future could be an exciting one. There is increasing interest in the idea of participatory budgeting and new experiments outnumber those that are being discontinued.

There needs to be an additional effort in terms of systematic analyses and concept building in order to undertake an overall analysis of the processes that we have studied and better elicit their macro-political effects. What is really at stake in European participatory budgeting as a whole? Do these innovations correspond at least in part to their initiators' stated ambitions to democratise democracy, invert social priorities to the benefit of the most disadvantaged and improve the effectiveness of public services?

# PART III

# CHALLENGES AND OUTCOMES
# OF CITIZEN PARTICIPATION

The panorama of participatory processes that we have described in the second part of this work shows that the development of participatory budgeting and the different shapes it can take vary, sometimes considerably, from one place to another. With the help of the six models, moreover, we could show that the underlying political, social and economic logic varies considerably. At this stage, it is already obvious that participatory budgeting in Europe has little in common with the Porto Alegre model, although this procedure arrived on the Old Continent via the 'return voyage of the caravels' that set sail from Brazil. It is not only the forms that differ, but also the socio-political dynamics and, along with them, the very meaning of the processes that have become implanted. Very few experiments can really be considered close to those of the capital of Rio Grande do Sul.

We are now in a position to take another look at the cross-cutting assessment we undertook in Part I. This time, we can widen our reflections on participatory budgeting to include the problems, challenges and outcomes of citizen participation and of democracy in general. We would like to put forward a three-pronged hypothesis. We are dealing with a significant movement that is still going on, but whose development represents more than a fashionable trend. The examples we have looked at can be considered forerunners to this development. Looking beyond the various characteristics of the cases, all the experiments that we have analysed in this work so far are linked to three kinds of objective: managerial, social and political (Bacqué and Sintomer 2001). In this third part, we systematically analyse the results and challenges of participatory budgeting (and participatory instruments in general) in relation to these goals. We begin with the link to public service modernisation (Chapter 9); then we focus on the issue of social justice, analyzing also the impact on economic development and ecological sustainability (Chapter 10); and finally we discuss the issue of 'democratising democracy' (Chapter 11). This analysis will enable us to conclude with an assessment of participatory budgeting as a whole.

9

# PUBLIC SERVICES SERVING
# THE PUBLIC?

Can participation contribute to a modernisation of public services? Even if the idea of modernisation is only implicit in the Porto Alegre experiment, it constitutes an explicit aim of many participatory budgets in Europe. In contrast to a model where public service modernisation is mainly based on privatisations, we explain the idea of a 'participative modernisation'. The first section shows the general strategy of this approach that aims at integrating laypersons' competencies in public administrations work. The second section discusses different roles for laypersons' inclusion linked to possible benefits and obstacles. The last section is about technical democracy, which gives a broader theoretical foundation to citizen participation in public administration.

## 1. 'Making Public Services Competitive In Order To Avoid Privatisation'

As we have seen at the international level, public action in recent decades has undergone a wave of reform in a variety of aspects. In this field, as in others, privatisation has become a powerful trend. Although it may have a positive impact in certain contexts, particularly where public administrations are highly corrupt or inefficient, this evolution includes major and clearly identifiable risks: it reinforces inequalities, focuses only on those who are solvent, is rational only in the short term and workers lose out power to the benefit of shareholders. This is also why, in addition to the introduction of market criteria, a second reform movement concerns the internal modernisation of administration, particularly in countries where public authorities seek to play an active role. However, these changes to the administrative machine tend to encounter a number of obstacles.

The first is that in public bodies it is difficult to achieve the consensus required to vote through reforms, particularly due to bureaucratic or corporatist inertia, and also because, in a context of austerity, civil servants legitimately fear that reforms will first and foremost provide a means of introducing cutbacks at their expense. The second is that the rationale underlying the new modes of organisation is far from clear. It is true that traditional bureaucratic rationality, as developed by Max Weber, has become outmoded. Weber's model, based on the Prussian state, is one of a hierarchical structure composed of devoted civil servants who conscientiously obey orders. However, the enhanced value of administrative deconcentration, of networks and partnerships, and of the systematic use of evaluation and internal competitiveness in the public sector all pose considerable problems: partnerships and networks sometimes lead to an even greater complexity of decision-making processes, whereas the introduction of the criteria of evaluation and genuine control mechanisms are the Achilles heel of the new management procedures (Bogumil, Jann and Nullmeier 2006). A third obstacle is linked to the fact that legitimate acceptance of civil service management reforms first of all has an impact on service delivery. Although this is important, its excessive dominance tends to reduce citizens to simple users/clients. Is this technocratic managerial logic really adapted to what is at stake?

One thing is certain: the status quo in many Western democracies is untenable.[1] The traditional way in which civil services operate is increasingly coming up against its internal limitations and provoking user dissatisfaction. Putting off reforms for too long generally leads to their being implemented under the worst possible conditions, and market-economic logic then seems to become the order of the day. This was clearly perceived by the German trade unions when they formulated the slogan: 'Making public services competitive in order to avoid privatisation'. This idea is debatable, because the reference to competitiveness appears to consider the market as supreme judge; nevertheless, it does have the merit of underlining the urgency and extent of the change required.

In this context, using citizen-users as a stepping-stone – which constitutes a 'third way' of modernisation – can prove useful. It can contribute to the legitimising of public action and to enhancing the principle that the final decision on policy choices should be made by the citizens themselves; it is up to the users to decide whether public services really serve the public. At both ends of the scale, citizen-users are then called upon to 'voice' their claims (Hirschmann 1990). Considering the perspectives of lay persons in determining criteria for the evaluation and control of political and administrative decisions is crucial in reducing the risk of purely technocratic initiatives that are disconnected from reality, helping to integrate users' knowledge and to consider perspectives that reach beyond the input of experts. In addition, the involvement of citizen-users who have been mobilised and are bringing pressure to bear to improve services is likely to create favourable conditions for Modernising civil services. Increased contacts between citizens and civil servants at all levels of responsibility encourage the latter to further query the mechanisms and logic of their actions. The simple fact of establishing regular contact between users and managers

---

1 The situation in the former countries of the Soviet zone should be analysed in a separate investigation, even though some aspects of the 'democratic crisis' are shared by the former East and West.

in charge of services or in contact with reality on the ground frequently creates profound changes in the way the latter work, and a well-thought-out reorganisation of administration has immediately perceptible effects.

This third path of modernisation is also likely to provide a counterbalance to the weight of the logic of market economy and to prevent solvable needs from becoming the sole focus. It encourages public debate on the choices that are made by imposing a degree of transparency on the activities of public enterprises and by limiting the concentration of power in the hands of private enterprise. The participatory trend involves a logic which potentially contradicts that of the market economy. However, in the overwhelming number of cases studied, the development of participatory budgeting occurs in parallel to that of privatisation. In many cases, the budget of companies whose capital is municipally owned, but that operate independently and often under private law (for example, water distribution companies), is equivalent to the municipal budget; so far only in a few cases have these companies developed a participatory strategy, including the Andalusian town of Puente Genil and some council house authorities in France. All in all, the participatory trend is far from being the strongest. The core mechanisms and channels of influence in today's societies (legal institutions and rules, lobbying work by organised interests, party politics and so on), at local and national level, remain largely unchallenged. All we can observe is that institutional participation is tending to become a regular means in addition to other existing channels. This represents a fundamental shift that has been taking shape over recent years, and that can be observed almost everywhere. It appears to be potentially decisive in establishing a more democratic form of public administration reform. The analysis of European participatory budgeting enables us to shed some light on this question.

## 2. The Roles of Citizens in the Modernisation of Public Services

What roles can laypersons play in the modernisation of public services? Academic scholars and political actors have developed a broad range of categories in order to analyse the different ways in which citizens can take part in defining public policy. We would like to offer a summary that brings together a progressive version of New Public Management, as developed in Germany, the more political approaches developed in France and Latin America and the Anglo-Saxon versions that favour community development. From this perspective, it is possible to draw an analytical distinction between four roles that citizens can have when becoming involved in participatory measures.

As *consumers*, they are essentially interested in the kind and quality of services delivered and do not become involved in the way in which they are delivered. As *joint decision-makers*, they can be involved in designing services offered or projects implemented, and may be involved to a greater or lesser extent in the decisions taken. This can go as far as the de facto delegation of decision-making powers in the most radical cases. As *joint managers* they are involved in the implementation of projects or services, which may even be self-managed. This ranges from different forms of voluntary work in public institutions, through the devolution of some task to citizens and associations, to the independent management of sectorial policy by professional NGOs and Third Sector organisations. Finally, as *controllers* or *evaluators*, they may exercise a role that is normally reserved for actors within the civil services or for external civil services or auditors.

In addition to these roles, it is possible to distinguish the scales of participation within each role. Whereas Arnstein's (1969) famous typology relates mainly to the role of joint decision-maker, we also distinguish between different scales in relation to the other roles. Table 9.1 provides an overview of the roles and scales of participation in public policies.

*Table 9.1* Roles and scales of participation in public policies

| Roles | Scales |
| --- | --- |
| Consumer | – Information of users/clients<br>– Consultation (for example, surveys, user panels and so on)<br>– Full integration of user/client reaction (mechanisms guaranteeing the responsiveness of civil services or companies to requests made, ombudsman, quality guarantee that may allow for subsequent compensation) |
| Joint decision-maker | – Consultation<br>– Joint planning<br>– Joint decision-making |
| Joint manager | – Marginally associated with management of services/delegation of tasks tightly controlled by public authorities<br>– Genuine joint management, delegation of tasks based on programmes provided by public authorities<br>– Self-management, third sector (social economy, community development) |
| Controller and evaluator | – Transparency<br>– Right to summon<br>– Formalised evaluation*<br>– Ability to apply sanctions* |

*Note:* * This exists only in rare cases in which public authorities voluntarily renounce the right to evaluate or the monopoly of applying legal sanctions, handing it over to citizens.

*Source:* authors' elaboration

The roles people are called upon to play vary depending on the participatory process. The panorama outlined in the previous section shows how people have so far been mobilised in participatory budgets in Europe, essentially assuming the role of consumers or joint decision-makers (all the participatory models go down this road sooner or later). They have not, however, been deeply involved in joint implementation, which is a feature, essentially, of models close to the community development model. This contrasts sharply with the situation in Latin America and the countries of the Global South, where joint management or self-management of resources by inhabitants is often the touchstone of the process, particularly when they address the poorest communities. Finally, the role of controller or evaluator has proved to be marginal (it is generally a by-product of claims made by mobilised people).

Another aspect in the framework of this discussion, which adds a historical dimension, concerns the issue of workers' participation. In most modern participatory processes, the possibilities available to workers for getting involved are not clearly settled. In the 1960s and 1970s, to the contrary, the participatory process occurred essentially in companies. The ideal of self-management was particularly widespread in France. In Germany and Northern Europe, the joint management of companies enabled workers to exert considerable influence on company policy. At the end of the 1990s and in the 2000s, there is a striking contrast: in the private sector, new management techniques do not appear to have included much prior criticism. Although employees might get involved in decision-making processes, they have no real impact on them (Boltanski and Chiapello 2005); it is the shareholders who have asserted their ability to control the way companies work. The themes discussed in participatory processes have shifted to local concerns and science and other technical domains in which citizens are more involved as consumers of services than as workers in companies. There is a potential tension between local civil service employees and citizens as consumers of the said services. To overcome this and to create a virtuous circle that would enable local civil service workers and citizens to cooperate in a positive way is an issue that must be addressed within the framework of the modernisation of public services. It is also a major challenge in terms of participatory processes. How do participatory budgeting in Europe addresses this question?

Generally speaking, it is understating the matter to declare that trade unions are not a driving force in the domain of citizen participation. Germany is the exception. The multi-service trade union Ver.di has shown a genuine interest in the question, and the Hans Böckler Foundation, which is linked to the unions, has been a key partner in several pilot schemes. In Italy and in the northern European countries, there has also been a certain interest, although at continental level trade union involvement has proved rather disappointing. This can be partially explained by corporatist hesitancy, as the introduction of participatory measures can undermine certain aspects of municipal workers' employment and complicate their work by introducing a new actor, in a context in which cohabitation with elected representatives is not always easy.

Over and above these purely defensive or routine reflexes, there is a genuine risk that can cause legitimate worries for the workers in question: the organisers frequently fail to recognise or appreciate the additional workload created when the participatory approach is introduced. Most people are available for participating only outside standard office hours. Even the most fervent volunteers cannot overcome the long-term need for recognition of the importance of this new dimension of work, especially when there is no major reorganisation of services, which would enable a rationalisation of tasks. The high school participatory budget in Poitou-Charentes, which is one of the most dynamic processes of its kind in terms of the modernisation of civil services, initially ran into criticisms from those in charge of drawing up financial estimates and following up on work in progress. When they are taken seriously, and have an impact on public decisions, participatory instruments are added to existing procedures and change established habits. This issue cannot be avoided, because it may have negative knock-on effects on other aspects of civil servants' work and on the efficiency of public services in general. Unless there is an in-depth reorganisation, it can lead to disappointment and even become counter-productive. Even the showcase example of Porto Alegre ran into serious difficulties on this issue. In the high school participatory budget in Poitou-Charentes, the reorganisation of the flow-chart of work and responsibilities helped to resolve the initial difficulties and considerably improved the operational abilities of departments. However, only a handful of experiments have been implemented in such a decisive manner.

Without waiting for deeper change to occur, a small fraction of municipal employees does, however, become involved in the managing of participatory procedures, sometimes with great enthusiasm. They are an indispensable link in the process: they often have a history of activism and are motivated by their political, ethical or professional convictions. In many cases they are people from the outside, specifically recruited to do the job and are the incubators of a process that takes time to become established as well as to motivate long-standing employees. An increasing percentage of civil servants involved have also received training (either initial or ongoing) that emphasises the themes and techniques of citizen participation. It is essential to roll out this practice if participation is to become an integral part of administrative routine, particularly in the case of people who occupy leading positions in the public administration.

## 3. An Empirical Evaluation

Over and above all this, can the study of European participatory budgeting provide us with reliable empirical data on the real impact of participation on the modernisation of civil services? On both this question and that of the social and political stakes that we shall be examining in chapters 10 and 11 of this third part, we need to be cautious, because the processes that we analysed were still quite recent. Their outcomes can truly be measured only over the medium term (Font, Della Porta and Sintomer 2014). It is also difficult, methodologically speaking, to separate the participation variable from other factors, in both qualitative and quantitative analyses. The results we present here are essentially based on qualitative ones; it was not possible to corroborate them with closely defined quantitative surveys. This is the reason why our results have to be treated cautiously; and they should be compared to other results or 'tested' within future research projects. Having taken these precautions, the impact of the European participatory budgets on the modernisation of civil services appears to vary widely. Six major trends can be identified: improved services, better responsiveness, problem-solving, devolution, 'joint-up-thinking' and transparency.

The first, which concerns most of the towns involved in the process, is the *sustainable improvement in the quality of services delivered*, thanks to the input of the expertise of certain NGOs or of people's user know-how. Gaps or needs that local civil services had overlooked or had been unable to correctly identify thus far, or to which they had been unable to respond in a suitable manner, are receiving improved coverage. Urban infrastructure, local police forces or socio-cultural activities for young people have improved. In the town of Albacete, for example, local NGOs carried out a detailed survey of all the neighbourhoods in 2004. They examined the state of the infrastructure and health needs, as well as safety and housing. This 'grassroots' survey enabled the civil services to target their actions, based on information hitherto unavailable. This progress is the result of proximity management and does not only involve experiments close to the ideal-type of the same name. Participatory budgeting is, in this respect, similar in its outcomes to other measures that we have studied, such as those of Hämeenlinna or Utrecht.

The second and third trends are also linked to proximity management. In many cases, the *responsiveness of the administration* has greatly improved. Civil servants are more accessible; participatory budgeting enables people's requests to be transmitted far faster than under traditional bureaucratic procedures; and the introduction of feedback mechanisms enables suggestions and complaints made by local people to be more effectively included. Participatory budgeting has also, in a significant number of places, helped create a *specific problem-solving ability* to respond to the needs of certain social groups (see also DCLG 2011). The civil service had previously been unable to solve these problems because of a lack of knowledge. This generally concerns micro-local issues, such as questions of clean streets or neighbourhood conflicts. These two trends particularly involve experiments that are close to proximity models, participatory democracy and community development.

The fourth improvement, which is more markedly present in community development and multi-stakeholder participation, involves the *devolution to NGOs or residents' groups* of certain projects that have public funding. They implement the projects far more quickly than the civil service could, and with better value for money and quality of service. In European participatory budgets, this kind of development concerns only micro-local projects involving relatively low sums, but it is indeed these 'little things' that contribute to greatly improving or upsetting the day-to-day lives of groups or members of a local community.

The fifth trend concerns *improved 'joined-up thinking' on the part of civil services*. Faced by requests from citizens affecting different departments of the civil service at the same time, the latter are encouraged to create team coordination mechanisms that facilitate an integrated approach and a cooperative response. The many innovations range from the creation of multifunctional units or one-stop centres at neighbourhood level, to establishing thematic standing committees (working groups) and improving communication between the heads of departments or the introduction of more across-the-board programmes. Most participatory budgeting models have to face these issues sooner or later.

The final trend is that of *greater transparency in matters of local finance*, from the point of both the public and local political leaders. The requirement to present the town budget in a way that can be understood by all citizens encourages those in charge to publish brochures or other documents that present the budget in simple terms; often, the elected representatives discover that they too develop a better understanding and clearer view of things. In Germany, participatory budgeting almost always involves creating a brochure that presents the town budget, providing the detailed costs. In the case of Berlin-Lichtenberg, the costs of the various services (playgrounds, park benches and so on) are outlined, neighbourhood by neighbourhood. When faced by questions from 'laypersons' who do not pay much heed to the budget lines of civil services, and who are far more interested in the products or services that are on offer to them, civil servants and elected political representatives are forced to examine closely whether to introduce a budget that is based on specific products or on general programmes.

Shifting away from everyday routines, combined with confronting concrete requests, encourages a certain distancing from ordinary bureaucratic reflexes and can be a source of innovation. While this trend includes cases that are close to all our participatory models, participatory modernisation has a systematic influence on the whole town, whereas the other models concern usually micro-local projects.

## An Instrument for Playing Catch-up?

It is difficult to evaluate the extent to which these various kinds of progress in the modernisation of civil services are interlinked. Transparency also has its limits: its impact is most frequently visible at the micro- rather than the town level, even though in almost every other case both levels are affected. Furthermore, the most controversial projects are more often than not outside the scope of participatory budgeting. Puente Genil in Andalusia was the only town in which a complete reform of the administrative machine took place. To a lesser extent, Berlin-Lichtenberg and Emsdetten in Germany have set up a similar dynamic by introducing participatory budgeting at the same time as they introduced a budget-by-product process; moreover, the city of Emsdetten has introduced a highly elaborate project for calculating and controlling costs. In other places, there has been considerable reorganisation of public action as a outcome of the introduction of participatory budgeting. But cases such as this are still in a minority. Most processes have a tangible impact, which leads to improvements in certain sectors or the modification of existing practices, but rarely involve major qualitative change.

Although the overall effects of participatory budgeting appear to be fairly limited in terms of the modernisation of civil services, this can be partially explained by the relatively short lapse of time since these procedures were introduced. It is also worth noting that in all the experiments with regard to which we carried out an in-depth qualitative survey, we were able to identify some modernisation impacts. If we look at the real cases, most impact on modernisation was surprisingly observed in the European cities that follow an adaption of the Porto Alegre model. And these outcomes are much more important than those we observed in the social or political spheres.

In most cases, the importance and sustainability of participatory budgeting in terms of the modernisation of civil services depends on how closely they are linked to the public administration. We have already stated that this is far from generally the case; the process is most frequently managed by a marginal department or policymaker (such as a deputy mayor in charge of participation). The various participatory models have also produced contrasting results. The greatest paradox is that the model of participatory modernisation, which is the one we might expect a priori to produce the most significant outcomes in this area, has proved disappointing as far as participatory budgeting is concerned. As the German experiments that we analysed in the second part of this work have shown, they have proved rather unsuitable for initiating administrative reform.

We need to add an observation here that might appear fairly banal to supporters of citizen participation, but which is generally controversial in the world of politics, amongst technical experts and in the academic arena.

At no point has the introduction of participatory budgeting led to negative impacts in terms of managerial rationality. This again runs counter to the dire predictions of elitist or technocratic theories that proclaim that involving citizens to a greater extent in public management can lead only to confusion. We must, however, recognise that European participatory budgets have often been created in towns that have not been the first in introducing a process of administrative reform. An initial hypothesis in this regard is that participatory budgeting represented a means of playing 'catch-up' and that it allowed local governments that were neither particularly behind nor particularly ahead in the race to modernise and to speed things up. This means that the future of the procedure is somewhat uncertain and could be set aside in favour of other instruments if and when local authorities have successfully achieved a sufficient level of modernisation. Another hypothesis is that this was just a passing phase. As the process becomes more popular, it will doubtless affect an increasing number of local authorities that are at the cutting edge in this field. This idea appears plausible, given the fact that Nordic towns are starting to show a serious interest in participatory budgeting (they are the leaders in the modernisation of civil services); the UK has started to mainstream it; and in the Latin American context, participatory budgeting has often been introduced by towns that represent the avant-garde of innovation in civil services. The future is certainly open. If the technical considerations with regard to the advantages and limits of the approach do have some weight, the political choices that link the interest in public administration to considering the social and political impacts of participation will prove decisive.

## 4. Towards Technical Democracy

Is it at all legitimate to establish a close link between administrative modernisation and democracy? Is the former not just a managerial question, linked to the 'police', whereas the democratic stakes are part of the 'political' (Rancière 2004): that is to say, the radical review of the right to govern and the reasons that establish social hierarchies and unequal distribution of resources? We shall come back to this question in Chapter 10 and in the Conclusion. We can nevertheless demonstrate here that the clear-cut division between management and politics deserves to be considered with greater moderation. The first reason for this is that the modernisation of public administration is indispensable if we are to protect its role in contemporary society, particularly from being sidelined by commercial considerations. This key issue is linked to a fundamental choice in terms of the type of society we want – and not just to a discussion on good management practice. Such reasoning does not, however, establish a clear link between administrative modernisation and political issues: it is through improved technical efficiency of public services, potentially supported by participatory institutions, that modernisation can have an impact on the type of democracy we have.

## Technical Issues and Politics

A second, complementary argument goes further than this, putting forward the idea that citizen participation can help to redefine the political dimension of technical and managerial choices, thus providing the means for asserting political authority over bureaucrats and technicians. Participatory budgeting is very promising in this respect, as it reaches beyond the micro-local level and goes right to the heart of the matter by addressing financial issues. It is very much in the interest of elected representatives to play along with this, and to take citizen-users into account. The following extremely positive conclusions were drawn by a member of the regional government of Poitou-Charentes and Chairman of the Poitiers Council Housing Authorities (OPARC). He is also the initiator of a participatory budgeting process that involves people living in council housing in Poitiers:

> Participatory democracy gives me far greater power as an elected representative, contrary to what one might be tempted to think. An elected representative who operates on the basis of representative democracy has power, but he/she shares this in an unequal way with civil servants. Civil servants come to work every day, they manage things and they have the technical know-how. So sometimes the elected representative is somewhat on his own. If he limits himself to running clinics and saying 'do something about Mrs Jones' or Mr Smith's problem', the civil servant will take care of the issue for you. That does give you some power, but not a whole lot. Whereas if you are supported by all the people who have something to contribute, you organize their contributions, their expression and you also give them part of the power, [things are different. In this instance,] people listen to the elected representative when he explains his non-participatory decisions, because he isn't trying to pretend that other people have decided [on everything]. This confers a huge legitimate power on the elected representative. I believe that this is a fantastic role, and it is ten times more interesting than that of the classical system.

Is this positive affirmation of a politician also representative of other groups of actors? When we questioned civil servants, many of them complained that elected representatives regularly disrupted their work, interfering with aspects with which they were not familiar, imposing strange decisions. They also criticised the fact that they were often motivated by electoral concerns or cronyism and were sometimes very ideological in nature. They complained even more when

177

their work got disturbed by citizen participation. Civil servants can perceive this as undermining their expertise. In order to avoid this potentially negative influence of the political on the administrative function, while at the same time reinforcing the authority of the former over the latter, the supporters of New Public Management frequently propose a clear division of labour. This was only sketched out in the traditional relationship between elected representatives and their civil servants: orders are placed by the politician, who needs to be able to present his objectives clearly; the work is then executed just as clearly by the technical operators. This clear separation tends to facilitate evaluation and the operational role can just as easily be implemented by a private company as by public services – a similar motivation is doubtlessly important in promoting a clear division of labour between those responsible for placing orders and those responsible for executing any work.

But things become less clear in participatory modernisation projects, where citizens become involved in day-to-day management, as in the case of Hämeenlinna: is the user's input linked to the political decision or to its implementation? When citizens are involved in the technical design of projects – in citizen's conferences on scientific and technical issues, when users' associations or patients are involved in designing a project of urban development or an experimental protocol for new medication – the division of labour between the political order and technical expertise appears to be breached.

Within the framework of 'technical democracy' (Callon, Lascoumes and Barthes 2001), the same participatory rationale lies behind the decision-making process and the implementation phase of projects. Theoreticians of technical democracy have been reproached for underestimating the question of power and attaching excessive empirical importance to processes of technical democracy, which are politically desirable but still limited to relatively restricted fields. One of their main advantages, however, is that they undermine the excessive division between political decisions and their execution; this idea is unavoidable in modern participatory processes. The claim of technicians to haver the monopoly of expertise is more than debatable.

## Citizens' Knowledge

Expressions such as 'citizens' knowledge' and 'ordinary knowledge' or 'customary expertise' are increasingly used by political leaders, as well as within NGOs, foundations, universities and consultancies. Although the semantic vagueness is undoubtedly one of the reasons behind their success, they do testify to a large-scale change. In order to analyse this correctly, we need to differentiate between various dimensions.

The idea of 'citizens' knowledge' and equivalent terms refers, first, to the idea of 'ordinary reasoning', accessible to one and all. There are two variations.

(i) *User knowledge* is the most common. The American philosopher John Dewey developed this paradigm, writing: 'The man who wears the shoe knows best if and where it pinches, even if the expert shoemaker is the best judge of how the trouble is to be remedied ... A class of experts is inevitably so removed from the common good as to become a class with private interests and private knowledge, which in social matters is not knowledge at all' (Dewey 1954: 207).

User knowledge is part of the proximity paradigm, in a triple sense. First, geographical proximity, as it is local or micro-sectorial. The local then becomes the heart and springboard of democracy in general. This idea was already present in John Dewey: 'Democracy must begin at home, and its home is the neighbourly community' (1954: 213). Proximity is also present in the communication between decision-makers and users, in the case of elected representatives or civil servants who work 'hands-on' rather than shut up in an office. Finally, proximity can also sometimes mean sociological likeness between decision-makers and their electorate.[2] The different facets of user knowledge constitute a noteworthy input that complements the technician's knowledge.

In other participatory processes, it is not mainly in the aspects of usage that citizens' knowledge comes into play but rather in calling on them to exercise their (ii) *common sense*. This term refers to the ordinary capacity of good judgement, to the 'ability to judge well, without passion, on problems that cannot be resolved by scientific reasoning' (*Le petit Robert*). This non-systematic and non-party politically interested knowledge is typically called upon during jury duty, in citizens' juries or in consensus conferences where ordinary citizens are asked to express their opinions on questions that do not necessarily directly concern them. Using random selection in this way guarantees the impartiality of verdicts handed down by juries (Röcke 2005, Sintomer 2011a). In order to achieve this, common sense requires sufficient information and controversial debates bring people to exchange points of view, as well as giving everyone enough time to decide 'with a clear conscience'. This is therefore closely linked to deliberation, which helps to develop an enlightened opinion. Without this common sense, it would be difficult to accept the legitimacy of the very concept of democracy, which is based on the idea that everyone has the right to participate in the way things are defined, even if only by voting for their own representatives.

---

2 This is an old idea, originating in the mid-nineteenth century worker's movement, when workers held discussions on fielding working class candidates in the election: 'The workers know their needs and their resources. Who can tell us better than they themselves what they need or want? Wealthy people imagine that they alone have the power to solve social problems, that they alone have the knowledge to do it, but at the least intervention on their part, they only just manage to place the plaster next to the wound' (quoted in Rosanvallon 1998: 84).

'Citizens' knowledge' as form of 'ordinary reasoning' cannot, however, be reduced to user knowledge and common sense. People sometimes use the expression 'user expertise': this is used to grant citizens the status of 'experts on their everyday lives'. The term plays on the original meaning of the word, which comes from Latin, where 'expert' means 'a person who has obtained great skill through experience' (*Le petit Robert*). The word has undergone an historical evolution, however, with the increasing division of labour and the rise of experimental science. It increasingly refers to technical knowledge that reaches beyond mere experience and practical knowledge, whether it is of a systematic character or involves abstract concepts. The noun, which dates back to the sixteenth century, has basically taken on this second connotation: the expert has become 'a person selected for his/her technical knowledge, who is responsible for examining, reporting on or evaluating on a fact or a specific subject' or 'a specialist in charge of solving a technical problem' (*Le petit Robert*). Experts are opposed to non-specialists, to persons whose knowledge does not fall into the category of a systemic technical approach, to the 'uninitiated'; that is to say, the person who 'is not initiated in an art, a science, a technique, a way of life' (*Le petit Robert*). As we have just seen, it is precisely as non-specialists that 'ordinary' citizens are most often called upon to participate, their non-formalised user knowledge or their common sense being supposed to complement the technical knowledge that would prove inadequate if it were the sole basis. This participation of ordinary citizens is anchored in an attempt to fight the increased division of labour that tends to limit non-specialists to an increasingly marginal role.

Nevertheless, certain types of 'citizens' expertise' imply that systematic knowledge and techniques can also be involved in participatory processes. *Professional knowledge* (iii) is increasingly common in participatory initiatives: citizens who become involved as inhabitants are also workers with professional knowledge that they can reinvest outside their jobs. This can take the form of architects objecting to an urban development project; a social worker who becomes involved in discussions on public policy youth or immigrant issues; or a teacher who becomes involved as the parent of a student in a parent–teacher meeting at his or her child's school. This form of knowledge tends to increase as the 'knowledge society' develops and is linked to the important role played by the intellectual middle classes of modern society that characterises the new social movements. This trend contributes to breaking down the classical division of labour between representatives and represented.

(iv) *Expertise by delegation* corresponds to another logic. It designates technical or professional knowledge that results from the state delegating certain tasks to NGOs or the recognition by the state of the public usefulness of a given activity. The extent of this orientation can be considerable, particularly when it involves the community development model, and the knowledge that is developed can be technically of a high standard.

(v) *Counter-expertise* is based on a different dynamic. It typically occurs in the case of a technical or scientific controversy, when certain actors express the need to open up the discussion beyond the usual circle of decision-makers. In recent decades, there have been many such examples in various fields: drawing up alternative plans for urban development or community plans proposed by grassroots, mobilizing patients' associations in establishing new treatments, fighting the introduction of GM crops and so on. Calling upon this counter-expertise is a fundamental dimension of technical democracy, far more so than expertise that has been delegated. To go back to the image conjured up by John Dewey, it reaches beyond user knowledge inasmuch as it undermines the delegation of the technical solution to the cobbler: it is not enough to simply explain to him where the shoe hurts; nor is it enough that some participants may themselves be cobblers, as in the case of diffuse professional knowledge, or to create a community association aimed at repairing old shoes, as is the case of expertise by delegation. Rather what is needed is to carry out several examinations or audits of the shoes, to develop several different possible ways of repairing them and even to go so far as to contribute to their initial design.

Finally, there is potential for developing (vi) *political knowledge* through participatory approaches. This knowledge presupposes the ability to make judgements, which is symbolically linked to the status of citizens; but is also linked to the exercise of citizenship without which this status remains a formality, just as rights need to be exercised in order to prove them. Some theoreticians of participatory democracy, such as Carole Pateman or C.B. MacPherson, suggest that *political common sense* (as a faculty that all citizens are supposed to possess in principle) and *civic-mindedness* (as a knowledge that results from education and socialisation) can come together to form a virtuous circle. But there are also other opinions on this point. In ancient democracies, the aristocratic reclaimed that persons with political responsibilities should be nominated according to their competences; which constitutes an important restriction on the idea of political equality. This tension was reinforced in modern democracies dominated by the principle of representation – and therefore the delegation of decision-making to elected representatives who were supposed, according to the ideas upon which the concept was founded, to be wiser than simple citizens. The suspicion of inability that hovered in the minds of the masses in the nineteenth century was not the reserve of the conservative or liberal thinkers, and was shared by the republican left and socialists – with regard to which ambivalences concerning universal suffrage (Rosanvallon 1992) or the avant-garde were most revealing. The tension between 'common sense' and the political 'profession' took a particular turn and became increasingly important from the point at which politics became a profession. The progressive emergence of professional politicians in the second half of the nineteenth century, reinforced by the creation of mass parties, countered the slow accession of individual adults to playing their role as citizens by restricting their status to that of uninitiated lay persons.

Nevertheless, many people ranging from republicans to liberals, and to socialists, considered that in order to increase the legitimacy of the state it was necessary to develop citizens' knowledge of the state, of how the institutions work and of overall questions of politics and common good. The state was supposed to take on the role of educating people, for example through the introduction of public schools and civic education. It was in the same spirit that it was considered justified to call upon lay persons to take part in juries because this helped members of civil society to learn the law, to practice it and to lay claim to it (Hegel 1986: §228; Sintomer 2011a). Even nowadays it is still the spirit in which participatory processes are introduced: they enable citizens to gain a fuller understanding of the complexity of professional politics and the way the state works.

'Civic culture' that has been obtained in this manner has first and foremost a function of legitimisation. Political knowledge developed by an active commitment to local affairs may take on a meaning that reaches beyond this pedagogical framework where the division of labour between those 'who know' and those who are learning appears to remain untouched. In more radical examples, the idea of participation as a 'school of democracy' (Talpin 2011) or as empowerment aims to emancipate citizens, to help them to gain access to knowledge that will progressively enable them to take control of their own affairs. If the knowledge in question is partly anchored in user knowledge, born of the contact with institutions, it also includes collective forms of expertise by delegation and counter-expertise that contribute to the creation of countervailing powers (Fung and Wright 2001).

All forms of citizens' knowledge certainly run into difficulties and have their limits. User knowledge tends to limit participation to proximity or sectorial levels, which is why elitist theories may take it up, conceding that citizen participation can extend beyond the act of voting to the local public sphere. But as soon as one goes beyond this to address more global issues, it would be ridiculous to take citizens' perspectives into consideration (Schumpeter 1946). Common sense has obviously its limits. In public meetings for example, citizens with a greater cultural capital or who are simply more used to public speaking are more likely to have their voice heard than others. Professional knowledge is also unequally spread and valued. Participatory meetings have different dynamics depending on whether they are held in working class or in rich neighbourhoods. There is an inherent tension in expertise by delegation: the more the managers of NGOs become professionals and experts, the greater their separation from their own grassroots; the division between experts and ordinary citizens thereby reappears within civil society.

This problem also affects the use of counter-expertise, which in any case is still rare. Whole areas of scientific practice have no equivalent development to the mobilisation of AIDS victims or North American women's groups for treatment of the menopause, which are emblematic but also very specific cases (Gaudillière 2006). For every 'grassroots' community plan with a real outcome, how many neighbourhoods have totally changed shape and population as the outcome of real estate deals made without the involvement of any counter-expertise? Are 'political common sense' and 'civic culture' not a source of constant potential conflict? These are obvious questions in the case of participatory budgeting, as soon as they reach beyond micro-local neighbourhood issues and become involved in complex financial issues that far exceed user knowledge:

> For participatory budgeting, you put your name down for a working group, which involves attending a certain number of meetings, and the problem is that, as usual, when you get to the meeting, you haven't read the file you have just been given. Suddenly you find yourself with a pile of documents, figures all over the place that are presented by the civil servants who prepared the file ... But how can you take a decision or express an opinion when the case has just been presented? It isn't even possible to ask other people from the neighbourhood for their opinion, ... and if you are talking about another neighbourhood that you don't know, all you can do is express your own ideas ... When we are supposed to work on the budget, we should be able to study the file beforehand. In order to be able to express an opinion, you need to have thought about things, and what's more the amounts of money at stake are huge ... I think we should have a bit of training. (Member of the Allende neighbourhood tenant's association, in the French town of Saint-Denis)

Some of the problems raised by this activist could be solved easily enough if the work were better organised. One could introduce training mechanisms that enable the participants to obtain a better understanding of the background and that help the civil servants to become familiar with the participatory approach, using language that ordinary people can grasp. The tensions that affect all these dimensions of 'citizens' knowledge' would still not be resolved, however, as there would still tend to be a distance between activists who had received training and other citizens.

Nevertheless, are not these tensions characteristic of politics in general? The knowledge of those who are professionally involved in politics can be judged first and foremost by the strategic and tactical skills they use in the struggle for power, but this skill in isolation produces politicians only in the negative sense of the term. Professional politicians also need some know-how with regard to public policies, so that politics is not reduced to pure demagogy. However, when faced by experts whose technical expertise is – inevitably – greater than theirs, political leaders should demonstrate the ability to lead group actions and emphasise the political issues of the files under study in order to reach beyond the technocratic aspects, and link management of the present to the defence of major ethical and social causes (Weber 1919). All in all, should not the emphasis be on 'competence acquired through experience' rather than on purely scientific or professional skills? From this point of view, there is no knowledge gap, just a difference in the degree of this kind of political knowledge between citizens and elected representatives. This difference in no way justifies the historical monopolisation of power by elected representatives.

The objective of technical democracy in this regard is to suggest a different kind of articulation that is both desirable in normative terms and superior with regard to how knowledge is regarded. As we have seen, this is not easy to achieve, but given the stakes and the dead ends of technocratic methods, it is worth making the effort. The empirical conclusions we can draw concerning participatory budgeting, although modest, point in this direction. Each of the different models of participation is anchored specifically in one or another type of citizens' knowledge and confronts specific difficulties that should be studied systematically. Globally, citizen participation does contribute to the modernisation of civil service, but this should not be restricted to a purely managerial dimension: technical democracy has also a deep political dimension.

# 10

# AN INSTRUMENT OF
# SOCIAL JUSTICE?

Do the interesting developments in terms of administrative modernisation and technical democracy have any equivalent with regard to social justice? In the discourse of the alter-globalisation movement, the Porto Alegre instrument was presented as a springboard for an alternative to neoliberalism. Serious studies show that the Latin American participatory budgets have had a remarkable social impact (Marquetti, de Campos and Pires 2008, BIRD and BM 2008), both because they include criteria of distributive justice that encourage the allocation of resources to the most disadvantaged, and because the latter become involved in the process. Participatory budgeting there has generally come to be considered an instrument of the poor. What is the situation in Europe?

## 1. An Alternative to Neoliberalism?

What is striking in comparison to Porto Alegre is that the empirical impacts of European participatory budgets on social questions are fairly limited. In many experiments, no noteworthy social outcome can be observed: in some of them, the question has not even been brought up; in others, it has been addressed rhetorically, but without practical impact. In less than half of the cases examined, the effects are perceptible but remain limited in scope.

When European participatory budgets deal with the allocation of public budgets, either de facto or by formal delegation, this tends to make the process credible. But the social impact is generally less if the procedure is restricted by the limited funding available and by a failure to distribute the resources in a way that would help reduce inequalities. Over and above this overall observation, major differences exist. In the cases that we studied, there were two noteworthy experiments where the budget allocated exceeded 100 euros per inhabitant or per user of an institution with participatory budgeting: Pieve Emanuele (approximately 130 euros per inhabitant, more than 10 per cent of the town's budget until 2010) and the 'high school participatory budget' in Poitou-Charentes with over 300 euros per pupil (which represents 2 per cent of the regional budget and 9 per cent of the budget dedicated to schools). On this scale, widespread action becomes possible and, if it is aimed at enhancing social justice, it can have a considerable impact.

In Pieve Emanuele, there have been fairly positive outcomes: apart from aspects that concern the town as a whole, the majority of work that has been carried out under the participatory budget has been centred on two outlying neighbourhoods that were affected by a singular lack of services. This outcome is essentially due to the particularly intense mobilisation of the inhabitants of these neighbourhoods, and to the favourable response of the executive, even though the inhabitants in question did not correspond to their traditional electorate.

A second group of processes has dedicated sums ranging from 15 euros per inhabitant to the participatory budget: Cordoba (28 euros), Morsang-sur-Orge (24 euros) and Seville (17 euros). This is a relatively small amount, but the absolute sums can be very high: 9 million euros in Cordoba, almost 12 million euros in Seville in 2004 (corresponding, respectively, to 4.3 per cent and 1.4 per cent of the towns' budgets). Participatory budgets were not vectors of social justice, however. This was particularly clear in the case of Morsang-sur-Orge, where this objective did not appear on the agenda of those responsible for the project. At first sight, the situation appeared to be very different in the Spanish towns of Cordoba and Seville. Social justice was listed as a key objective in the participatory process which, as in Porto Alegre, was based on formalised criteria of redistribution that favoured disadvantaged groups (this was the case in Cordoba), as well as neighbourhoods that suffered from a lack of infrastructure or services (in both Cordoba and Seville). The concrete outcomes were ambiguous, however. Although the participatory budget undoubtedly encouraged the implementation of social projects, it is difficult to pretend that it 'changed things'. In Cordoba, the poorest neighbourhoods benefited less from additional investment than the outlying neighbourhoods that lack infrastructure but whose inhabitants tended to have a more comfortable socio-economic background. The participants did not appear to belong to socially disadvantaged groups or neighbourhoods either. In Seville one of the poorest neighbourhoods in the town, Polígono Sur, which has several tens of thousands of inhabitants, took advantage of the distributive justice criteria of the participatory budget applied on city level for large-scale projects, but the sums involved seem almost derisory: 10.90 euros per person as opposed to 8.70 if criteria would not have been applied. Polígono Sur got a 'bonus' of 70,000 euros (350,000 euros in total).[1] By comparison, the resurfacing of a road or the development of a sports' park costs several hundred thousand euros. A more significant amount was dedicated to the neighbourhood within a separate participatory process,

---

1 A further sum – approximately the same amount – was dedicated through participatory budget for small-scale projects. This money was not distributed through social justice criteria. Hence, at the end Polígono Sur got in total 700,000 euros from participatory budgeting.

which receives funding from the European Union's Structural Funds. This form of conventional neighbourhood renewal had no links to social distribution and did not differ from conservative neighbourhood policies. The idea of linking these funds to participatory budgeting was frequently discussed, but was not implemented. Even in these bastions of the radical left, where the influence of Porto Alegre was strongest, then, the effects of European participatory budgeting were far from comparable with the Brazilian equivalent.

A third group is those participatory budgets where less than 10 euros per capita was available, as in Saint-Denis (8 euros), Pont-de-Claix (5.5 euros), Bradford (2.18 euros, but triple that if community funding for disadvantaged neighbourhoods is included) or Płock (1.91 euros). In the case of the two French towns, we can repeat the observations we made concerning Morsang-sur-Orge. The situation was somewhat different in Bradford. The funding allocated to participatory budgeting was essentially used for the benefit of the most disadvantaged, and part of the funding was drawn from national programmes specifically aimed at urban regeneration. In Bradford (or the process in the London Borough of Tower Hamlets) it seems indeed to be the working classes or their delegates who have become involved in the process; ethnic minorities have also been actively involved. The sums at stake have, however, been very low: compared to the budget of the borough as a whole, it comes to a few euros per person. Płock was involved in a somewhat similar process, but with even less impact inasmuch as some of the funded projects were not social, and the participants were not members of disadvantaged groups. In such experiments, there is little hope of changing major social imbalances by the introduction of participatory budgeting. The process can, at best, act as a lever in attempts to launch a positive dynamic via a process of empowerment of the disadvantaged groups to try to reverse negative spirals of social regression.

If we include the impact of participatory budgets that were merely consultative, it changes little. Emsdetten in Germany was close to the second group that we have just considered. The participatory budget had no budget line of its own, but the increase in tax proposed by the inhabitants in the context of this procedure helped raise 610,000 euros in additional annual funding, and thus preserved public services. The allocation of these new reserves was not, however, aimed at helping the poorest, and the sums involved were modest. It worked out at less than 20 euros per inhabitant, whereas the town budget was 1,600 euros per person. In Albacete in Spain, the projects were concentrated on the most marginalised members of the community, particularly the gypsies, who were the most stigmatised and disadvantaged members of the ethnic minority community. The outcomes achieved were significant, but the population involved is a minority group. On the Old Continent, the small Italian town of Grottammare was the only local authority that can lay claim to undertaking social action that was comparable with the Brazilian participatory budgets.

If we consider European participatory budgeting as a whole, there have been some social outcomes, but apart from some exceptions, they have been on a fairly small scale. They have usually involved affirmative action aimed at the most disadvantaged and occasionally allowing for some improvement for specific groups, but the macro-social balance has remained unchanged. The 'small steps forward' or progress in a given sector that follow should not be overlooked, because at local level they can be the starting point for greater development, symbolically opening up new horizons with regard to 'another possible world'. But they should not be overestimated, either. It is in the experiments that are closest to the models of participatory democracy and community development that we find the greatest likelihood of seeing a broad social impact, although the empirical results are fairly disappointing overall. This observation is reinforced if we consider that, in most cases, the companies with public capital but operating independently or under private law are not affected by participatory budgeting. Small towns such as Puente Genil in Spain and, to a lesser extent, Groß-Umstadt in Germany, or Bobigny and Poitiers in France (two towns in which independent participatory budgeting for lodger of the public owned housing stock) are exceptions to the rule.

How can we explain this situation? First, what we have observed with regard to participatory budgeting also holds true *a fortiori* of other participatory approaches on the Old Continent. Most frequently, citizen participation is introduced to serve the hypothetical idea of 'increasing social capital'.[2] It also regularly allows affirmative action to take place. Exceptionally, it is used to achieve distributive justice. Most of the time, the real impact is very limited.

Participatory budgeting is potentially a powerful mechanism in terms of social justice, but this potential has, to date, not really been exploited in Europe. Is this just because it is only in its infancy? Maybe not. If we examine the Latin American and European processes, five factors appear to be particularly important in turning participatory processes into instruments of social justice: a genuine political desire to work in this direction; the fact that discussions involve important issues and consequential amounts of money; transparency that enables precise calculation of the social impact of public policies and the priority groups at which they are aimed; criteria of redistributive justice or targeted measures that favour the allocation of resources to lower social strata; and finally, social mobilisation of these classes so that their voice can be heard, their interests taken into account and social recognition achieved.

These five criteria do not necessarily all have to be present for participation to have a genuine impact, but the more present they are, the greater the likelihood that a virtuous circle will emerge. In Europe, however, this situation

---

2 In the evaluation report on the UK (DCLG 2011), 'increased community cohesion and increased self-esteem and confidence' were the most common outcomes cited.

is exceptional, and it is hardly surprising that participatory budgeting does not stand out compared to other participatory instruments.

## 2. Further Dimensions

One of the aspects most overlooked when analysing the social impact of a process or institution is that it is difficult to perceive who currently benefits from public policies given the methods of public accounting and traditional ways of thinking. Budgeting by product, which enables a relatively fine-tuned definition of the needed service and its cost, is only a first step in this direction. In addition, figures have to be aggregated and interpreted in terms of social criteria in order to get an exact idea of precise benefits to the groups in question. One of the most interesting experiments in this field is the 'social budget' that was introduced fairly widely in Italy at the end of the 1990s and which is aimed precisely at introducing and promoting such developments. Measuring the social effects of public policies enables leaders to evaluate the outcomes of the programmes that they have been promoting and to improve how they target their efforts. It also allows both governors and citizens to get used to examining the socio-territorial impacts of politico-administrative action in a precise way. In more advanced experiments, such as Castel San Pietro Terme, near Rimini, the emphasis was on providing the requisite technological means so that measures like this could become stable aspects of civil service 'routine' rather than one-off operations. These technical instruments are often the outcome of preoccupations centred on socio-economic groups; they may also be used if the motivation is environmental or related to gender equality.

At this stage of our argument, we might also mention two further objectives, in addition to the three that we discuss more in depth (Modernising the administration, social justice and the democratisation of politics). One of these uses participation to contribute to economic development, particularly by helping to build mutual trust between actors; the other, which is particularly prevalent in the case of local Agenda 21s, is aimed at using participation as a privileged means of implementing sustainable local development. The idea here is that this cannot be achieved in an authoritarian way, as it involves changing the practices of all the actors involved (public authorities, companies, NGOs and citizens). The latter two objectives are relatively marginal in European participatory budgeting, and this explains why, in both this and the two subsequent chapters, we concentrate on the managerial, social and political aspects, highlight the stakes involved and ask questions about the extent to which we can perceive tangible outcomes.

## Gender Mainstreaming

This sort of development seems all the more important in Europe as participatory budgeting almost never contributes to changing the social roles of men and women. At a time when the theme of gender equality is taking on increasing importance, participatory processes rarely appear to contribute. And yet almost everywhere, women appear to be involved in them to a considerable degree. In almost all the experiments we studied, they represented between 30 per cent and 50 per cent of those involved, with an upward trend when the process becomes more institutionalised. The gender inequalities are, all in all, fairly small, even if the quality is far from perfect and, in most cases, men speak up more or tend to become delegates more frequently. This situation contrasts strongly with the persistent lack of female representation in the traditional political system. Specific measures sometimes foster the presence of women. This is the case in both Pieve Emanuele and Seville, where child-minding facilities are provided to coincide with the meetings of assemblies for the participatory budget; in the Andalusian capital, there are programmes to help women enter the labour market, managed by women themselves, and linked to participatory budgeting. Nevertheless, in most cases, nothing is done to facilitate equal participation. It is certainly no coincidence that the two political figures in Europe who are attempting (or have attempted) to carry the idea of the participatory budgeting forward at national level, and who have constructed their political profile on the basis of the participatory theme – Segolène Royal in France and Hazel Blears in the UK – are both women.

In a number of experiments, public policies aimed at women use participatory tools. In Spain in particular, many towns have an 'office for women's affairs' that is actively involved in participatory budgeting. In some towns, such as Albacete, there is a women's participatory council. Many projects under discussion aim to help specific groups of women, who may, for example, be of immigrant origin. These praiseworthy initiatives, however, often approach women as a homogeneous group (compare the expression 'office for women's affairs'), do not challenge gender roles and are restricted to single areas. They rarely lead to the development of overall policies aimed at achieving a gender balance between men and women and using participation as a means of achieving this aim.

The extent to which participatory budgeting and gender mainstreaming remain mutually exclusive processes in Europe is striking. At least until 2010, there was no visible connection between them in the cases that we analysed. This is all the more surprising, as the two processes seem to be quite similar. They require and encourage improved transparency in the allocation of public resources and encourage budgeting by product and by programme. The current situation of mutual lack of recognition is therefore not the result of the structural incompatibility of participatory budgeting with the objective of gender mainstreaming. This situation could change quite quickly, however, given the rapid expansion of participatory budgeting and of institutions that are in the process of adopting gender mainstreaming procedures. Significant cross-pollination could then occur. It may be symbolic that Freiburg in Germany, which has a Green Party major, had decided to link the two procedures, suspended the experiment of participatory budgeting after one year and restarted it exclusively on internet, with a weak gender dimension. In this way, the convergence between the two procedures represents one of the most important challenges that European participatory processes will face in coming years.

## Local Development: Between the Third Sector and Public–Private Partnerships

The gap between Latin America and Europe is also discernible when one comes to analyse the economic impact of participatory processes. In the Southern hemisphere, these are often aimed at supporting local development, particularly the development or consolidation of communities and the voluntary sectors (they differ from both the state and the market economy). In Europe, these sectors include many different organisational forms and activities, ranging from authentic mutualism to associative economic activities. They are less developed than in the countries of the Global South – with little legal underpinning – and so far they have not been fully recognised (although the UK represents a notable exception in this regard). As seen in the previous chapter, participatory processes can address citizen-users as joint developers of public policies, with the state delegating some of its tasks to NGOs or financially supporting activities initiated by groups of citizens (when it considers that the activities represent a public interest). Once they receive this kind of institutional support, community and voluntary sector activities become part of a participatory process that can be considered part of the community development model. In the Western world, this orientation is particularly prevalent in the Anglo-Saxon countries, but it tends to emerge sooner or later in all countries. Some participatory budgets can play a role in these developments. This is the case in several British experiments, where delegates from local community groups discuss which projects deserve to be supported by a public fund. In Europe, experiments such as these have been very limited so far.

The other connection between participatory approaches and economic development differs strongly from the former, inasmuch as it is based on the supremacy of market mechanisms in the form of the introduction of multi-stakeholder participation. As we have seen, the idea of involving citizens in public–private partnerships is fairly recent. It is based on the conviction that the involvement of citizens in such partnerships strengthens their legitimacy and therefore helps to create an environment that is more favourable to economic development. This functionalist hypothesis is sometimes accompanied by genuine goodwill aimed at democratising political-administrative institutions by including new actors. The example of Płock showed that participatory budgeting can be used in this way and also that its impact has so far been fairly limited on the Old Continent. More generally, it is difficult to say whether multi-stakeholder participation will develop much more in the future or whether it will remain a marginal phenomenon in Europe. It is also difficult to say whether there will be more support for it as compared to the third sector (that is active in participatory institutions).

More indirectly, other participatory models can be fairly important for local economic development, supporting more efficient or more legitimate 'good governance' and thus contributing to the development of a more favourable institutional environment. Even towns whose discourse was fairly radical, such as Saint-Denis or Bobigny in France and Porto Alegre in Brazil, can attract companies if their geographical position and infrastructure make them attractive – and they do everything they can to encourage this, given the tax revenues and social benefits that it brings. This involves participation in only a marginal way, however, except when it includes a strategic participatory planning process or similar measures. In most cases, they are top-down processes that bring the relevant actors together around the local government table. It is quite rare for strategic planning to be linked to participatory budgeting. The experiment of Santo André, in the suburbs of São Paulo, where delegates had a mandate to take part in the participatory budget council and where funds are reserved for long-term actions in strategic participatory planning processes, is almost unique (even though towns such as Belo Horizonte in Brazil or Villa El Salvador in Peru also linked participation, planning and annual budgetary decision-making). In Europe, towns such as Bobigny also took steps in this direction, despite the limitations imposed by procedures based on proximity. The Andalusian town of Puente Genil was outstanding in this regard: it is the only one to tried to formally link strategic planning and participatory budgeting.

### Sustainable Development

At the end of the day, it is more by asserting the logic of sustainable development than by contributing to economic development stricto sensu that participatory processes appear to make their real contribution. Strategic participatory planning and community plans developed at neighbourhood level in a bottom-up dynamic can have considerable impact. The citizens who mobilise are generally worried by the medium-term social and environmental consequences of economic activities; economic actors, on the other hand, focus increasingly on short-term profits and technocrats are often unaware of the knock-on effects of 'progress'. Since the end of the 1980s, participation has increasingly been perceived as the key to sustainable development at international level. The local Agenda 21 processes are the most prominent example in this regard.

Several participatory budgets have had a noteworthy impact in terms of sustainable development. The Grottammare experiment in Italy is the most spectacular, as uncontrolled development that resulted from real estate speculation was stopped thanks to participatory budgeting. This enabled the newly elected team in the town hall to be considered sufficiently legitimate to confront the real estate developer lobby; to accept that they would have to forgo the prospects of juicy high local taxes; and to obtain acceptance for plans based on more sustainable development. The evolution of this town, which is a tourist destination, reminds us somewhat of Calvia in Spain, where the participatory instrument was the local Agenda 21. Grottammare's context is quite specific, however, and participatory budgeting is not the most suitable in this field, even though it can occasionally make a useful contribution to some specific issues. A far more promising approach is to link an Agenda 21 and participatory budgeting. This means that annual budgetary discussions can be considered in conjunction with more long-term considerations. Puente Genil was one of the few European towns that had started to go down this road.

# 11

# DEMOCRATISING DEMOCRACY?

What about the political impact of participatory budgeting and other instruments of citizen participation? Have they led to a democratisation of democracy in the sense given above (see Part I, Chapter 3), that is the combination of traditional mechanisms of representative government with direct or semi-direct democratic procedures for ordinary citizens? We have seen how important the political results were in the Porto Alegre. It is true that the party system has only been marginally modified, at least to the extent that party bureaucracy, internal and external power struggles and personal competitions have remained more or less the same. On that level, the main effect has been the hegemony of the Workers Party during three terms, a kind of exception in Brazilian cities. More decisively, the process of participatory budgeting has led to a marked reduction in cronyism; civil society has emerged as a new countervailing power; a plebeian public sphere has been created; and an institutionalised fourth power has been supported by participatory budgeting.[1] In other Latin American cases, even though it is fairly common to observe only some of these transformations, participation is rarely limited to a mere institutional mechanism. It has been part of a broader emancipation process involving the lower classes and their empowerment in politics. The multiplication of participatory budgets and the swing to the left in most South American countries have been part of the same development. The working class, who is often mixed-race, is starting to become socially accepted and to move beyond the 'internal colonialism' that had previously relegated it to a totally subordinate position (Brisset et al. 2006).

Participatory budgeting has encouraged this swing to the left. It has proved the possibility of progressive management; has given concrete shape to the idea that another sort of politics is possible; and has helped to reduce corruption and to consolidate independent working class movements. In like fashion, the advances of the left in politics have made a decisive contribution to popularising the participatory theme, as well as to the flourishing number of processes that now exist. Over and above the social impact, participatory budgets in Latin America are an integral part of a deep change in the balance of power and relations between the political elite and citizens. And despite very marked differences from one experiment to another, there is little doubt that they are

---

1 All these are further elements that sustain the model of participatory democracy (see also glossary).

making an overall contribution to the democratisation of democracy. Can the same be said, even on a more modest scale, of Europe?

## 1. Towards a Deliberative Democracy?

In light of the observations in previous pages, the reader may not be surprised if our reply is somewhat clouded by scepticism. But before going into detail, it is important to underline another important aspect of the Latin American processes. We have already spoken about the fact that they are generally based on clear and often highly complex rules. Participatory democracy such as that developed in Porto Alegre is procedural democracy, and this exerts a strong influence on how it resonates: to give just one example, the book by Tarso Genro and Ubiratan de Souza (1998) is as much a handbook for practitioners as a theoretical work. Participatory budgeting in the capital of Rio Grande do Sul is explicitly opposed to participatory populism, and the spontaneous version of participatory democracy of the 1970s. In some ways it provides an answer to the question that had remained unanswered by the theoreticians of participatory democracy of the 1970s: Carole Pateman (1970), C.B. MacPherson (1977) or Nikos Poulantzas (1978), who were not really able to outline the institutional forms that would be suitable for the political regime that they were suggesting.

### Procedural Rationality

Despite all the contrasts that exist, the overall trend is to take procedural rationality more seriously. The procedural turning point is not specific to Latin American participatory budgeting; it is applicable more broadly to all participatory processes that have sprung up all over the world since the second half of the 1990s. The practical developments have found an echo in political theory. The idea of procedural democracy has been widely developed, particularly since the work of Jürgen Habermas (1993, 1997). From the 1980s, the Frankfurt philosopher distanced himself from the excessively spontaneous nature of the paradigm of communicative action that he had developed in the course of the previous decade. Initially, he had derived the rationality of democratic deliberation from anthropological structures linked to the pragmatic use of language. From the 1980s onwards, he insisted that institutions and democratic procedures constitute necessary supports as well as a materialisation of deliberative rationality.

A number of critics have viewed this evolution positively. However, they also believe that it is necessary to take things further, particularly by taking into account the fact that discussion needs to be organised in order to limit the asymmetrical power that tends to result in structural deformations (Fraser 1997,

Phillips 1995). In addition, deliberation needs to be understood in a broader sense of the term. It needs to include arguments and logical demonstrations as well as other registers, such as testimony or cries of moral indignation that enable certain actors to speak up more easily, and to enrich an exchange that would otherwise prove too narrow if it were to be limited to pure discussion. Political deliberation that has been developed with this in mind is nonetheless a dialogical exchange that creates interests, values and identities. It cannot be reduced to a strategic confrontation where all the speakers use language in an instrumental manner. Based on a critical appreciation of Habermas and other authors, as well as the analyses that we have developed, the deliberative quality of a participatory process can now be considered according to three main principles (Blondiaux 2005: 126–27).

*A principle of discussion*: Democratic debate should enable an exchange of reasoning; this therefore implies organising procedures that enable the best arguments to come to the surface, and to move away from an aggregative conception of legitimacy. It is important that discussions help to create the common good and are not limited simply to defending private interests. In order to successfully reach this point, it is essential that sufficient time be allocated for discussion and that those taking part have access to relatively complete information. It is also important that other forms of expression, such as testimony or moral cries of indignation, be heard, and that these other registers include cognitive and normative content that could be justified in a different framework, or at another moment in time. Deliberation should be based on clear procedural rules and clearly defined responsibilities; it also needs to allow for conflicts and disagreements to be resolved, and to carry out a balanced synthesis. Discussion facilitators help to centre the discussion, as well as enabling consideration of technical issues without falling into the trap of using ultra-specialised vocabulary.

*A principle of inclusion*: The discussion should be open to the greatest possible number of people, and ideally to all those who may be affected by any given decision. It is fundamental that people participate on an equal footing, irrespective of their social group or origins. Organising the discussion in small groups is important from this point of view. Likewise, the deliberative quality of a participatory procedure is all the better if the discussion takes place not just between civil servants and citizens, but between the latter, too.

*A principle of publicity*: Deliberation is also linked to public debate. To be more explicit, a certain transparency in the discussion and in the follow-up is part of the quality of a democratic type of participatory process that differs from that of cronyism or lobbying.

If we evaluate it in this light, the deliberative quality of European participatory budgeting is quite variable. In the experiments that we have studied closely, it was relatively mediocre in four out of twenty cases where comparative data was available. This was essentially where participation was concentrated in an extremely short period of time (as in many German participatory budgets). In two other cases it was quite high, due to the fact that a participatory budgeting council or the equivalent supported the discussion over a long period of time (the paradigmatic case is that of Albacete). In most processes, the deliberation was of medium quality.

### Deliberative Democracy or Participatory Democracy?

So, are we witnessing the progressive emergence of deliberative democracy? This question leads us to examine the parallels and differences between two ideas, participatory democracy and deliberative democracy. In the more common versions that have developed in Anglo-Saxon political philosophy, with reference to the work of philosophers John Rawls and Jürgen Habermas, the idea of deliberative democracy is anchored in three principles that we have mentioned as the criteria of deliberative quality, although in a limited sense. The principle of discussion is reduced to the dimension of exchange of arguments through dialogue. In the principle of inclusion as interpreted *a minima*, the opening to all people concerned can, for example, occur via a representative sample of the population rather than the genuine participation of the greatest possible number of people. Finally, the principle of making something public is played down, and some deliberative spaces can operate behind closed doors. These elements point to a conceptual tension. Does using deliberation as the entry point to the question of democracy not lead to minimising participation, if only because the greater the numbers taking part in discussions, the more difficult it becomes to achieve high quality deliberation? Conversely, does the participatory imperative not lead to minimising the deliberative quality? After all, revolutions or social movements are based on political mechanisms that are far away from the ideal deliberative speech situation. The idea of deliberation is certainly linked to a certain degree of publicity, and this implies reaching an audience whose limits are, a priori, difficult to define. In like manner, it is difficult to ground long-term participation in an insurrectional and fusional way. For these reasons, deliberation seems to be an indispensable complement.

Certain normative perspectives do, however, stand between the two. We are obliged to observe that deliberation has not always proven to be a key aspect of participatory democracy. And on the other hand, the partisans of deliberative democracy insist that they often do not consider the transfer of decision-making competences, which remain in the hands of the elected representatives. Studying the deliberative processes of the constitutional assemblies of France and the United States at the end of the eighteenth century, Jon Elster put forward the idea that working behind closed doors tended to favour quality of debate, because making debate public leaves greater room for rigid confrontation and one-upmanship (Elster 1994: 249). As for Habermas, he explicitly states that his concept of procedural democracy makes civic commitment a secondary matter (Habermas 1998), whereas participationist theories found their approach on this idea. Finally, social conflict plays a central role in the theories of participatory democracy, whereas it is far more secondary in deliberative democracy.

These conceptual tensions are accentuated by the fact that the two ideas – deliberative democracy and participatory democracy – are not used by the same actors, and do not always designate the same practice. Even if there is relative convergence between them, the processes that are linked to them are different. A series of deliberative spaces, such as constitutional courts, always carry out their deliberations behind closed doors and refuse to allow (even silent) participation of citizens. On the contrary, processes aimed at encouraging grassroots participation in decision-making, such as general assemblies and referenda are not ipso facto deliberative procedures. This makes it difficult to assimilate these two ideas (Held 2006, Sintomer 2011c, Pateman 2012). Some convinced supporters of participatory democracy tend to overlook deliberative democracy, which they suspect may be too technocratic. Likewise, many partisans of deliberative democracy who mainly advocate for mini-publics are fairly reserved about participatory democracy, which they suspect of hindering the creation of enlightened opinion. These conceptual tensions are well illustrated by the gap that exists between the ideas of public sphere, plebeian public sphere and hybrid forum (see Glossary). These practical and theoretical conflicts reveal deep-seated tensions as regards the normative basis of democracy. Many theoreticians have certainly tried to create a synthesis, either by working on the deliberative quality of participatory processes, or on the participatory extension of deliberative mechanisms, by balancing the two conceptual approaches or by developing hybrid models. Nevertheless, we are still a long way from seeing the birth of a unified paradigm, even if processes such as participatory budgeting in Porto Alegre or the 'forum form' used by the World Social Forum provide some basis for the conceptualisation that still, for the most part, has yet to be invented.

### Participation and Populism

Before asking ourselves about the potential contribution of European participatory budgets to this synthesis, one additional point needs to be considered. The reader will remember that, in the first part of this book, we noted that the strengthening of the powers of mayors and the introduction of participatory measures frequently coincided. We asked whether this pointed to a growing personalisation of power anchored in a sort of charismatic domination and linked to poorly organised processes, or whether it might also allow the implementation of 'serious' participatory instruments. Can we now answer this question?

Critics of citizen participation often condemn it on the grounds that, together with the media and opinion polls, it could favour the development of populism, for which the democratic rationale is lower than for parliaments and parties. There is much to support this. The development of participatory processes and the spread of direct democracy procedures are undoubtedly anchored in a period, which is marked by the weakening of political parties and legislative bodies. Political leaders have tended to avoid conventional instruments of mediation by calling on public opinion in a more direct manner, and encouraging the implementation of participatory processes. Tony Blair in the UK strongly encouraged the implementation of participatory instruments, while at the same time keeping local government under strict control and leading the Labour Party during an all-time historical low with regard to party activism. Segolène Royal clearly stood out from the French Socialist Party and its apparatus in 2006–2007 by looking for support from public opinion, supporters and new members, as well as from those involved in participatory approaches of all kinds. At local level, a certain number of mayors who introduced participatory budgeting have somewhat difficult relationships with their own town councils. This was the case in Rheinstetten and in Berlin Marzahn-Hellersdorf in Germany. Participatory innovations are almost always launched by the executive authority, with the role of local legislature taking second place or even being marginal. For these reasons, the strongest resistance often comes from legislative bodies inside the political system.

Although it is true that the link between the legislative and participatory procedures requires further strengthening, it is important to refute the idea that citizens' participation is merely an expression of 'audience democracy'. In Europe, and despite their limitations, these processes are making an overall contribution to the creation of a more enlightened public opinion, not popular manipulation. Although the deliberative quality in many cases is insufficient and their impact on decision-making and on big-league politics is often relatively limited, participatory budgets, nevertheless, play an important role in the development of a more deliberative form of democracy. The underlying procedural logic is opposed to that of opinion polls, which suggest that citizens should respond instantly to questions that they have often never asked themselves and whose formulation they are not in a position to query. Drawing freely on Max Weber (1921 [1978]), we can argue that in times characterised by the direct election of mayors and the establishment of more direct links between leaders and citizens, participatory and deliberative approaches could, by contrast, minimise political domination which delegates the essential aspects of decision-making power to a political class that is markedly cut off from the citizens. Participatory approaches could help to modify Benjamin Constant's diagnosis of representative democracy, according to which electors do not govern and when they exercise their sovereignty 'at certain rare moments' it is only to renounce it immediately (Constant 1986: 269).

## 2. A Governo Largo?

Do European participatory budgets have any real impact on the traditional party system? To what extent do they encourage the independence of civil society? Do they represent a new arena of expression and action for the working classes or social movements?

The answers need to be nuanced and, as we have seen, they depend to a great extent on the participatory models at stake. It is in the participatory democracy model that we find the greatest possibility of combining non-conventional mobilisation and participation in the institutional political system. Conversely, it is in the community development model that there is the strongest trend of participatory politics supplanting the traditional political system. There is a high risk of instrumentalising participation in order to claim greater legitimacy in proximity democracy, whereas participatory modernisation and multi-stakeholder participation involve the possibility of a purely managerial approach that has a low impact on politics.

All in all, it cannot be said that European participatory budgeting has had a positive impact on the number of people turning out to vote.[2] These figures were dropping in the towns we studied. More importantly, the rate of abstention was often higher than in cities of similar social structure but without participatory budgeting. On this same point, participatory budgeting would appear to be relatively representative of participatory approaches in general. They do not seem to be of much use in reducing abstention despite the faith political leaders have often placed in them (Rey 2005; Blanco and Font 2005). Nor does introducing a participatory budget provide any guarantee of improved results for the elected city council: the figures are still too contrasted to show a general trend. Emblematic towns such as Cordoba, Albacete or Seville in Spain, Pont-de-Claix and, to a lesser extent, Saint-Denis in France, Venice and Pieve Emanuele in Italy and Berlin-Lichtenberg and Rheinstetten in Germany have seen their town councils suffer severe defeats, sometimes after initial successes. Some other town councils, such as Grottammare in Italy, have, on the contrary, proven very successful and have achieved sustained support. The situation in Europe, like that in the capital of Rio Grande do Sul, has shown that introducing a participatory structure often has little impact on the internal organisation of the institutional political system. At electoral level, participatory approaches appear like a magnifying glass that contribute to transparency and help to make the success stories and difficulties of the ruling majorities more clearly visible.

---

2 For the situation in the UK, where positive results existed in some cases, see DCLG 2011.

Whatever their limits might be, participatory budgets cannot be considered to be instruments that the majority can manipulate to their hearts' content. In Porto Alegre, after 2002, the supporters of the former local government and other civil society actors used participatory budgeting to undermine the authority of the new mayor. In a more subdued way, the joint session of the town council and participatory budget participants that was organised in Saint-Denis in 2004 gave rise to a clear challenge to the local executive, and participatory budgeting in Seville regularly caused political upheaval, including between the two left-wing parties who governed in coalition. If there have not been more incidents of this kind, it is because the institutional initiators try to exert fairly strict control over most participatory budgets; it is also because these instruments are still in their infancy and they are often done away with if the opposition come to power. But more fundamentally, it is because politicising the approach along party-political lines tends to be perceived poorly by the participants. This is something about which we can generalise.

Over and above the considerable local differences that exist in local contexts, participatory processes seem to appeal to a kind of political involvement that is not linked to political parties. There are strong reactions to 'political' manoeuvres in the negative sense of the term.[3] It is thus especially by contributing to the creation of a new project that is halfway between 'image politics' and the creation of a new identity that participatory budgeting has had a political impact on some traditional political actors; this concerns, for instance, the post-Communist groups that are in total disarray after the collapse of bureaucratic socialism, as well as some social democrats. Participatory budgeting helped them to reformulate political goals and left-wing parties were able to demonstrate their will to political renewal through participative experiments.

This renewal, however, also has its limit. As shown in the second part of this book, participatory budgets could not prevent left wing governments from being swept away from power in the context of the European financial crisis. Moreover, one could argue today that alternative left parties and post-communist parties have failed in modernising themselves through participatory politics. In the face of the European financial crisis, voters have opted for conservative parties (one noticeable exception being the January 2015 Greek elections). One reason for this may be the fact that the left could not offer credible solutions for the crisis, but also their participatory policy at the local level could not mobilise sufficient support to maintain power in the municipalities. This is most visible in Spain, where in 2011 the left was defeated in several places. Consequently, participatory budgeting has stopped in Seville, Albacete, Getafe, and other lighthouse experiences in the country. The effect is less visible in Portugal,

---

3 Popular initiatives (referenda) are an exception from this point of view, with political parties often playing a decisive role.

because the post-communist and alternative left have never shown high interest in participatory politics. In Germany, the *Linke* is also in decline. The post-communist mayor of Lichtenberg lost the election and has been replaced by a social democrat. Participatory budgeting has not ceased, but it has lost its dynamic. In all, the German post-communists vaguely support participatory politics, but have not established a strong agenda on these grounds. If they support participation, it is often for strategic reasons and more linked to referenda that are likely to stop governmental projects. Participatory budgeting remains important in Germany, however, because it has been supported from the beginning by parties of all political colours and because it is now used for making cost reductions.

The impact on the political culture of civil society is more perceptible, which might seem paradoxical for an approach that has been initiated top-down. In most of the cases that we studied, the associative culture and the citizens who participated had been able to take advantage of this new political sphere. For instance, they strengthened the ability to influence the policies that were being implemented, increased their contacts with other civil society actors and improved their knowledge of the workings of the political system and the civil service machine. We should not be too quick to draw conclusions on any increase in democracy or strengthening of countervailing powers. The overall independence of civil society in the processes varies a lot according to the procedure and from one experiment to another. In like manner, the link between an institutional structure like participatory budgeting and social movements is far from being universal. As we have already underlined, before 2008, no social movement in Europe was calling for the introduction of participatory budgeting. And what is more, in most cases, the social movements – in particular, the alter-globalists – are not very active in European participatory budgeting. Some movements even query the idea of participatory democracy, as this does not represent a sufficiently radical upheaval in terms of changing the existing power structure or, on the contrary, in some cases, because the authoritarian structure of local authorities does not fit in with this idea. In most cases, however, once the process has been introduced, participatory budgeting makes the politico-administrative system more open to citizens' requests. In certain cases, the bottom-up dynamics then meet the top-down ones that were responsible for introducing the process. The reasons for this are often contextual. It can be linked to the existence of an independent and organised civil society movement, or to the personality of a leader or the opening up of a window of opportunity for a given social movement. The organisation of an open-access process with formal rules and the independence of the actors involved then become favourable factors.

All in all, it is only in rare cases that participatory budgeting in Europe has enabled the emergence of a countervailing power, most frequently in processes that are close to the participatory democracy or community development models. This also tends to be on a far more limited scale than in Porto Alegre. This modest political impact is all the more marked by the fact that a countervailing power is not necessarily synonymous with the empowerment of subaltern groups. In Europe, it is most frequently the middle class and the already organised citizens that seize the opportunities provided by participatory processes and not the working class or subaltern groups, and participatory budgets are no exception to this rule. It is thus only in a few places that we can witness the emergence of a plebeian public sphere.

At the same time, we can see the hesitant appearance of a fourth power in certain European participatory budgets, where citizens can decide about a consequent amount of money or where they have a strong institutional position in the decision-making process. This has happened mainly in Spain (where the designation *presupuesto participativo* implies the existence of a decision-making power for most of the actors) and in Italy, and also concerns the French High school participatory budgeting. Even in these most advanced European experiments, the weight of the fourth power cannot be compared with that of the three other powers (executive, legislative, judicial). It does, however, make a difference to representative government: the latter implies a monopoly on decision-making, which lies in the hands of elected representatives who remain independent from those they administer. This is not the case with regard to participatory budgeting delegates. If the logic of representation is still present, it is of quite another kind, based on spokesmen who are either selected at random or who have a semi-imperative mandate, or with a de facto constraint to obtain consensual support at grassroots level. So far, these premises of a fourth power have remained secondary or marginal. This situation does not, however, indicate how things will progress, and the future remains uncertain. After all, wasn't the introduction of parliaments also problematic before the modern democratic revolutions occurred?

European participatory budgets can currently be situated halfway between a deliberative reorientation of representative democracy and the emergence of a genuine participatory democracy that would combine the institutions of representative government with a fourth power that enables citizens to take decisions, either directly or through delegates. The common ground on which these experiments could flourish is supported by the idea of enlarging the decision-making process beyond that of the sphere of elected representatives. The normative changeover already appears to be massive, even if the practice is somewhat slow and unequal in impact. The traditional organic metaphors tended to follow Durkheim in considering the state as the brains of society and speaking of other institutions as the 'limbs' of a social organism. Nowadays, authors such as Antonio Negri and Michael Hardt compare all of society to a brain, working like a coordinated whole, a network of neurons that have no clearly identifiable centre (Hardt and Negri 2001). Can this metaphor be applied to participatory budgeting and, beyond it, to other participatory approaches? In line with Negri and Hardt, some authors question this, putting forward the idea that these structures remain centred around the state or local governments, which consult, deliberate and even delegate some decisions, but remain the supreme instance of regulation. They oppose institutional participation to radically democratic practices, for instance groups within the alter-globalist movement or free-software activists. If there is a grain of truth in this idea, this opposition needs to be played down, if only because even the most apparently democratic or cooperative networks are also marked by an imbalance of power, information and ability to take the initiative.

It is therefore as wrong to idealise participatory approaches as to reduce them to marginal arrangements of the political system. They are helping to broaden the methods of governing, and the borders have not been set in stone. In order to analyse them, the idea of *governo largo* that was developed by Italian cities in the Middle Ages and the Renaissance can have a certain heuristic value (Röcke 2005). The 'broad government' in which Florence took so much pride, differed from the 'narrow government' (*governo stretto*) that characterised the aristocratic or despotic governments of the time. But it was not synonymous with genuine democracy: the working class was excluded from civic participation, and were not granted institutional recognition except for during brief revolutionary periods. Women were always excluded from institutional politics and participation in the public sphere. Although quite broad for the times, the type of self-government in Florence did not prevent the real power from being monopolised by a fairly limited elite. Nevertheless, there were continuous controversies concerning the borders of the sphere that included people entitled to actively exercise the civil rights and to take part in self-government. During the first Renaissance, the political system of the Florentine Republic was strongly opposed to the absolute regimes that were starting to appear, as well as to the oligarchic republics that, like Venice, once and for all closed the limited circle of those considered worthy of taking part in the decision-making process.

The differences between the social, cultural and political contexts of the Florentine Republic and those of the current approaches to institutionalising participation are clear. But is there not some sort of *governo largo* emerging in the latter, which is different from the *governo stretto* of classical representative government – even if it involves only a small minority of the population and therefore remains far from genuine self-government? Whereas representative government is tending to reduce democracy to the right to cast a vote for a small elite with a power monopoly, participatory processes tend to enlarge the circles of discussion and decision-making to a far broader public, even if it is still quite limited compared to the population as a whole. At the same time, the pretended ability of some elected representatives to monopolise the definition of the common good and decision-making is losing credibility. Moreover, the political system's resistance to the demands of citizens is increasingly considered obsolete whereas the idea of enhanced citizen participation is gaining more and more legitimacy. This evolution testifies to different paths of development, procedural forms and outcomes. They counterbalance mere plebiscitary mechanisms, the spread of 'image politics' and the development of forms of governance where private companies and expert groups have more influence than ordinary citizens. However, they do not automatically provoke a 'democratisation of democracy'.

# CONCLUSION
## Housing, Building and Painting

What is the impact of participatory instruments in Europe today? We can provide only a partial answer to the question. However, our study does enable us to pronounce a verdict on the three interpretations mentioned in the introduction. As a reminder, the first interpretation is the view that participatory budgeting represents a democratisation of democracy – an initial step towards implementing another possible world. The second is the idea that institutionalised participation is primarily a means for the system to recuperate – participation, according to this view, contributes to the pursuit of their goals by some politicians who try to legitimate their own policies through participatory budgeting. The third hypothesis represents a intermediate view between these two radical interpretations: participation and deliberation are seen as regulatory reference points and pragmatic sources of experimentation that are increasingly being used to criticise and justify public policies, to the point that they are progressively becoming the new spirit of democratic institutions.

Our conclusion does not represent a definitive judgement. This is due to the difficulties involved in carrying out an empirical appraisal given that the processes we have studied are still new and very much still under way. A few hypotheses can nevertheless be proposed.

So far, the first interpretation is at best wishful thinking and at worst an ideological self-justification. In Europe, participatory budgeting is not currently an alternative to neoliberal globalisation because it does very partly produce recognition of the working classes or subaltern groups and is only a relatively weak vector for social justice. Participatory budgeting in Europe is not much different from other participatory tools on this point and this is without a doubt a major reason why participatory budgeting has not so far sparked a strong grassroots movement in Europe.

The second interpretation also appears far too much of a caricature to encompass a reality that extends beyond simplistic analysis. There can be no doubt that significant administrative changes have occurred to the benefit of users; the citizens involved have taken part in institutions that initially were designed from above; and the political impact of participatory processes concerns civil society at least as much as politicians. In addition, the fact that participation is used as a strategy with the aim of producing political gains is a tribute to its virtue, in that it reflects the constraints that developments in democratic legitimacy have placed on professional politicians.

Is the third interpretation, the intermediate view on the modification of the spirit of democratic institutions, then, the correct one? Generally speaking, yes, but we have also seen that European participatory budgets differ considerably with regard to the ideal-type models they resemble and the contexts in which they emerge. Developments are taking place, but the scope of the movement is uncertain and it is going in a wide variety of very different directions.

To take things a step further, we can base ourselves on an analytical distinction suggested by Peter Hall (1993). This differentiates between three degrees of public policy transformation. In the *first degree*, the intensity of the action varies, but the instruments used and the objectives pursued remain the same. For example, investing more financial resources in a programme would merely reflect a routine adjustment to a political-administrative activity. The *second degree* of change implies the introduction of new public policy instruments, while the objectives pursued remain the same. Generally, this can also be interpreted as merely an internal political-administrative bureaucratic change. The *third degree* of change implies a change in the reasoning that guides public action, rather than merely a change in the intensity with which it is carried out or the introduction of new tools into a strategy whose goals remain unchanged. This kind of change cannot take place in a routine manner; it occurs only in specific circumstances, when existing frameworks appear unable to deal with (new) major problems. It implies wide-ranging social discussion that spreads much further than the narrow circle of political or administrative decision-makers and produces a change in the balance of power in society. This is not merely a learning process, but also an empowering process that is to the benefit of some groups and the detriment of others. The change is therefore political, in the purest sense of the term.

By this measure, European participatory budgets, in the first decade of their existence, sometimes introduced a second-degree change, especially when they come close to the Porto Alegre model. More broadly, increased citizen participation – participatory budgeting is part of this process – represents a second-degree change from traditional public policies. The question is whether these changes should also be described as third-degree – that is, a paradigm change. Is the change political or purely management-related? Does it imply a change in the balance of power? Going on the evidence, the answer depends more on the context than on the participatory system used. Taken as a whole, the ideological and institutional changes do produce subtle changes in the balance of power, but they do this in very different ways. For example, the emergence of a cooperative civil society countervailing power can be observed only in participatory democracy and community development models. On the flip side of the coin, in the cases described, economic actors, such as private companies, had an influence on the political-administrative system only in participatory budgets close to the multi-stakeholder participation model.

Reasoning in less technical terms, John Parkinson (2004) used the following metaphor: when citizens are involved in decision-making, the process can affect *housing,* in the sense of structural issues. It can also concern *building,* in the sense of issues that are important but secondary. Finally, it can focus on *painting,* in the sense of additional and relatively minor issues. Parkinson added that all too often English participatory instruments have been designed to produce discussion on painting and to make people forget about building and housing. Taken in isolation, almost all European participatory budgets at the time of our study dealt with either painting or building, but very rarely with housing. This is even more the case given that their area of influence was limited to the local level. Nevertheless, a more general overview of all the participatory systems established over the past two decades produces a more positive diagnosis. Wide-ranging change does exist: administrative action has been influenced in so many areas that its reasoning is undergoing profound changes, despite resistance and counter-tendencies. Speaking purely politically, the development is more uncertain. The time when party machines were dominant and unopposed is almost certainly over and a more participatory and deliberative democracy is gaining credibility. However, it faces an 'audience democracy' and authoritarian trends whose influence is also increasing. Socially speaking, participatory instruments essentially remain limited to internal decoration, and sometimes totally abandon even this area. This is one of their main weaknesses in Europe and also the factor that most differentiates European processes from those emerging in numerous places in Latin America.

# GLOSSARY

*Accountability:* Accountability is the fact of being responsible for one's actions and decisions to those affected by them, or who have taken part in the decision-making process or to the people one is supposed to represent. Being accountable is one of the core dimensions of democratic regimes and even more so of *participatory budgeting.*

*Active citizens:* see *Citizens (types concerned).*

*All citizens:* see *Citizens (types concerned).*

*Associative democracy:* This is a model of democracy related to Tocqueville's theory, in which the strength and legitimacy of democracy is proportionate to the weight of organised *civil society.*

*Audience democracy:* According to Bernard Manin, the history of *representative government* can be analysed in terms of three successive ideal-types. In the first, democracy of dignitaries (or parliamentarianism); this representative regime is based on a rather limited social class, with the parliament at its heart. In the second, party democracy, the mass parties enable popular classes of society to be included in the political system. In the third ideal-type, audience democracy, the weakening of classical organisational mediation is linked to the emergence of the media as the new centre of the political system and the representatives that come to the fore are those who know how to use or to influence new communication techniques. In another conceptual vocabulary, audience democracy is called '*opinion-based democracy*'. It is opposed to *participatory democracy:* although it may play on certain forms of citizens' participation, it does not guarantee them any real procedural independence or enable good quality *deliberation* to take place; it also fails to allow any *countervailing power* to be created. *Citizens' juries* or *participatory budget* committees differ from the panels of *ordinary citizens* that political programmes on television most frequently include.

*Benchmarking:* This expression imported from the field of economics refers, in the case of public policy, to an approach that aims to establish a cost/benefit comparison between various suppliers of services or products. Benchmarking enables best practice to be identified; that is, the cases that are the most *efficient and effective,* and that can be used as a reference model. The idea of Benchmarking can also be used in relation to participatory institutions. Although Benchmarking does theoretically facilitate the improvement of public services, it is contested, when the services to be compared are based on a uniform definition. In like manner, Benchmarking can be applied to *budgeting of products* in different towns, when the products are defined in the same way.

*Best practice*: see *Benchmarking*.

*Budgetary procedure*: The budgetary procedure involves the drafting, approval and implementation of the budget, as well as reporting back. *Participatory budgeting* generally takes place in the drafting stage, but may also involve the other stages.

*Budgeting by objective*: see *Incremental budgeting*.

*Budgeting by product*: see *Incremental budgeting*.

*Citizens' jury*: This procedure consists of a public authority bringing a small group of citizens (10 to 25 people) together by random selection in order to discuss a given theme for several days. In Germany this initiative is better known under the name of 'planning cell' ('Planungszelle').

*Citizens (types concerned)*: A participatory approach can be addressed to citizens as members of social groups (women, children, disabled, foreigners and so on). It is frequently aimed at active citizens (those who have mobilised), by opening up all meetings and basing participation on a voluntary basis. Organisers of a participatory instrument increasingly often choose to involve ordinary citizens, selected on a random basis, because they are considered statistically more representative of the population. Finally, all citizens may be involved via referenda or popular initiatives.

*Civil society*: The idea of civil society has at least two meanings. In the traditional definition, civil society includes all organised bodies outside the state, particularly companies in the market economy and economic actors. In the neo-Tocquevilian or neo-Gramscian sense that we use, however, it refers to the sphere that can be distinguished from both the market economy and the institutional political system. It is based on the association and mobilisation of *citizens* in the public sphere.

*Client*: see Roles of citizens in the modernisation of civil services.

*Commissioning*. The process of designing which services are required to deliver on government or local authority planned expenditure or policy. This includes gathering evidence and intelligence to design the right procurement strategy. Commissioning can be open to *citizen* influence to varying degrees, but is often a highly technical process conducted solely by trained professionals.

*Community*: A community describes a group of *citizens* brought together by a feeling of belonging, particularly when they live in a given area. In urban and local policies this might be an association defined on geographical or ethnic criteria, an interest group, or inhabitants of a region.

*Community development*: Community development refers to economic, social or cultural activities that are created by local inhabitants (rather than the state or the market economy), in areas with socially disadvantaged populations. These activities may be initiated bottom-up or by public services that have delegated certain tasks to local groups. One of the important instruments used are *community funds*. In a more limited way, community development is one of the six ideal-types of participation that we propose in this book. The key characteristics are that participation is essentially aimed at project implementation, in a context in which the participatory process is separate from weak local government, as well as strong bottom-up mobilisation and not just top-down implementation. In this model, the margins of action for local representative government are relatively limited. The institutional *fourth power* and countervailing power that emerge are therefore not closely linked to local political institutions. This model differs from that of *participatory democracy*.

*Community funds*: see *Neighbourhood funds*.

*Community sector*: see *Third sector*.

*Consumer*: see *Roles of citizens in the modernisation of public services*.

*Controller*: see *Roles of citizens in the modernisation of public services*.

*Countervailing power*: The notion is situated at the level of de facto social power rather than that of the institutional division of powers. The concept was created by Archon Fung and Erik Olin Wright. 'Countervailing power' can be differentiated from 'counter-power' by the fact that it emphasises two dimensions at once: *countervailing power* exists when *civil society* has genuine independence from institutional representatives and, more generally, when there are a series of mechanisms that can weaken or neutralise the power and the political prerogatives of the normally dominant social actors. Countervailing power can, however, be exercised in the cooperative resolution of conflicts rather than in a purely agonistic perspective. The emergence of a *fourth power* constitutes a favourable condition for the development of a countervailing power, but it is neither a prerequisite nor a sufficient condition. The existence of a countervailing power facilitates the fact that the *fourth power* can have more than a purely formal impact; as the latter also looks to the institutions for support, however, countervailing power is in itself neither a sufficient condition nor a prerequisite for the development of a *fourth power*.

*Decentralisation*: Decentralisation implies that the state delegates a part of its responsibilities to a lower level of government, with a devolution of decision-making powers, separate civil services and independent political management, generally through an electoral mandate. Deconcentration involves only the geographical transfer of a part of central civil services to regions so that they are closer to the *citizens* who are the users of these services. The decision-making process is not fundamentally modified, and the decision-making body remains centralised.

*Deconcentration*: see *Decentralisation*.

*Deliberation*: In English as in the accepted meaning given it by contemporary political philosophy the word 'deliberation' refers to a careful consideration or discussion about all the dimensions of an issue. This may resemble ideal scientific discussion, with communication based on the strength of the best argument, or as a process aimed at convincing people, including arguments but also testimonies and other types of expression that involve an emotional dimension. It is in the latter sense that the notion is used in the present book. In Old French and other Neo-Latin languages, this word is synonymous with decision-making, and this meaning is still partly present today.

*Deliberative democracy*: Deliberative democracy is based on three basic principles. A principle of debate: democratic debate should first and foremost consist of an exchange of reasoned argument; this means that discussions need to be organised to enable the best arguments to come to the fore, and to create a distance from an aggregative conception of legitimacy that is restricted to the sum of individual points of view. A principle of inclusion: the discussion needs to be open to the greatest possible number of people and ideally to all those who are liable to be affected by any given decision. Finally, a principle of publicity: *deliberation* needs to undergo a process of public discussion. Thus defined, deliberative democracy shows certain similarities with *participatory democracy*. The latter may, however, favour certain forms of mass participation, such as general assemblies that are not particularly effective in terms of their deliberative qualities; and participatory practices create more space for conflict and social struggles. Conversely, deliberative democracy mainly rests on mini-publics, on small groups of persons, often behind closed doors, which implies limiting the number of participants and the role of public opinion. Finally, the supporters of deliberative democracy frequently put forward the idea that it constitutes a useful complement to *representative government*, inasmuch as it enables the introduction of more enlightened decision-making by governors and consent of the governed, whereas *participatory democracy* insists on the *empowerment* of *ordinary citizens* to participate in the decision-making process.

*Opinion-based democracy*: see *Audience democracy*.

*Direct democracy*: A political system in which *citizens* are directly responsible for exercising power rather than conferring power on representatives. The institutional mechanisms of direct democracy are general assemblies, random selection (which together with a rapid turnover of responsibilities in a small group guarantees that everyone takes their turn at being governor and governed) and *referenda* (or popular initiative). A semi-direct democracy may include strictly controlled delegates.

*Effectiveness*: The fact that decisions are followed by effects and are genuinely implemented.

*Efficiency*: The fact that the organisation of a project meets its stated goals with a positive ratio of material, financial or human investment to results obtained.

*Electronic democracy (E-democracy)*: This term has two meanings. It can refer to the democratisation of access to new means of electronic communication. More frequently it implies that the latter enables democracy to enter a new age, characterised by greater communication between decision-makers and *citizens*, greater interactivity and more horizontal communication, as is the case with the Internet. Most of the time, this vision, which is not particularly critical, grossly overestimates the impact of these techniques of communication and fails to consider that they are inevitably linked to very varied socio-political dynamics. Nevertheless, the new interactive possibilities that are emerging with electronic media are obviously of great importance for the further development of participatory practices.

*Empowerment*: The idea of empowerment describes the learning curve whereby dominated social actors acquire greater social or political capital and power and reinforce their ability to act. This idea can be conceptualised in an agonistic perspective that underlines the power and domination that structure society, or in a more consensual perspective according to which the gain in power for certain groups implies self-improvement more than a modification of the balance of power with other groups.

*Fourth power.* This concept is part of theories of the separation of powers. Since the eighteenth century, this has focused essentially on *representative democracy*, and the instruments lack heuristic scope to analyse contemporary development of participatory processes. But there is at least an embryonic emerging fourth power, when *citizens* participate in the decision-making process, either directly (in general assemblies or via *referenda*) or in small randomly selected groups (*citizen's juries*) or via strictly controlled delegates (*participatory budgeting, community development* structures). This fourth power is linked to the three classical powers (legislative, executive, judicial). Its emergence testifies to the fact that the process goes beyond mere consultation or a communicative reformulation of *representative democracy*. It contributes to establishing a *participatory democracy* in which the structures of *representative government* are linked to forms of *direct or semi-direct democracy*. It represents a specifically form of mixed government. The idea of a fourth power also differs from the *countervailing power* that refers essentially to a de facto power.

*Gender budgeting:* see *Gender mainstreaming.*

*Gender mainstreaming.* Gender mainstreaming was first introduced at the third World Conference on Women in Nairobi in 1985 and was officially launched at the Beijing Conference in 1995. Its aim is to question and change the traditional roles of men and women in order to promote gender equality. Policies of Gender Mainstreaming encourage the development of programmes aimed at both men and women. They also systematically analyse concrete measures in terms of their impacts on both men and women (by asking, for example, whether the development of part-time work or parental allowances consolidate sexual discrimination or not). One important aspect of this question is *Gender budgeting,* which aims to measure the way in which public budgets support existing differences between men and women and how they reinforce or change traditional gender roles. Gender mainstreaming has been promoted by feminist lobbyists and international organisations, particularly by the United Nations and the Council of Europe. Although increasingly accepted, it still remains a minority practice.

*Governance.* Governance is a concept that is both cognitive and normative. Political and economic actors, as well as academics use the term. It describes an on-going process and indicates recommended developments. At political level, the term involves four elements. Governance can be said to exist (i) when various public actors are involved in an action; (ii) when a *public–private partnership* has been formalised; (iii) when public policy is guided by a pragmatic experimental approach rather than based on merely implementing decisions taken by the relevant hierarchical bodies; and finally (iv) when the decision-making process is a somewhat more informal affair and partially disconnected from legislative institutions. If these four conditions are met, it is legitimate to talk of a shift from government, which is supposed to be rigid and authoritarian and ill-suited to the new complexity of our societies, to governance. Critics claim that governance dispossesses *citizens* of their sovereignty by using paths other than the democratically elected assemblies to the advantage of lobbies. The idea of 'participatory governance' implies that *citizens* are considered legitimate actors in the decision-making process and that they have become involved via innovative measures. The theme of governance now seems to have replaced that of *neo-corporatism*. However, whereas the latter underlines the central role of the state in measures that associate the forces of *civil society* with decision-making, theories of governance generally attach considerable importance to the role of private enterprise.

*Hybrid forum*: This idea is related to participatory processes involving actors with different skills and status, enabling *technical democracy* to be established at institutional level. It is fairly similar to the idea of the *public sphere*, although the two can be distinguished in several ways: the heterogeneous nature of participants is crucial in hybrid forums, whereas certain *public spheres* are made up of actors whose social or functional status is identical. This heterogeneity leads to an emphasis on the exchange of different kinds of knowledge (there is genuine participation on the part of everyone involved in the exchange). The topics dealt with in hybrid forums are essentially scientific and technical. Meetings are not necessarily held in public. Finally, hybrid forums are generally aimed at consensus building, whereas the *public sphere* is generally prone to conflict-ridden dynamics.

*Incremental budgeting*: According to the traditional budgeting procedure, financial means are determined department by department via inter-departmental negotiations based on the previous year's budget. Every department considers costs related to personnel, overheads and investment separately, but is unable to calculate the exact cost of any given item when different departments contribute to its financing. This calculation is even more difficult at inter-governmental level. For example, a French nursery school involves teachers' salaries that are paid by the state, technical staff salaries paid by the town hall, maintenance costs that may be covered by various municipal departments, road maintenance covered by the relevant local authorities and so on. Comparing the cost of one nursery school with another, and querying the reasons and legitimacy of the difference in running costs is almost impossible. The new budgetary methods are aimed at merging labour costs, overheads and investment on a product-by-product basis in order to calculate the exact cost of every service and implement the corresponding reforms (*budgeting by products*). Over and above the gain in *efficiency* with regard to management, this transparency enables far more precise management and far greater *responsiveness*. This approach is reinforced when it is possible to group products according to broad programmes that involve various departments (for example, *sustainable development* or the fight against poverty). This enables a precise discussion of major priorities of public action (*budgeting by objectives* that represent an additional step forward compared to *budgeting by products*). Without the transparency of these new approaches to budgeting, *participatory budgeting* runs the risk of enabling only a limited democratisation of budgetary choice.

*Ideal-types of participation*: In this volume we propose six models of participation: (a) *participatory democracy*, (b) *proximity democracy*, (c) *participatory modernisation*, (d) *multi-stakeholder participation*, (e) *neo-corporatism* and (f) *community development*.

*Joint decision-making*: see *Roles of citizens in the modernisation of civil services*.

*Joint development*: see *Roles of citizens in the modernisation of civil services*.

*Local Agenda 21*: Participatory instruments established in the context of a strategy for sustainable local development launched by the United Nations at the Rio Conference on environment and development in 1992. They enable very diverse actors – ranging from private companies to *NGOs* – to come together with local authorities. This procedure can be considered a variant on strategic participatory development and can also be categorised under the neo-corporatist model. By 2004, over 10,000 towns had introduced an Agenda 21. It is a voluntary approach and local Agenda 21s do not generally include constraining measures. As a result, their impact varies considerably from one town to another, with some just listing good intentions and others going as far as a complete reorientation of their development model.

*Neighbourhood association*: see *Neighbourhood council*.

*Neighbourhood committee*: see *Neighbourhood council*.

*Neighbourhood council*: Neighbourhood councils are structures recognised by the local governments that created them as having a certain competence at micro-local level. They are at least partially composed of local inhabitants and facilitate communication between political or administrative decision-makers and *citizens*; their role is to provide a place for discussion and to call upon *citizens* to become involved. They differ from neighbourhood committees, which are independently organised by local inhabitants to deal with micro-local issues and from neighbourhood associations which are also independent of local government but which may additionally deal with very varied themes reaching beyond micro-urban issues.

*Neighbourhood democracy*: The English term, which is based on the geographical dimension of citizen involvement, does not fully convey the complexity of the French term 'démocratie de proximité'. There are many related terms in other languages: 'bürgernahe Verwaltung' ('citizen-orientated civil service') in German, 'pieni demokratia' ('small democracy') in Finnish and 'wijkaanpak' (neighbourhood approach) in the Netherlands. The key characteristic of *proximity democracy* is that it takes both geographical proximity and communication between policymakers and *citizens* into account, while consistently leaving the decision-making power in the hands of the former. *Proximity democracy* is based on informal rules and the independence of *civil society* is severely limited. It is based on *selective listening (cherry-picking)* that institutionalises regular dialogue. However, this is done on the basis of informal procedures that leave the decision-makers with sole responsibility for whether or not to include suggestions put forward in discussions.

*Neighbourhood funds*: Neighbourhood funds enable local inhabitants to spend small sums of money for micro-local projects. We restrict our use of this term to projects where inhabitants only take decisions on the projects selected, with the authorities being responsible for their subsequent implementation. Neighbourhood funds can be distinguished from *community funds* where it is the inhabitants themselves who implement the projects with the funds made available to them.

*Neo-corporatism*: This term was very commonly used in the 1970s and 1980s, and aims to describe the development of structures designed to mediate the interests that had emerged outside the parliamentary political system and parties. The state selects areas for which it delegates responsibility to the social partners and designates the structures entitled to participate. The powers that are invited to take part in the neo-corporatist structures are supposed to represent specific interests. They represent intermediate milieus between private individuals and the state and it is in this capacity that they have legally recognised powers to influence positions in public policy in certain sectors. The introduction of neo-corporatist structures is linked to the development of the welfare state. It represents a break with the authoritarian trend that marked the corporatist approach to the first part of the twentieth century, while representing a sort of 'third path' situated between state socialism and classical liberal capitalism, as well as simultaneously providing a means of compensating for the weaknesses of *representative democracy*. At local level, neo-corporatist structures were developed on a proportionately smaller scale than at national level. Neo-corporatism is one of the six *ideal-types of participation* that we propose in this work. Its key trait is that local government asserts itself by enabling the participation of organised groups, social sectors and various local institutions. It aims to enable broad consultation with the 'powers that count' and the tendency is to achieve broad consensus through the mediation of the interests, values and need for recognition of the most significant components of society.

*New Public Management.* Over the past three decades a broad movement inspired by management transformations in private enterprise has aimed at reforming traditional public administration. On the one hand, the movement involves increased use of market mechanisms, the introduction of profitability criteria, the sub-contracting of some activities and competitiveness between private and public providers of services, establishing independent companies using public capital but with private legal status, multiplying *public–private partnerships* and even privatisation. Another dimension is the internal modernisation of the civil service. This involves reducing the hierarchical strata, changing accounting systems and emphasising analytical accounting and *budgeting by product* or *by objectives*, 'joined-up thinking' and new methods of personnel management with increased personalisation of careers. In a further step, a third kind of modernisation has introduced close contact with *citizens* as an essential part of public action, whereby the participation of citizen-users is called upon to contribute to improve the *efficiency* of management through various means: mechanisms to provide user feed-back, quality charters, councils involving users in the management of certain facilities or amenities, delegation of public services that can go as far as *community development*, meetings enabling face-to-face discussions to be held between civil servants, politicians and local inhabitants, use of new technologies such as the Internet and so on. Although New Public Management is essentially characterised by a neoliberal orientation, social democratic versions that consider the role of the state in a more positive manner have been developed, particularly in the Scandinavian countries and Germany.

*NGO*: Non-Governmental Organisations differ from both the civil service and companies. Their objectives are matters of common good and they are non-profit-making. It is necessary to distinguish them from Quangos – Quasi-autonomous non-governmental organisations – which, although they do not have governmental status, function as the mouthpiece of the civil service or government.

*NGO sector.* see *Third sector.*

*Ombudsman.* A person responsible for defending the rights of users of public services.

*Ordinary citizens.* see *Citizens (types concerned).*

*Organised citizens.* see *Citizens (types concerned).*

*Participatory budgeting.* In Portuguese, orçamento participativo; in Spanish, presupuesto participativo; in Italian, bilancio partecipativo; in French, budget participatif; and in German, Bürgerhaushalt. Participatory budgeting is, generically speaking, an approach that enables non-elected *citizens* to take part in the planning or sharing of public finance. In order to study European examples, five additional criteria need to be mobilised: (i) The budgetary and/or financial dimension needs to be explicitly discussed. (ii) Participatory budgeting needs to be implemented at town level (or a decentralised district that has an elected assembly and a certain measure of control over public services). Neighbourhood level per se is not enough. (iii) It should be a repeated procedure over a period of time: a single meeting or referendum on budgetary issues does not constitute participatory budgeting in the sense implied in our work. (iv) The process should include certain forms of public deliberation in assemblies or specific forums. (v) The moderators of the participatory approach should report back on the results achieved, at least in the form of a report or follow-up to discussions (notion of *accountability*).

*Participatory democracy.* In some countries, the term participatory democracy has come to be used to qualify most approaches that associate *citizens* with the decision-making process in one way or another. It is, however, preferable to use the idea in a more precise way. Generally speaking, participatory democracy consists of associating a procedure of *direct democracy*, where inhabitants (or their delegates who are subject to a semi-imperative mandate) have a decision-making mandate conferred upon them, as a complement to the classical mechanisms of *representative government*, where only the representatives have a decision-taking mandate. In more specific terms, participatory democracy constitutes one of the six *ideal-type models of participation* in Europe. It designates approaches in which *civil society* plays an important part and has a *countervailing power*, based on the mobilisation of voluntary *active citizens* and the election of delegates who operate under strict control or clearly established rules, jointly developed by the *citizens* and decision-makers, where participation and social justice are closely connected. This enables a *fourth power* to emerge.

*Participatory modernisation.* Participatory modernisation consists of one of the six *ideal-types of participation* that we propose in this work. The key characteristic is that participation is considered merely as an aspect of the modernisation of public services in a context where the state is attempting to modernise to avoid privatisation of its services. This process is not politicised, has only consultative value and the normative frames are participatory versions of *New Public Management*.

*Party democracy.* see *Audience democracy*.

*Plebeian public sphere:* This expression designates spheres dedicated to discussion created by the working class, initially in parallel to those created by the enlightened bourgeoisie in the eighteenth century, and regularly renewed in the course of the history of modern democracies. The plebeian public sphere shares characteristics with the *public sphere* of the 'Enlightened', particularly the idea of public exchange of views to validate or criticise collective decisions. The difference is that they are linked to emancipation movements of the lower classes and large-scale social struggles because the subjects discussed are specific (social questions play an important role), and finally because their sociological make-up tends to encourage the kind of expression and discussion that is far-removed from the stilted discussions held in salons, and gives way to other forms of expression. There is a close link in this sense between the plebeian public sphere and *participatory democracy* as defined in this work.

*Procurement:* The legal procedures used to establish new contracts for public service delivery, most often through forms of competitive tendering. Procurement is often constrained by rules designed to allow for fair competition across the European Union. There are limited opportunities to include special conditions, such as guaranteed local employment within procurement processes, but these are still rare.

*Proximity democracy:* see *Neighbourhood democracy.*

*Proximity management:* see *Proximity democracy.*

*Public sphere:* According to Habermas, the public sphere in the political sense refers to the historical emergence of an open discussion sphere where the acts and decisions of the state and the authorities are subject to criticism and require justification. The idea per se goes back to the period of the Enlightenment. It designated a sphere in which the educated bourgeois were supposed to set aside their characteristics and their private interests and exchange arguments for the common good, in a process where the only decisive factor was the best argument. This concept of public sphere, has been extended from the educated bourgeoisie to all *citizens*. It defers from *deliberative democracy* because it does not rest mainly on mini-publics. It has been criticised however, as it fails to take minority public spheres (particularly *plebeian*) into account. It also fails to take a position on significant exclusions, such as that of women, and presupposes that these private individuals are easily able to take the common good into account. It also tends to exclude certain 'private' issues from public debate (specifically, the social question and the patriarchal family). It can also be said that it is anchored in an excessively rationalist vision of public debate. Nevertheless, irrespective of how we definite it, the emerging public sphere is clearly linked to the affirmation of republican democratic regimes and it represents a historical invention that is of equal importance to the introduction of the modern bureaucratic state.

*Public-private partnerships/Multi-stakeholder participation*: Partnerships between public authorities and private enterprises became common after the crisis of the 1970s and even more so after the downfall of communism in the Eastern Bloc countries. They are particularly widespread in the Anglo-Saxon world and in the countries of the South, and are often anchored in neoliberal thinking. They are supposed to prove particularly suitable in times when public finance is undergoing stress, when the market can provide additional capital and where involving the private sector is believed to improve the *efficiency* of public services. In the 1980s and 1990s public-private partnerships became part of the action programmes of almost all international organisations. The very varied success of the proposed economic policies of these bodies and the increase in inequalities that they imply have led to increased opposition. In order to respond to these concerns and to defuse the situation, one of the suggested paths in the early 2000s was to involve *civil society* organisations. The resulting participatory public-private partnerships constitute the ideal-type of multi-stakeholder participation. The key characteristic is that *citizens* are merely one of the actors alongside companies and local government authorities in a process in which the private fund-givers set the tone and where politics can play only a small part.

*Referendum*: In political vocabulary we often distinguish between plebiscites, which are procedures initiated from above and which call on *citizens* to vote for or against a leader (either directly or via a measure that is considered particularly symbolic), classical referenda on a piece of legislature (such as the European Constitution) and popular initiatives. These are implemented as the outcome of a bottom-up initiative based on petitions by a significant number of *citizens*. All these procedures enable the involvement of *all citizens* in the decision-making process. In most countries, 'referendum' and 'popular initiative' have decision-making impact.

*Representative democracy*: We agree with Bernard Manin who characterises *representative government* according to four criteria: the election of governors at regular intervals by the governed; the independence of the governors (once elected) in their decision-making; the corresponding freedom of public opinion; and finally, the fact that the decision-making process should, at some point, undergo public discussion. In this manner, *representative government* constitutes a mixed regime, partially 'aristocratic' inasmuch as the governors maintain the essential aspects of decision-making powers and partially democratic, as these representatives are elected and the *citizens* are able to bring pressure to bear on them through public opinion. The term representative democracy can be used as a synonym for *representative government*, at least at a formal level. Various models of *representative government* have succeeded each other historically (see *audience democracy*). Supporters of *participatory democracy* criticise a concept of democracy based only on the idea of representation and call for the introduction of a more participatory style of politics.

*Representative government*: see *Representative democracy*.

*Responsiveness*: The responsiveness of civil services is their ability to reply quickly and adequately to the requests made by users, particularly in the context of participatory processes.

*Roles of citizens in the modernisation of civil services*: It is possible to distinguish analytically between several roles whereby *citizens* (in the generic sense of the word) can be involved in participatory processes. (i) As *consumers*, they are essentially concerned by the quality of services provided and do not become involved in the way in which this works. The users of public services are essentially similar to the customers of market products. Although the French often make a clear-cut distinction between 'users' and 'clients' (using the latter term generally implies a neoliberal viewpoint) this is not the same in English or German (where only one word exists, 'Kunde'). (ii) As joint *decision-makers* they are involved to a greater or lesser extent in decisions taken (this is where the *scales of participation* come in). (iii) As *joint managers* they are involved in implementing projects or services, even to the extent of self-management. (iv) Finally, as *controllers* or evaluators who may exercise a role normally reserved for local or national civil servants or auditors.

*Scale of participation*: The scale of participation constitutes variations based on an article by Sherry R. Arnstein in 1969. The idea is to locate the potential intensity of participation on a graph that can range from simple manipulation to citizens' control, and includes information, consultation, partnership and delegation of power. The advantage of this graph is its simplicity; the disadvantage is that it represents a single dimension and fails to take into account the fact that participation can involve *citizens* in different capacities, which may each include participation to a variable extent.

*Selective listening (cherry-picking)*: The idea refers to a participatory procedure whereby civil servants and elected representatives carry out a synthesis of discussions, but without having to abide by any specific rules. This frequently leads to their retaining only those suggestions that fit in with the decision-makers' own opinions and projects. This procedure characterises the model of *proximity democracy*, but is also present in *participatory modernisation* and sometimes occurs in neo-corporatist projects. Selective listening (cherry-picking) is diametrically opposed to *direct democracy*, where citizens' opinions form the basis for the decisions taken. Nevertheless, even if the project is consultative, the limits of selective listening (cherry-picking) are partially overcome when *citizens* are given the possibility of creating a hierarchy of their proposals through voting or when they are able to independently write a report on the discussions that were held and the decision-makers are also required to justify their reasons for accepting or refusing the recommendations that were made (process of *accountability*).

*Social sectors*: see *Citizens (types concerned)*.

*Stakeholder*: This term is increasingly commonly used, particularly by international organisations. It is applied to all people or entities that are involved with, or potential stakeholders in an issue, over and above responsibilities and legal rights. The idea is often used with neoliberal overtones, implying a negotiation bringing different interests together rather than a justified construction of the common good.

*Technical democracy*: Michel Callon, Pierre Lascoumes and Yannick Barthe developed the idea of technical democracy. According to them, the stakes of the modern world require going beyond the double delegation that *citizens* traditionally granted to elected representatives, on the one hand, and to technical staff and experts, on the other. This perspective takes the theories of *participatory democracy* into consideration, but is even more based on history, social sciences and the sociology of risk developed by Ulrich Beck. Science and technology are grounded in broader practice, and the wide range of scientific and technical choice is linked to society's preferred options. Furthermore, the dynamics of innovation include retroactive cycles that include practical experimentation, developing standardised procedures and users' and consumers' reactions to the products. In order to manage this complexity, it is advisable to establish *hybrid forums* involving actors who have varying forms of knowledge and status. Technical democracy does not imply doing away with the disparate forms of knowledge, but it does require the pooling of knowledge and points of view and a cooperative approach that includes technical, ethical and political perspectives. Political choice cannot be achieved in a realistic manner without paying attention to the technical constraints that appear progressively as projects are implemented. Conversely, the implementation of projects not only raises technical issues, but includes a series of micro-choices and paths that include social and political dimensions. Techniques are objective inasmuch as the material and logical constraints, the instruments and situations in question cannot be manipulated by political interests at will – but this objectivity is not synonymous with neutrality, as it is rarely the one and only technical solution to a given problem. Including lay *citizens* in hybrid forums introduces other forms of knowledge than that of academics, civil servants or politicians. It is political: it contributes to making technical issues less technocratic, underlining the societal stakes and providing *citizens* with the means of influencing fundamental collective choice at a time when science and technology is weighing more heavily than ever before.

*Third sector.* This economic sector is separate from the state (it does not fall under the rules of the civil service) and from the market economy (it is non-profit-making). It is also known as the 'solidarity economy' sector. It covers a broad range of realities, from genuine mutual societies to the *NGO sector*. This often includes groups and organisations of the local community sector, the voluntary sector made up of more formal *NGOs* and charity-based organisations that work at neighbourhood level from the outside and generally on a scale that reaches beyond the micro-local.

*Voluntary sector.* see *Third sector.*

# BIBLIOGRAPHY

## General Bibliography

Albert, M. 1993. *Capitalism against Capitalism*. London: Wiley.

Allegretti, G. and Herzberg, C. 2004. *Participatory Budgets in Europe. Between Efficiency and Growing Local Democracy*. Amsterdam: TNI Briefing Series 5.

Amable, B. 2003. *The Diversity of Modern Capitalism*. Oxford: Oxford University Press.

Arato, A. and Cohen, J. 1992. *Civil Society and Political Theory*. Cambridge: MIT Press.

Archibugi, D. and Held, D. (ed.) 1995. *Cosmopolitan Democracy. An Agenda for a New World Order*. Cambridge: Polity Press.

Aristote, 1995. *Politics*. Oxford: Oxford University Press.

———— 2005. *Rhetoric*. Stilwell: Digireads.

Arnstein, S.R. 1969. A Ladder of Citizen Participation. *Journal of the American Institute of Planners*, 35, 216–224.

Bacqué, M.-H., Rey, H. and Sintomer, Y. (eds) 2005. *Gestion de proximité et démocratie participative. Une perspective comparative*. Paris: La Découverte.

Balibar, É. 1994. *Masses, Classes, Ideas: Studies on Politics and Philosophy Before and After Marx*. London/New York: Routledge.

Barber, B. 1984. *Strong Democracy, Participatory Politics for a New Age*. Berkeley: University of California Press.

Beck, U. 1992. *Risk Society. Toward a New Society*. London: Sage.

Benford, R. 1997. An Insider's Critique of the Social Movement Framing Perspective. *Sociological Inquiry*, 67, 4, 409–430.

Biewener, C. and Bacqué, M.H. 2013. *L'empowerment, une pratique émancipatrice*. Paris: La Découverte.

Blondiaux, L. 1998. *La Fabrique de l'opinion*. Paris: Seuil.

———— 2008. *Le nouvel esprit de la démocratie. Actualité de la démocratie participative*. Paris: Seuil/La République des idées.

Blondiaux, L. and Sintomer, Y. 2002. L'impératif délibératif. *Politix*, 15, 17–36.

Bohman, J. and Rehg, W. 1997. *Deliberative Democracy*. Cambridge: MIT Press.

Boltanski, L. and Chiapello, E. 2005. *The New Spirit of Capitalism*. London: Verso.

Boltanski, L. and Thévenot, L. 2006. *On Justification. The Economies of Worth*. Princeton: Princeton University Press.

Bourdieu, P. 1984. *Distinction: A Social Critique of the Judgement of Taste*. Cambridge (MA): Harvard University Press.

—————— 1998. *Practical Reasons.* Cambridge: Polity.

Callon, M., Lascoumes, P. and Barthe, Y. 2001. *Agir dans un monde incertain. Essai sur la démocratie technique.* Paris: Seuil.

Castells, M. 1977. *The Urban Question. A Marxist Approach.* London: Edward Arnold.

Chakrabarty, D. 2007. *Provincializing Europe: Postcolonial Thought and Historical Difference.* Princeton/Oxford: Princeton University Press.

Che Guevara, E. 1977. *Escritos y discursos.* La Habana: Editorial de Ciencias Sociales.

Cohen, J. and Rogers, J. 1995. *Associations and Democracy.* New York/London: Verso.

Crouch, C. 2004. *Post-Democracy.* Cambridge: Polity.

Della Porta, D. 2007. *The Global Justice Movement: Cross-National and Transnational Perspectives.* Boulder: Paradigm Publishers.

Desrosières, A. 2000. *La Politique des grands nombres. Histoire de la raison statistique.* Paris: La Découverte.

Dewey, J. 1954. *The Public and its Problems.* Athens (Ohio): Swallow Press/Ohio University Press.

Dias, N. (ed.) 2014. *Hope for Democracy. 25 years of Participatory Budgeting Worldwide.* São Brás de Alportel (Portugal): In Loco.

Dryzek, J. 1990. *Discursive Democracy. Politics, Policy and Political Science.* Cambridge: Cambridge University Press.

—————— 2000. *Deliberative Democracy and Beyond: Liberal, Critics, Contestations.* Oxford: Oxford University Press.

Eder, K. 2007. The Public Sphere and European Democracy: Mechanisms of Democratisation in the Transnational Situation, in *The European Union and the Public Sphere. A Communicative Space in the Making?*, edited by J.E. Fossum and P.R. Schlesinger. London: Routledge, 44–64.

Elster, J. (ed.) 1998. *Deliberative Democracy.* Cambridge: Cambridge University Press.

Engels, F. 1907. *Landmark of Scientific Socialism: Anti-Duehring.* Chicago: C.H. Kerr.

Esping-Andersen, G. 1990. *The Three Worlds of Welfare Capitalism.* Princeton: Princeton University Press.

Feld, L.P. and Kirchgässner, G. 2001. Does Direct Democracy Reduce Public Debts? Evidence from Swiss Municipalities. *Public Choice,* 109, 3–4, 347–370.

Fishkin, J. 1997. *The Voice of the People. Public Opinion and Democracy.* London/New Haven: Yale University Press.

Font, J. 2001. *Ciudadanos y decisiones públicas.* Barcelona: Ariel.

Font, J., Della Porta, D. and Sintomer, Y. (eds) 2012. Methodological Challenges in Participation Research. *Revista internacional de sociología,* 70, extra 2, 9–18.

Font, J., Della Porta, D. and Sintomer, Y. (eds) 2014. *Local Participation in Southern Europe: Causes, Characteristics and Consequences*. Washington D.C: Rowman and Littlefield.

Fraser, N. 1997. Rethinking the Public Sphere. A Contribution to the Critique of Actually Existing Democracy, in *Justice Interruptus. Critical Reflections on the 'Postsocialist' Condition*, edited by N. Fraser. New York/London: Routledge, 69–98.

Fung, A. and Wright, E.O. (eds) 2001. *Deepening Democracy. Institutional Innovations in Empowered Participatory Governance*. London/New York: Verso.

Gamson, W. 1992. *Talking Politics*. Cambridge (England)/New York (USA): Cambridge University Press.

Gaxie, D. 1978. *Le Cens caché. Inégalités culturelles et ségrégation politique*. Paris: Seuil.

Goffman, E. 1974. *Frame Analysis. An Essay on the Organisation of Experience*. New York: Harper Colophon.

Habermas, J. 1991. *The Structural Transformation of the Public Sphere*. Boston: MIT Press.

———— 1998. *Between Facts and Norms: Contributions to a Discourse Theoriy of Law and Democracy*. Boston: MIT Press.

———— 2000. *Inclusion of the Other: Studies in Political Theory*. Boston: MIT Press.

Hall, P. 1993. Policy Paradigms, Social Learning, and the State. *Comparative Politics*, 25, 274–296.

Hall, P.A. and Soskice, D. (eds) 2001. *Varieties of Capitalism*. Oxford/New York: Oxford University Press.

Hardt, M. and Negri, T. 2001. *Empire*. Cambridge (MA): Harvard University Press.

Hegel, G.W.F. 1991. *Elements of the Philosophy of Rights*. Cambridge: Cambridge University Press.

Held, D. 2006. *Models of Democracy*. Cambridge: Polity Press.

Hirschmann, A.O. 1990. *Exit, Voice and Loyalty: Responses to Decline in Firms, Organisations and States*. Cambridge (MA): Harvard University Press.

Hirst, P. 1994. *Associative Democracy: New Forms of Economic and Social Governance*. Cambridge: University of Massachusetts Press.

Ismayr, W. (ed.) 2003. *Die politischen Systeme Westeuropas*. Opladen: Leske und Budrich.

———— (ed.) 2004. *Die politischen Systeme Osteuropas*. Opladen: Leske und Budrich.

King, D. and Stoker, G. (eds) 2002. *Rethinking Local Democracy*. Basingstoke: Macmillan.

Lehmbruch, G. and Schmitter, P. (eds) 1982. *Patterns of Corporatist Policy-Making*. London: Sage.

Lewis, J. 1992. Gender and the Development of Welfare Regimes. *Journal of European Social Policy*, 2, 3, 159–173.

Macpherson, C.B. 1977. *Life and Times of Liberal Democracy*. Oxford: Oxford University Press.

Manin, B. 1997. *The Principles of the Representative Government*. Cambridge: Cambridge University Press.

Marx, K. 1993. *The Eighteenth Brumaire of Louis Bonaparte*. New York: International Publishers.

——— 2009. *The Civil War in France*. London: Verso.

Marx, K. and Engels, F. 1970. *Critique of the Gotha Program*. Moscow: Progress Publishers.

1992. *The Communist Manifesto*. Oxford: Oxford University Press

Negt, O. 2007. *L'espace public oppositionnel*. Paris: Payot/Rivages.

Offe, C. 1990. Reflections on the Institutional Self-Transformation of Movement Politics: A Tentative Stage Model, in *Challenging the Political Order. New Social and Political Movements in Western Democracies*, edited by R.J. Dalton and M. Kuechler. Cambridge: Polity Press, 232–250.

Orloff, A. 1993. Gender and the Social Rights of Citizenship: The Comparative Analysis of Gender Relations and Welfare States. *American Sociological Review*, 58, 303–328.

Passeron, J.C. and Revel, J. 2005. *Penser par cas*. Paris: EHESS.

Pateman, C. 1970. *Participation and Democratic Theory*. Berkely/Los Angeles/ London: Cambridge University Press.

——— 2012. Participatory Democracy Revisited. *Perspectives on Politics*, 10, 1, 7–19.

Pestre, D. 1995. Pour une histoire sociale et culturelle des sciences. *Annales HSS*, 50, 3, 487–522.

Pestre, D. 2006. *Science, argent et politique. Un essai d'interprétation*. Paris: INRA Éditions.

Philips, A. 1995. *The Politics of Presence*. Oxford: Oxford University Press.

Picketty, T. 2014. *Capital in the Twenty-First Century*. Cambridge (MA): Harvard University Press.

Pitkin, H.T. 1972. *The Concept of Representation*. Berkeley Los Angeles: University of California Press.

Poulantzas, N. 1980. *State, Power, Socialism*. London: Verso.

Rancière, J. 2004. *Disagreement: Politics and Philosophy*. Minneapolis (MN): University of Minnesota Press.

Röcke, A. 2005. *Losverfahren und Demokratie. Historische und demokratietheoretische Perspektiven*. Münster: Lit.

——— 2014. *Framing Citizen Participation. Participatory Budgeting in France, Germany and the United Kingdom*. Basingstoke (HA): Palgrave Macmillan.

Rosanvallon, P. 1998. (1992), *Le sacre du citoyen: Histoire du suffrage universel en France*. Gallimard, Paris.

——— 1998. *Le peuple introuvable*. Paris: Gallimard.

———— 2008. *Counter-Democracy: Politics in the Age of Distrust.* Cambridge: Cambridge University Press.

Sainsbury, D. 1999. *Gender and Welfare State Regimes.* Oxford: Oxford University Press.

Scharpf, F. 1999. *Governing in Europe, Effective and Democratic?* Oxford: Oxford University Press.

Schmitter, P. 1974. Still the Century of Corporatism? *Review of Politics*, 36, 1, 85–131.

———— 1984. *Neo-Corporatism and the State.* Working Paper 106, EUI, Florence.

Schumpeter, J. 1975. *Capitalism, Socialism and Democracy.* New York: Harper and Row.

Sintomer, Y. 1999. *La démocratie impossible? Politique et modernité chez Weber et Habermas.* Paris: La Découverte.

———— 2011a. *Petite histoire de l'expérimentation démocratique. Tirage au sort et politique d'Athènes à nos jours.* Paris: La Découverte.

———— 2011b. Intellectual Critique and the Public Sphere: Between the Corporatism of the Universal and the *Realpolitik* of Reason, in *The Legacy of Pierre Bourdieu. Critical Essays*, edited by S. Susen and B.S. Turner. London/New York: Anthem Press, 329–246.

———— 2011c. Délibération et participation: affinité élective ou concepts en tension? *Participations. Revue de sciences sociales sur la démocratie et la citoyenneté*, 1, 239–276.

Sintomer, Y., Herzberg, C. and Röcke, A. 2005. *Participatory Budgets in a European Comparative Approach. Perspectives and Chances of the Cooperative State at the Municipal Level in Germany and Europe, Intermediary Report.* Berlin: Centre Marc Bloch.

———— 2008. Participatory Budgeting, in Europe: Potential and Challenges. *International Journal of Urban and Regional Research*, 32, 1, 164–178.

Sintomer, Y., Herzberg, C., Röcke, A. and Allegretti, G. 2012a. Transnational Models of Citizen Participation: The Case of Participatory Budgeting. *Journal of Public Deliberation*, 8, 2, article 9, http://www.publicdeliberation.net/jpd/vol8/iss2/art9.

Sintomer, Y., Herzberg, C., Allegretti, G., Röcke, A. and Alves, M. 2012b. *Participatory Budgeting Worldwide – Updated Version.* Bonn: Engagement Global/Service Agency Communities in One World.

Sintomer, Y., Traub-Merz, R., Zhang, J. and Herzberg, C. (eds) 2013. *Participatory Budgeting in Asia and Europe. Key Challenges of Deliberative Democracy.* Basingstoke (HA): Palgrave Macmillan.

Smith, G. 2009. *Democratic Innovations.* Cambridge (UK): Cambridge University Press.

Snow, D. and Benford, R. 1988. Ideology, Frame Resonance, and Participant Mobilisation. *International Social Movement Research*, 1, 1, 197–217.

Subrahmanyam, S. 1997. Connected Histories – Notes towards a Reconfiguration of Early Modern Eurasia. *Modern Asian Studies*, 31, 3, 735–762.

———— 2011. *From Tagus to the Ganges: Explorations in Connected History*. Oxford University Press India.

Talpin, J. 2011. *Schools of Democracy. How Ordinary Citizens (Sometimes) Become More Competent in Participatory Budgeting Institutions*. Colchester: ECPR Press.

Tilly, C. 1978. *From Mobilisation to Revolution*. New York: Random House.

Tocal, M. and Montero, J.R. 2006. *Political Disaffection in Contemporary Democracies. Social Capital, Institutions, and Politics*. London/New York: Routledge.

Tocqueville, A. de 2003. *Democracy in America: And Two Essays on America*. Penguin.

United Nations Development Programme (ed.) 2002. *Human Development Report 2002. Deepening Democracy in a Fragmented World*. New York/Oxford.

Wainwright, H. 2003. *Reclaim the State. Experiments in Popular Democracy*. London/ New York: Verso.

Weber, M. 1919. [2004] *The Vocation Lectures: 'Science as a Vocation'; 'Politics as a Vocation'*. Indianapolis (IL): Hackett Publishing Co.

1921. [1978] *Economy and Society*. Berkeley: University of California Press.

Werner, M. and Zimmermann, B. (eds) 2004. *De la comparaison à l'histoire croisée*. Paris: Le Seuil.

Zald, M.N. and Ash, R. 1966. Social Movement Organisations: Growth, Decline, and Change. *Social Forces*, 44, 327–341.

## Gender Mainstreaming, Gender Budgeting

Akerkar, S. 2001. *Gender and Participation. Overview Report*. Brighton: Institute of Development Studies.

Council of Europe (ed.) 1998. *L'approche intégrée de l'égalité entre les femmes et les hommes. Cadre conceptuel, méthodologie et présentation des 'bonnes pratiques'*. Strasbourg.

Erbe, B. 2003. *Kommunale Haushaltsplanung für Frauen und Männer. Gender Budgeting in der Praxis. Konzepte, Erfahrungen, Perspektiven*. München: Gleichstellungsstelle für Frauen der Landeshauptstadt München.

Hofbauer Balmori, H. 2003. *Gender and Budgets. Overview Report*. Brighton: Institute of Development Studies.

Judd, K. (ed.) 2002. *Gender Budget Initiatives. Strategies, Concepts and Experiences*. New York: United Nations Development Fund for Women.

Reeves, H. and Sever, C. 2003. *Gender and Budgets. Key Texts, Case Studies, Tools, Guides and Organisations*. Brighton: Institute of Development Studies.

## Local Governance and Reform of Local Administration

Bäck, H., Heinelt, H. and Magnier, A. (eds) 2006. *The European Mayor. Political Leaders in the Changing Context of Local Democracy*. Wiesbaden: VS.

Baldersheim, H., Illner, M. and Wollmann H. (eds) 2003. *Local Democracy in Post-Communist Europe*. Wiesbaden: VS.

Bertelsmann Stiftung (ed.) 1994. *Carl Bertelsmann-Preis 1993. Demokratie und Effizienz in der Kommunalverwaltung*. Gütersloh: Bertelsmann Stiftung.

Bogumil, J., Holtkamp, L., Kißler, L., Kuhlmann, S., Reichard, C., Schneider, K. and Wollmann, H. 2007. *Perspektiven kommunaler Verwaltungsmodernisierung*. Berlin: Edition Sigma.

Bogumil, J.S., Grohs, J. and Kuhlmann, S. 2006. Ergebnisse und Wirkungen kommunaler Verwaltungsmodernisierung in Deutschland – Eine Evaluation nach zehn Jahren Praxiserfahrung. *Politik und Verwaltung (PVS – Politische Vierteljahresschrift)*, edited by J. Bogumil, W. Jann and F. Nullmeier, Special Issue 37/2006. Wiesbaden: VS, 151–184.

Boogers, M., Franzke, J., Ruano, J. and Schaap, L. (eds) 2007. *Tensions Between Local Governance and Local Democracy*. Den Haag: Reed Business.

Bouckaert, G. and Pollitt, C. 2004. *Public Management Reform. A Comparative Analysis*. Oxford: Oxford University Press.

Caulfild, J. and Larsen, H. 2002. *Local Government at the Millenium*. Opladen: Leske und Budrich.

Delcamp, A. and Loughlin, J. 2002. *La Décentralisation dans les États de l'Union européenne*. Paris: La Documentation française.

Delwit, P., Pilet, J.-B., Reynaert, H. and Steyvers, K. (eds) 2007. *Towards DIY-Politics. Participatory and Direct Democracy at the Local Level in Europe*. Bruges: Vanden Broele.

Denters, B. and Rose, L.E. (eds) 2005. *Comparing Local Governance. Trends and Developments*. Basingstoke (HA): Palgrave Macmillan.

Hoffmann-Martineau, V. and Sellers, S. (eds) 2007. *Politique et métropole*. Paris: CNRS édition.

Kersting, N., Caulfield, J., Nickson, R.A., Olowu, D. and Wollmann, H. 2009. *Local Governance Reform in Global Perspective*. Wiesbaden: VS.

Lazin, F., Hoffmann-Martineau, V., Wollmann, H. and Evans, M. (eds) 2007. *Local Government Reforms in Countries in Transition: A Global Perspective*. Lanham: Lexington Books.

Loughlin, J. 2001. *Subnational Democracy in the European Union: Challenges and Opportunities*. Oxford: Oxford University Press.

Muller, P. 2000. L'analyse cognitive des politiques publiques: vers une sociologie politique de l'action publique. *Revue française de science politique*, 50, 2, 189–208.

Reichard, C. 2001. New Approaches to Public Management, in *Public Administration in Germany?*, edited by K. König and H. Siedentopf. Baden Baden: Nomos, 541–556.

Reichard, C. and Röber, M. 2001. Konzept und Kritik des New Public Management, in *Empirische Policy- und Verwaltungsforschung. Lokale, nationale und internationale Perspektiven*, edited by E. Schröter. Opladen: Leske und Budrich, 371–392.

Reynaert, H., Steyvers, K., Delwit, P. and Pilet, J.-B. (eds) 2005. *Revolution or Renovation? Reforming Local Politics in Europe*. Brugge: Vanden Broele.

Warin, P. (ed.) 1997. *Quelle modernisation des services publics? Les usagers au coeur des réformes*. Paris: La Découverte.

Wainwright, H. and Little, M. 2009. *Public Service Reform ... But not as We Know it! A Story of How Democracy Can Make Public Services Genuinely Efficient*. Hove: Compass/Unison/TNI.

Wollman, H. 2003. *Evaluation in Public-Sector Reform*. Cheltenham/Northampton: Edward Elgar.

———— 2004. *European Local Government Systems under the Triple Impact of 'Traditional' Reforms, NPM-led Modernisation and Revolutionary Rupture: Convergence or Divergence?* Paper presented at 'Academic symposium held in honor of Harald Baldersheim and Larry Rose', Oslo, 26 November.

———— 2007. *Reformen in Kommunalpolitik und – verwaltung. England, Schweden, Frankreich und Deutschland im Vergleich*. Wiesbaden: VS.

## Belgium

Damay, L. 2010. *Construire le politique au cœur de l'action publique participative. Une analyse du budget participatif de la ville de Mons*, PhD Thesis, Universités Saint-Louis, Bruxelles.

Damay L. and Schaut C. 2007. Des justifications de politiques participatives: le cas des conseils consultatifs des locataires en Région de Bruxelles-Capitale et du budget participatif à Mons. *Espace et Sociétés*, 128/129, 1–2.

Delperée, F. 1999. Le fédéralisme de confrontation, in *Gouverner la Belgique. Clivages et compromis dans une société complexe*, edited by P. Delwit, J.D. Waele and P. Magnette. Paris: PUF, 53–69.

Di Rupo, E. 2001. Carte Blanche. Retour de Porto Alegre. *Le Soir*, 17 August 2001.

Elchardus, M. 2004. *La Démocratie mise en scène*. Bruxelles: Labor.

Mertens, S. *et al.* 1999. *Le Secteur non marchand privé en Belgique, Résultats d'une enquête-pilote: panorama statistique et éléments de comparaison internationale*. Bruxelles: Fondation Roi Baudouin.

Schaut, C. 2003. Une participation sur ordonnance: le cas des conseils consultatifs des locataires en Région de Bruxelles-Capitale. *Espace et Sociétés*, 112, 41–58.

## Brazil – Latin America

Abers, R. 2000. *Inventing Local Democracy: Grassroots Politics in Brazil.* London: Boulder.

Allegretti, G. 2003. *L'insegnamento di Porto Alegre. Autoprogettualità come paradigma urbano.* Florence: Alinea.

——— 2005. *Porto Alegre: una biografia territoriale. Ricercando la qualità urbana a partire dal patrimonio sociale.* Florence: Florence University Press.

Avritzer, L. 2002. *Democracy and the Public Space in Latin America.* Princeton/ Oxford: Princeton University Press.

——— 2009. *Participatory Institutions in Democratic Brazil.* Baltimore: The Johns Hopkins University Press.

Avritzer, L. and Navarro, Z. (eds) 2003. *A inovação democrática no Brasil: o Orçamento Participativo.* São Paulo: Cortez.

Avritzer, L. and Wampler, B. 2008. *The Expansion of Participatory Budgeting in Brazil.* Washington (DC): World Bank.

Baierle, S. 2006. Les ONG et l'insoutenable marchandisation de la solidarité. *Mouvements*, 47/48, 118–127.

Baiocchi, G. 2005. *Militants and Citizens. The Politics of Participatory Democracy in Porto Alegre.* Stanford: Stanford University Press.

BIRD (Banco International de Reconstrucao e Desenvolvimento) and BM (Banco Mundial). 2008. *Rumo a um Orçamento Participativo mais inclusivo e efectivo em Porto Alegre.* Working paper. Washington, February.

Brisset-Foucault, F., Lipietz, A., Saint-Upéry, M., Sintomer, Y. and Lipietz, A. 2006. Amérique latine: les racines du tournant à gauche. *Mouvements*, 47/48, 5–12.

Cabannes, Y. 2004a. *Participatory Budgeting: Conceptual Framework and Analysis of its Contribution to Urban Governance and the Millenium Development Goals. Concept Paper.* Quito: UMP-LAC/UN-HABITAT/UNDP.

——— 2004b. *Answers to 72 Frequently Asked Questions about Participatory Budgeting.* Quito: UMP-LAC/UN-HABITAT/UNDP.

——— 2005. *Presupuesto participativo y finanzas locales. Documento Base. Segunda versión ampliada. Red Urbal, 9.* Porto Alegre: Alcaldía Municipal de Porto Alegre, (www.portoalegre.rs.gov.br/urbal).

——— 2006. Les budgets participatifs en Amérique Latine. *Mouvements*, 47/48, 128–138.

Cassen, B. 1998. Démocratie participative à Porto Alegre. *Le Monde diplomatique*, August.

———— 2003. *Tout a commencé à Porto Alegre*. Paris: Mille et une nuits.

Castaneda, J.G. 2004. Presupuesto Participativo: la experiencia de Porto Alegre y su possible aplicación en Expaña. *Temas para el Debate*, 113.

Cidade (ed.) 2005. *De Olho no Orçamento*, 10/18, December.

———— 2007. *De Olho no Orçamento*, 11/21, Mayi.

Fedozzi, L. 1999. *Orçamento participativo. Reflexões sobre a experiência de Porto Alegre*. Porto Alegre: Tomo.

———— 2000. *O Poder da aldeia*. Porto Alegre: Tomo.

———— 2007. *Observando o Orçamento participativo de Porto Alegre*. Porto Alegre: Tomo.

Fedozzi, L., Furtado, A., Bassani, V., Macedo, C., Parenza, C. and Cruz, M. 2013. *Orçamento participativo de Porto Alegre. Perfil, avaliação e percepções do público participante*. Porto Alegre: Hartmann/Observa Porto Alegre.

Genro, T. 2001. Vers une nouvelle citoyenneté. Thèses pour une théorie démocratique de l'État du socialisme. *Mouvements*, 18, 32–37.

Genro, T. and De Souza, U. 1997. *Orçamento Participativo. A experiência de Porto Alegre*. São Paulo.

Gret, M. and Sintomer, Y. 2004. *The Porto Alegre Experiment: Learning Lessons for a Better Democracy*, New York: Zed Books.

Herzberg, C. 2001. *Der Bürgerhaushalt von Porto Alegre. Wie partizipative Demokratie zu politisch-administrativen Verbesserungen führen kann*. Münster: Lit.

Le Monde Diplomatique 2000. *Special Issue 'Ville'*, May.

Marquetti, A. 2005. *Which Brazilian Cities are Experiencing the Participatory Budgeting?* Working Paper. Departamento de Economia, PUCRS.

Marquetti A., De Campos, G. and Pires, R. (eds) 2008. *Democracia Participativa e Redistribuição: Análise de Experiências de Orçamento Participativo*. São Paulo: Xamã.

De Sousa, S. 1998. Participatory Budgeting in Porto Alegre: Towards a Redistributive Justice. *Politics and Society*, 26, 4, 461–509.

———— (ed.) 2005. *Democratizing Democracy. Beyond the Liberal Democratic Canon*. London/New York: Verso.

Wampler, B. 2010. *Participatory Budgeting in Brazil: Contestation, Cooperation, and Accountability*. Pennsylvania: Pennsylvania State University Press.

Whitaker, C. 2005. *O desafio do Fórum Social Mundial. Um modo de ver*. São Paulo: Loyola/Fundação Perseu Abramo.

## Finland

Auffermann, B. 2003. Das politische System Finnlands, in *Die politischen Systeme Westeuropas*, edited by W. Ismayr. Opladen: Leske und Budrich, 187–224.

Baldersheim, H. and Stahlberg, K. (eds) 1994. *Towards the Self-Regulating Municipality: Free Communes and Administrative Modernisation in Scandinavia*. Ashgate: Aldershot.

Stiftung Bertelsmann (ed.) 2000. *Service-Garantien in der Kommunalverwaltung. Customer Contracts, 'Reform der Kommune'*. Gütersloh: Bertelsmann Stiftung.

Kettunen, P. 2003. How Democratic are the Finnish Local Governments? *Finnish Local Government Studies*, 4, 271–278.

Kolehmainen, K. 1999. *Bürgerkommune realisieren: Kernaussagen*. Paper presented at 'Bürgerkommune realisieren', September, Berlin.

Naschold, F. 1999. *Hämeenlinna at the Cross-roads. The Challenge of Strategic Politics and Strategic Management*. Berlin: Wissenschaftszentrum Berlin.

Oulasvirta, L. 2003. Local Government Finance and Grants in Finland. *Finnish Local Government Studies*, 4, 340–348.

Pesonen, P. and Riihinen, O. 2002. *Dynamic Finland. The Political System and the Welfare State*. Helsinki: Finnish Literature Society.

Rose, L.E. 1990. Nordic Free Commune Experiments: Increased Local Autonomy or Continued Central Control?, in *Challenges to Local Government*, edited by D.E. King and J. Pierre. London: Sage.

Rose, L.E. and Stahlberg, K. 2005. The Nordic Countries: Still the 'promised land'?, in *Comparing Local Governance*, edited by B. Denters and L.E. Rose. Basingstoke (HA): Palgrave Macmillan, 83–100.

Ryynänen, A. 2002. Reformbestrebungen im finnischen Finanzausgleich, in *Finanzausgleich – Herausforderungen und Reformperspektiven*, edited by B. Rossmann. Wien: Kammer für Arbeiter und Angestellte für Wien, 69–76.

## France

Bacqué, M.-H. and Fol, S. 1997. *Le Devenir des banlieues rouges*. Paris: L'Harmattan.

Bacqué, M.-H and Sintomer, Y. 2001. Affiliations et désaffiliations en banlieue. Réflexions à partir des exemples de Saint-Denis et d'Aubervilliers. *Revue Française de Sociologie*, 42, 2, 217–249.

Blondiaux, L. 2005. L'idée de démocratie participative: enjeux, impensés et questions récurrentes, in *Gestion de proximité et démocratie participative. Une perspective comparée*, edited by M.-H. Bacque, H. Rey and Y. Sintomer. Paris: La Découverte, 119–138.

Braconnier, C. and Dormagen, J.Y. 2007. *La Démocratie de l'abstention*. Paris: Gallimard.

Castel, R. 1995. *Les Métamorphoses de la question sociale*. Paris: Fayard.

Craps and Curapp (ed.) 1999. *La Démocratie locale. Représentation, participation et espace public*. Paris: PUF.

Donzelot, J. and Estebe, P. 1994. *L'État animateur. Essai sur la politique de la ville.* Esprit.

Le Bart, C. and Lefebvre, R. (eds) 2005. *La proximité en politique. Usages, rhétoriques, pratiques.* Rennes: Presses Universitaires de Rennes.

Masclet, O. 1983. *La Gauche et les cités.* Paris: La Dispute.

Mazeaud, A. 2011. Un saut d'échelle vers la justice sociale. *Territoires*, June–July.

Neveu, C. (ed.) 1999. *Espace public et engagement politique.* Paris: L'Harmattan.

Offerlé, M. 1989. Mobilisation électorale et invention du citoyen. L'exemple du milieu urbain français à la fin du XIXe siècle, in *Explication du vote*, edited by D. Gaxie. Paris: Presses de la FNSP, 149–174.

Rey, H. 2005. Participation électorale et démocratie participative, in *Gestion de proximité et démocratie participative. Une perspective comparée*, edited by M.-H. Bacqué, H. Rey and Y. Sintomer. Paris: La Découverte, 217–227.

Sintomer, Y., Röcke, A. and Talpin, J. 2013. Participatory Democracy or 'Proximity' Democracy? The 'High School Participatory Budget in Poitou-Charentes France, in *Participatory Budgeting in Asia and Europe. Key Challenges of Deliberative Democracy*, edited by Y. Sintomer, R. Traub-Merz and J. Zhang. Basingstoke (HA): Palgrave Macmillan, 245–259.

Sintomer, Y. and Talpin, J. (eds) 2011. *La démocratie participative au-delà de la proximité. Le Poitou-Charentes mis en perspective.* Rennes: Presses Universitaires de Rennes.

Vidal, J.C. 1995a. Saint-Denis. Approche de la non-inscription sur les listes électorales. *Saint- Denis au fur et à mesure*, 14/02.

—— 1995b. Saint-Denis, Municipales 1995, analyse des résultats Secteur des études locales. Ville de Saint-Denis, 20 November.

## Germany

Banner, G. 1998. *Der Gemeindehaushalt – am Bürger vorbei?* Paper presented at 'Bürgermitwirkung am Haushaltsplan', Villingen, 12 November 1998.

—— 1999. Die drei Demokratien der Bürgerkommune, in *Demokratie vor neuen Herausforderungen*, edited by H.-H. Arnim. Berlin: Duncker und Humblot, 133–162.

Bertelmann Stiftung and Landesregierung Nordrhein-Westfalen (eds) 2004. *Kommunaler Bürgerhaushalt: Ein Leitfaden für die Praxis.* Gütersloh: Bertelsmann Stiftung.

Bogumil, J., Holtkamp, L. and Schwarz, G. 2003. *Das Reformmodell Bürgerkommune.* Berlin: Edition Sigma.

Bundeszentrale Für Politische Bildung (ed.) 2005. *Bürgerhauhalt in Großstädten. Arbeitsmaterialien für die Umsetzung.* Bonn: Bundeszentrale für politische Bildung.

Cuny, C. and Herzberg, C. 2012. Bürgerhaushalt und die Mobilisierung von Bürgerwissen, in *Der Bürgerhaushalt: von Porto Alegre nach Europa*, edited by C. Herzberg, Y. Sintomer and H. Kleger. Frankfurt/New York: Campus, 255–279.

Deutsches Institut Für Urbanistik (ed.) 2002. *Die Soziale Stadt. Eine erste Bilanz des Bund-Länder-Programms 'Stadtteile mit besonderem Entwicklungsbedarf – die soziale Stadt'*. Berlin: DIFU.

Herzberg, C. 2003. Bürgerhaushalt für Berlin. *Sozialwissenschaften 21*.

Herzberg, C. 2009. *Von der Bürger- zur Solidarkommune*. Hamburg: VSA.

Herzberg, C., Sintomer, Y. and Kleger, H. 2012. *Hoffnung auf eine neue Demokratie. Bürgerhaushalte in Lateinamerika und Europa*. Frankfurt/New York: Campus.

Holtkamp, L. 2004. Bürgerhaushalt Kontrovers. Beteiligen ohne Spielraum? *Forum*, 5, 12–13.

Hombach, B. 1998. *Aufbruch: die Politik der neuen Mitte*. München/Düsseldorf: Econ-Verlag.

Kate, E.V. (ed.) 2006. *Learning Community. Local Agenda 21 and Participatory Budget*. Stuttgart: Kate.

Koehl, E. and Sintomer, Y. 2002. *Les Jurys de citoyens berlinois. Rapport final*. Berlin: Centre Marc Bloch/DIV.

Naschold, F. 1997. Umstrukturierung der Gemeindeverwaltung: eine international vergleichende Zwischenbilanz, in *Innovative Kommunen: internationale Trends und deutsche Erfahrungen*, edited by F. Naschold, M. Oppen and A. Wegener. Stuttgart: Kohlhammer, 15–48.

Plamper, H. 2000. *Bürgerkommune: Was ist sie? Was soll sie sein? Was ist zu tun?*, Arbeitspapier 32, Düsseldorf: Hans-Böckler-Stiftung.

Reichard, C. 1997. Deutsche Trends der kommunalen Verwaltungsmodernisierung, in *Innovative Kommunalen: internationale Trends und deutsche Erfahrungen*, edited by F. Naschold, M. Oppen and A. Wegener. Stuttgart: Kohlhammer, 49–79.

Roth, R. 1998. Lokale Demokratie 'von unten', in *Kommunalpolitik. Politisches Handeln in den Gemeinden*, edited by H. Wollmann and R. Roth. Bonn: Bundeszentrale für politische Bildung, 2–22.

Stadt Essen (ed.) 2010. *Rechenschaftsbericht zur bürgerbeteiligten Haushaltskonsolidierung*. Essen: Stadt Essen Stadtkämmerei.

Stadt Essen (ed.) 2012a. *Essen kriegt die Kurve. Die bürgerbeteiligte Haushaltskonsolidierung 2011*. Essen: Stadt Essen Stadtkämmerei.

Stadt Essen (ed.). 2012b. *Essen kriegt die Kurve. Die bürgerbeteiligte Haushaltskonsolidierung 2011. Fortschreibung des Rechenschaftsberichtes*. Essen: Stadt Essen Stadtkämmerei.

Wollmann, H. 1999. Kommunalpolitik: Mehr (direkte) Demokratie wagen. *APuZ*, 24–25, 13–22.

## Italy

Allegretti, G. and Frascaroli, E. 2006. *Percorsi condivisi, Contributi per un atlante delle pratiche partecipative in Italia.* Florence: Alinea.

Allulli, M. 2006. *Il municipio globale. Culture e strategie del neomunicipalismo,* PhD Thesis. Rome: Università La Sapienza.

Amura, S. 2003. *La città che partecipa.* Rome: Ediesse.

Bobbio, L. 2003. *I governi locali nelle democrazie contemporanee.* Bari/Rome: Laterza.

D'albergo, E. (ed.) 2005. *Pratiche partecipative a Roma. Le osservazioni al piano regolatore e il bilancio partecipativo.* Rome: Università La Sapienza.

Fanesi, P. 2004. *Democrazia deliberativa e politiche pubbliche: il caso di Grottammare.* Master Thesis: Università di Macerata.

Laini, M. and Andreozzi, P. 2004. *Il valore dei soldi. Viaggio attraverso la cultura del lavoro e del denaro nel territorio bergamasco.* Rome: Ediesse.

Magnaghi, A. 2004. Il Nuovo Municipio: un laboratorio di democrazia partecipativa per una economia solidale, in *MAUSS. Quale altra mondializzazione?,* edited by A. Caillé and A. Salsano. Turin: Bollati Boringhier.

Mariani, F. 2005. *Il Bilancio partecipativo.* Rome: Aracne.

Ravazzi, S. 2007. *Civicrazia. Quando i cittadini decidono.* Rome: Aracne.

Smeriglio, M. 2006. *Città comune. Autogoverno e partecipazione nell'era globale.* Rome: DeriveApprodi.

Sullo, P.L. (ed.) 2002. *La democrazia possibile.* Rome/Naples: Carta/Intra Moenia.

Universita Di Roma 'La Sapienza' and Commune Di Roma (eds.). 2005. *Metodi e procedure di partecipazione alle trasformazioni urbane e alle scelte urbanistiche* Rome: Aracne.

## Netherlands

Davelaar, M., Duyvendak, J.W., Graaf, P.V.D. and Swinnen, H. 2001. *Good Governance and 'The Social Pillar of the Major-Cities Policy': Attributes and qualities of a successful local governmental strategy.* Utrecht: Verwey-Jonker Instituut.

Davelaar, M.E.A. (ed.) 2003. *Demos Project. Citizens'Participation and Interactive Policy; a Dutch Perspective.* Utrecht: Verwey-Jonker Instituut.

Denters, B. 2000. Urban democracies in the Netherlands, in *Urban Democracy,* edited by O. Gabriel, V. Hoffmann-Martinot and H. Savitch. Opladen: Leske und Budrich, 73–126.

Ketelaar, A. 2005. *How Democratic is Participatory Budgeting? Leiden and Porto Alegre Compared.* Master Thesis, London School of Economics and Political Science, London.

Meggeneder, O. 1981. Hypothesen zur Versäulung und Entsäulung – Dargestellt an den politischen Parteien in den Niederlanden. *Österreichische Zeitschrift für Soziologie*, 6, 80–91.

Swinnen, H. 2005. La démocratie participative dans le processus politique locale et le cas de la ville d'Utrecht (Pays-Bas), in *Gestion de proximité et démocratie participative. Une perspective comparée*, edited by M.-H. Bacqué, H. Rey and Y. Sintomer. Paris: La Découverte, 179–196.

Verwey-Jonker Instituut (ed.) 2003. *Community Boards on Trial*. Utrecht : Verwey-Jonker Instituut.

## Poland

Aissaoui, H. 2005. L'élargissement européen au prisme des fonds structurels: vers une européanisation de la gestion publique du territoire en Pologne? *Politique européenne*, 15, 61–84.

Dakowska, D. 2013. A Polish Case Study: Participatory Budgeting in the City of Płock, in *Participatory Budgeting in Asia and Europe. Key Challenges of Deliberative Democracy*, edited by Y. Sintomer, R. Traub-Merz and J. Zhang. Basingstoke (HA): Palgrave Macmillan, 198–209.

Raciborski, J. 2005a. Das System der territorialen Selbstverwaltung, in *Demokratie in Polen. Elemente des politischen Systems*, edited by J. Raciborski and J.J. Wiatr. Opladen: Barbara Budrich, 198–209.

——— 2005b. Wahlen und Wähler, in *Demokratie in Polen. Elemente des politischen Systems*, edited by J. Raciborski and J.J. Wiatr. Opladen: Barbara Budrich, 229–270.

Swianiewicz, P. 2005. Poland: A Time of Transition, in *Comparing Local Governance. Trends and Developments*, edited by B. Denters and L.E. Rose. Basingstoke (HA): Palgrave Macmillan, 100–118.

Wiatr, J.J. 2005. Entstehung und Wandel des Mehrparteiensystems, in *Demokratie in Polen. Elemente des politischen Systems*, edited by J. Raciborski and J.J. Wiatr. Opladen: Barbara Budrich, 197–228.

Ziemer, K. 2003. Parlament – Parteiensystem – Wahlen, in *Das moderne Polen*, edited by J. Franzke. Potsdam: Berliner Debatte Wissenschaftsverlag.

## Spain

Aguilar Rivero, R. 2004. La experiencia de los Presupuestos Participativos en Córdoba. *Temas para el Debate*, 113, 57–59.

Aviles Jimenez, F.J. 2004. Técnicas de organización de los Presupuestos Participativo. *Temas para el Debate*, 113, 45–48.

Ayuntamiento De Cordoba and Urb-Al 9 (eds) 2004. *Segundas Jornadas Internacionales sobre Participación Ciudadana. Segundo Encuentro Eurolatinoamericano sobre Presupuestos Participativos y Finanzas Locales.* Cordoba.

Ballersteros, F. 2004. *Modernización del Gobierno Local. Comentario Ley 57/2003.* Madrid: Angel.

Blanco, I. 2002. *Presupuestos Participativos y Democracia Local: Una comparación entre las experiencias brasileñas y españolas.* Available at: http://www.top.org.ar/Documentos/Blanco/.

Blanco, I. and Goma, R. 2002. *Gobiernos Locales y Redes Participativas.* Barcelona: Ariel.

Blanco, I. and Font, J. 2005. Los factores estructurales, instrumentales e ideológicos como explicaciones de la oferta institucional de participación, in *La participación ciudadana en grandes ciudades,* edited by M. Villoria and A. Godoy. Madrid: Dykinson, 147–172.

Brugue, Q. and Goma, R. 1998. *Gobiernos Locales y Políticas Públicas.* Barcelona: Ariel.

Castro, P. 2004. El Presupuesto Participativo en Getafe. *Temas para el Debate,* 113, 60–61.

Font, J. and Goma, R. 1999. *La participación ciudadana en la política local.* Madrid: Fundación Encuentro.

Font, N. 1998. *Democràcia i participació ciutadana.* Barcelona: Fundació Jaume Bofill.

Ganuza, E. 2007. *Tipologia y Modelos de los Presupuestos Participativos en España.* IESA Working Papers Series.

——— 2012. Ist ein Porto Alegre in Europa möglich? Die Bürgerhaushalte in Spanien, in *Hoffnung auf eine neue Demokratie. Bürgerhaushalte in Lateinamerika und Europa,* edited by C. Herzberg, Y. Sintomer and H. Kleger. Frankfurt: Campus, 223–238.

Ganuza, E. and Alvarez De Sotomayor, C. (eds). 2003. *Democracia y Presupuestos Participativos.* Barcelona: Icaria.

Ganuza, E. and Frances, F. 2012. *El Circulo Virtuoso de La Democracia: Los Presupuestos Participativos a Debate.* Madrid: Centro de Investigaciones Sociológicas.

Llamas, F. 2004. Participación y construcción de ciudadanía en Europa. *La Era Urbana (PGU-ALC),* March.

Navarro Yanez, C. 2002. *Democracia asociativa y oportunismo político. La política pública de participación ciudadana en los municipios españoles (1979–1993).* Valencia: Universidad Pablo de Olavide.

Perez Castell, M. 2004. La experiencia de los Presupuestos Participativos en Albacete. *Temas para el Debate,* 113, 54–56.

Pindado, F. 1999. *La partecipació ciutadana a la vida de les ciutats.* Barcelona: Serbal.

Sànchez, J. (ed.) 2000. *Participació ciutadana i govern local: els Consells Ciutadans*, Barcelona: Mediterrània.

Subirats, J., Blanco, I., Brugué, J., Font, J., Gomà, R., Jarque, M. and Medina, L. (eds) 2001. *Experiès de participació ciutadana en els municipis catalans*. Barcelona: Ed. Escola d'Administració Pública de Catalunya.

Villasante, T. 1995. *Las democracias participativas*. Madrid: HOAC.

Villasante, T. and Garrido, F.J. (eds) 2002. *Metodologías y presupuestos participativos (Construyendo Ciudadanía/3)*. Madrid: IEPALA.

Villasante, T. and Garrido F.J. *et al.* 1994. *Las ciudades hablan*. Caracas: Nueva Sociedad.

## United Kingdom

Barnes, M. 1999. *Building a Deliberative Democracy. An Evaluation of Two Citizens'Juries*. London: IPPR.

Blair, T. 1998a. *The Third Way. New Politics for the New Century*. London: Fabian Society.

——— 1998b. *Leading The Way. A New Vision for Local government*. London: IPPR.

Blakey, H. 2007. *Radical Innovations or Technical Fix? Participatory Budgeting in Bradford: How Latin American Participatory Traditions are Reinterpreted in the British Context*, 57th Political Studies Association Annual Conference: Europe and Global Politics, University of Bath.

Community Pride Initiative (ed.) 2000. *A Citizens' Budget. Regenerating Local Democracy Through Community Participation in Public Budgeting*. Manchester: CPI.

——— 2005. *Margins to Mainstream. Using Devolved Budgets and Community Action Plans to Influence Mainstream Spending*. Manchester: CPI.

Department for Communities and Local Government (DCLG) (ed.) 2006. *Strong and Prosperous Communities. The Local Government White Paper*. London: DCLG.

——— 2008. *Participatory Budgeting: A Draft National Strategy. Giving More People a Say in Local Spending*. London: DCLG.

——— 2009. *Empowering Communities to Influence Local Decision Making*. London: DCLG.

——— 2011. *Communities in the Driving Seat: A Study of Participatory Budgeting in England. Final Report*. London: DCLG.

Department for the Environment Transport and the Regions (DETR) 1998. *Modern Local Government: In Touch with the People*. London: DETR.

——— 2000. *Preparing Community Strategies*. London: DETR.

——— 2001. *Strong Local Leadership: Quality Public Services*. London: DTLR

Giddens, A. 1994. *Beyond Left and Right: The Future of Radical Politics*. Stanford: Stanford University Press.

Lavan, K. 2007. *Participatory Budgeting in the UK: an Evaluation from a Practicioner Perspective*. Manchester: The Participatory Budgeting Unit.

Lowndes, V., Pratchett, L. and Stoker, G. 2001. Trends in Public Participation: Part 1 – Local Government Perspectives. *Public Administration*, 79, 205–222.

Marlière, P. 2001. Le public au service du privé. Mondialisation néo-libérale et privatisation des services publics en Grande-Bretagne. *Les Temps Modernes*, 615–616.

Milburn, A. 2004. Active Citizenship: The Ten-year Agenda. Community Consultation Conference, London, March.

Office of the Deputy Prime Minister 2000. *Local Government Act 2000*. London: ODPM.

Parkinson, J. 2004. *Deliberative Democracy in Great Britain: The NHS and Citizen Juries*. Paper presented at 'Instruments d'action publique et technologies de gouvernement', IEP Paris, December 2001.

Power Inquiry (ed.) 2006. *Power to the People. The Report of Power, an Independent Inquiry into Britain's Democracy*. Yorck: The Power Inquiry.

Pratchett, L. 2004. Local Autonomy, Local Democracy and the New Localism. *Political Studies*, 52, 358–375.

Rallings, C. and Thrasher, M. 1996. *Local Elections Handbook*. Plymouth: LGC Elections Centre.

Röcke, A. 2010. Royaume-Uni – Budget participatif: des initiatives locales à l'ordre du jour national, in *La démocratie participative inachevée. Genèse, adaptations et diffusions*, edited by M.-H. Bacqué and Y. Sintomer. Paris: Yves Michel, 43–60.

Scarbrough, E. 2000. The Two Faces of Urban Democracy in Britain, in *Urban Democracy*, edited by O. Gabriel, V. Hoffmann-Martinot and H. Savitch. Opladen: Leske und Budrich, 127–186.

Skelcher, C., Weir, S. and Wilson, L. 2000. *Advance of the Quango State*. London: Local Government Information Unit.

Stewart, J. 2003. *Modernising British Local Government*. Basingstoke (HA): Palgrave Macmillan.

Stoker, G. (ed.) 1999. *The New Management of British Local Governance*. Basingstoke (HA): Palgrave Macmillan.

——— 2004. New Localism, Progressive Politics and Democracy. *The Political Quarterly*, 75, 1, 117–129.

Wilson, D. and Game, C. 2002. *Local Government in the United Kingdom*. Basingstoke (HA): Palgrave Macmillan.

——— 2011. *Local Government in the United Kingdom. Fifth Edition*. Basingstoke (HA): Palgrave Macmillan.

Wollmann, H. and Schroter, E. 2000. *Comparing Public Sector Reform in Britain and Germany: Key Traditions and Trends of Modernisation*. Aldershot: Ashgate.

# INDEX

Printed in the United States
by Baker & Taylor Publisher Services